PRENTICE HALL MATHEMATICS

ALGEBRA 1

Algebra 1A and 1B Lesson Plans

PEARSON

Prentice
Hall

Needham, Massachusetts
Upper Saddle River, New Jersey

ISBN: 0-13-125095-7
4 5 6 7 8 9 10 07 06 05 04

Algebra 1A and 1B Lesson Plans

Contents

Chapter 1

Chapter 2

Chapter 3

Chapter 4

Introduction

The *Algebra 1A and 1B Lesson Plans* provides you the information you need to teach *Prentice Hall Algebra 1* in a two-course sequence. This booklet is designed to help you manage your time. It serves as a guide to many elements of the *Prentice Hall Algebra 1* program, including the Student Edition, Teaching Resources, transparencies, and Technology.

This booklet has these sections:
- Pacing Guide
- Activities in Algebra 1A and Algebra 1B
- Algebra 1B—Getting Started
- NAEP and NCTM standards
- Lesson Plans by Objective
- Mid-Course and Final Tests

Pacing Guide
The Pacing Guide is designed to assist you in effectively planning instruction time for teaching the course over two-years in 45–55 minute periods or on a block schedule.

Activities in Algebra 1A and Algebra 1B
This section lists by lessons the Investigations, Technology activities and Hands-On activities that you can use to enhance student understanding.

Algebra 1B—Getting Started
This section gives you suggestions for using the Diagnostic Test to determine the concepts students need to review from Algebra 1A.

NAEP and NCTM Standards
Each lesson plan indicates the NAEP (2005) and NCTM (2000) standards covered by the lesson. For your convenience, pages T14–T17 give you a statement of those standards.

Lesson Plans
The Lesson Plans provide a detailed outline for the lessons by objective and include these components.
- **Objective**
- **New Vocabulary**
- **Standards**—NAEP (2005) and NCTM (2000)
- **Pacing**
- **Introduce** includes Check Skills You'll Need, Vocabulary, and for the second objective of a lesson, review for the first objective, with targeted resources.
- **Teach** points out the examples and the targeted resources available as you teach a lesson.
- **Practice** lists suggested exercise assignments for an objective and the targeted resources that will support you and your students. You can use the Mixed Review with either objective.
- **Assess** points out the Lesson Quiz, targeted resources, and the Computer Test Generator for creating a quiz by objective.

Mid-Course and Final Tests
Two forms of the mid-course and final tests, with answers, are provided for Algebra 1A and Algebra 1B. Also there is a Diagnostic Test for Algebra 1B.

How to Use Lesson Plans

Pacing is based on the Pacing Guide. See pages T8–T9.

NAEP objectives and **NCTM** Standards for each lesson are shown.

Record Your **Local Standards** for each lesson.

The **Introduce** section describes the prerequisite skills reviewed for the lesson objective and suggests how to teach new vocabulary.

The **Teach** section suggests how you can teach the objective, with emphasis on the Key Concepts.

The **Practice** section, based on Objective, contains exercises for both core and extension.

Write in your **Homework** assignment.

The **Assess** section describes the content of the Lesson Quiz and identifies, where applicable, the Checkpoint Quiz.

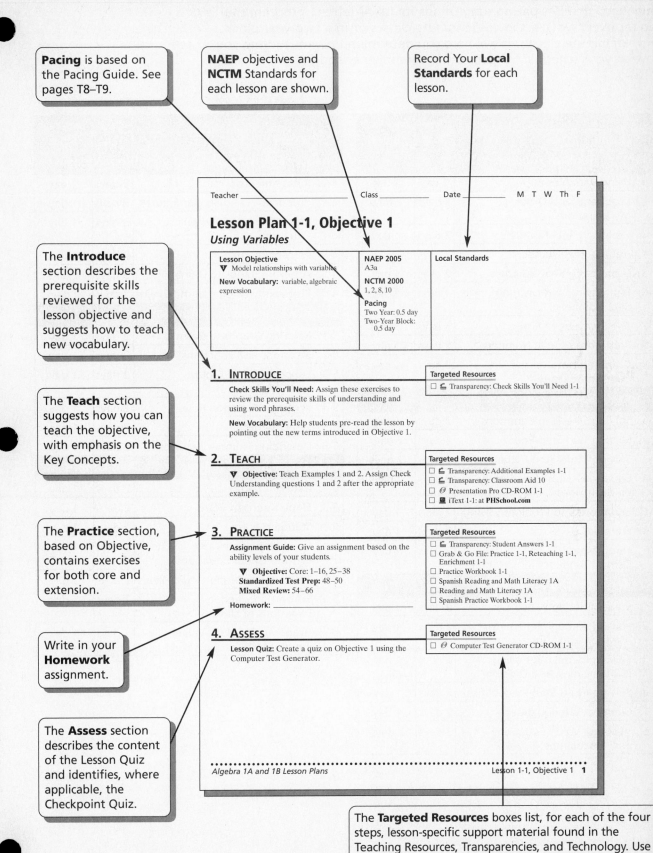

Teacher _____ Class _____ Date _____ M T W Th F

Lesson Plan 1-1, Objective 1
Using Variables

Lesson Objective	NAEP 2005	Local Standards
▼ Model relationships with variables **New Vocabulary:** variable, algebraic expression	A3a **NCTM 2000** 1, 2, 8, 10 **Pacing** Two Year: 0.5 day Two-Year Block: 0.5 day	

1. INTRODUCE

Check Skills You'll Need: Assign these exercises to review the prerequisite skills of understanding and using word phrases.

New Vocabulary: Help students pre-read the lesson by pointing out the new terms introduced in Objective 1.

Targeted Resources
- ☐ Transparency: Check Skills You'll Need 1-1

2. TEACH

▼ **Objective:** Teach Examples 1 and 2. Assign Check Understanding questions 1 and 2 after the appropriate example.

Targeted Resources
- ☐ Transparency: Additional Examples 1-1
- ☐ Transparency: Classroom Aid 10
- ☐ Presentation Pro CD-ROM 1-1
- ☐ iText 1-1: at **PHSchool.com**

3. PRACTICE

Assignment Guide: Give an assignment based on the ability levels of your students.

▼ **Objective:** Core: 1–16, 25–38
Standardized Test Prep: 48–50
Mixed Review: 54–66

Homework: _____

Targeted Resources
- ☐ Transparency: Student Answers 1-1
- ☐ Grab & Go File: Practice 1-1, Reteaching 1-1, Enrichment 1-1
- ☐ Practice Workbook 1-1
- ☐ Spanish Reading and Math Literacy 1A
- ☐ Reading and Math Literacy 1A
- ☐ Spanish Practice Workbook 1-1

4. ASSESS

Lesson Quiz: Create a quiz on Objective 1 using the Computer Test Generator.

Targeted Resources
- ☐ Computer Test Generator CD-ROM 1-1

Algebra 1A and 1B Lesson Plans   Lesson 1-1, Objective 1 **1**

The **Targeted Resources** boxes list, for each of the four steps, lesson-specific support material found in the Teaching Resources, Transparencies, and Technology. Use the boxes to check off which resources you use.

Pacing Guide

This chart provides pacing suggestions for an Algebra 1 program that is taught over two-years in 45–55 minute classes or in a two-year block with 90 minute classes. It will help you determine how much time you have in your schedule to cover other components and for review and testing.

Lesson	Two Year	Two-Year Block
Chapter 1 Tools of Algebra		
1-1: Using Variables	1 day	1 day
1-2: Exponents and Order of Operations	3 days	2 days
1-3: Exploring Real Numbers	2 days	1 day
1-4: Adding Real Numbers	2 days	1 day
1-5: Subtracting Real Numbers	2 days	1 day
1-6: Multiplying and Dividing Real Numbers	2 days	1 day
1-7: The Distributive Property	3 days	2 days
1-8: Properties of Real Numbers	2 days	1 day
1-9: Graphing Data on the Coordinate Plane	2 days	1 day
Chapter 2 Solving Equations		
2-1: Solving One-Step Equations	2 days	1 day
2-2: Solving Two-Step Equations	3 days	2 days
2-3: Solving Multi-Step Equations	2 days	2 days
2-4: Equations With Variables on Both Sides	3 days	2 days
2-5: Equations and Problem Solving	2 days	1 day
2-6: Formulas	2 days	1 day
2-7: Using Measures of Central Tendency	2 days	1 day
Chapter 3 Solving Inequalities		
3-1: Inequalities and Their Graphs	2 days	1 day
3-2: Solving Inequalities Using Addition and Subtraction	2 days	1 day
3-3: Solving Inequalities Using Multiplication and Division	2 days	1 day
3-4: Solving Multi-Step Inequalities	2 days	1 day
3-5: Compound Inequalities	2 days	1 day
3-6: Absolute Value Equations and Inequalities	3 days	2 days

Lesson	Two Year	Two-Year Block
Chapter 4 Solving and Applying Proportions		
4-1: Ratio and Proportion	2 days	1 day
4-2: Proportions and Similar Figures	2 days	1 day
4-3: Proportions and Percent Equations	2 days	1 day
4-4: Percent of Change	2 days	1 day
4-5: Applying Ratios to Probability	3 days	2 days
4-6: Probability of Compound Events	3 days	2 days
Chapter 5 Graphs and Functions		
5-1: Relating Graphs to Events	2 days	1 day
5-2: Relations and Functions	2 days	1 day
5-3: Function Rules, Tables, and Graphs	2 days	1 day
5-4: Writing a Function Rule	2 days	1 day
5-5: Direct Variation	2 days	1 day
5-6: Describing Number Patterns	2 days	1 day
Chapter 6 Linear Equations and Their Graphs		
6-1: Rate of Change and Slope	2 days	1 day
6-2: Slope-Intercept Form	2 days	1 day
6-3: Standard Form	2 days	1 day
6-4: Point-Slope Form and Writing Linear Equations	2 days	1 day
6-5: Parallel and Perpendicular Lines	2 days	1 day
6-6: Scatter Plots and Equations of Lines	2 days	1 day
6-7: Graphing Absolute Value Equations	2 days	1 day

Lesson	Two Year	Two-Year Block
Chapter 7 Systems of Equations and Inequalities		
7-1: Solving Systems by Graphing	2 days	1 day
7-2: Solving Systems Using Substitution	2 days	1 day
7-3: Solving Systems Using Elimination	2 days	1 day
7-4: Applications of Linear Systems	4 days	2 days
7-5: Linear Inequalities	2 days	1 days
7-6: Systems of Linear Inequalities	3 days	2 days
Chapter 8 Exponents and Exponential Functions		
8-1: Zero and Negative Exponents	2 days	1 day
8-2: Scientific Notation	2 days	1 day
8-3: Multiplication Properties of Exponents	3 days	2 days
8-4: More Multiplication Properties of Exponents	3 days	2 days
8-5: Division Properties of Exponents	2 days	1 day
8-6: Geometric Sequences	2 days	1 day
8-7: Exponential Functions	2 days	1 day
8-8: Exponential Growth and Decay	3 days	2 days
Chapter 9 Polynomials and Factoring		
9-1: Adding and Subtracting Polynomials	2 days	1 day
9-2: Multiplying and Factoring	2 days	1 day
9-3: Multiplying Binomials	2 days	1 day
9-4: Multiplying Special Cases	3 days	2 days
9-5: Factoring Polynomials of the Type $x^2 + bx + c$	3 days	2 days
9-6: Factoring Polynomials of the Type $ax^2 + bx + c$	3 days	2 days
9-7: Factoring Special Cases	3 days	2 days
9-8: Factoring by Grouping	2 days	1 day

Lesson	Two Year	Two-Year Block
Chapter 10 Quadratic Equations and Functions		
10-1: Exploring Quadratic Graphs	2 days	1 day
10-2: Quadratic Functions	2 days	1 day
10-3: Finding and Estimating Square Roots	1 day	1 day
10-4: Solving Quadratic Equations	2 days	1 day
10-5: Factoring to Solve Quadratic Equations	2 days	1 day
10-6: Completing the Square	2 days	1 day
10-7: Using the Quadratic Formula	2 days	1 day
10-8 Using the Discriminant	2 days	1 day
10-9: Choosing a Linear, Quadratic, or Exponential Model	2 days	1 day
Chapter 11 Radical Expressions and Equations		
11-1: Simplifying Radicals	2 days	1 day
11-2: The Pythagorean Theorem	3 days	2 days
11-3: The Distance and Midpoint Formulas	3 days	2 days
11-4: Operations with Radical Expressions	4 days	2 days
11-5: Solving Radical Equations	3 days	2 days
11-6: Graphing Square Root Functions	3 days	2 days
11-7: Trigonometric Ratios	2 days	1 day
Chapter 12 Rational Expressions and Functions		
12-1: Inverse Variations	2 days	1 day
12-2: Graphing Rational Functions	2 days	1 day
12-3: Simplifying Rational Expressions	2 days	1 day
12-4: Multiplying and Dividing Rational Expressions	2 days	1 day
12-5: Dividing Polynomials	2 days	1 day
12-6: Adding and Subtracting Rational Expressions	4 days	2 days
12-7: Solving Rational Equations	3 days	2 days
12-8: Counting Methods and Permutations	1 day	1 day
12-9: Combinations	2 days	1 day

Activities in Algebra 1A and Algebra 1B

To enhance student understanding of the concepts, you may want to incorporate activities into your instruction. In addition to the Investigations within the lessons, there are numerous other opportunities for students to explore mathematics, either working as a whole class, in groups, or individually.

Use With	Type	Title	Source
Chapter 1			
1-1	Investigation	Order of Operations	Student Edition, p. 9
1-4	Hands-On	Zero Out	Hands-On Activities, p. 1
1-5	Hands-On	Subtracting Integers	Hands-On Activities, p. 2
1-6	Technology	Matrices	Student Edition, p. 45
1-6	Technology	Playing with Numbers	Technology Activities, pp. 34–35
1-7	Investigation	The Distributive Property	Student Edition, p. 46
1-7	Hands-On	The Distributive Property	Hands-On Activities, 3
Chapter 1	Chapter Project	Taking Stock	Ch. 1 Grab & Go File, pp. 28–31
Chapter 2			
2-1	Hands-On	Balancing Act	Hands-On Activities, p. 4
2-4	Investigation	Modeling Equations	Student Edition, p. 95
2-4	Technology	Graphing to Solve Equations	Student Edition, p. 102
2-4	Hands-On	Modeling Equations	Hands-On Activities, p. 5
2-4	Technology	Finding Real Roots of Equations	Technology Activities, pp. 36–38
2-6	Hands-On	Time to React	Hands-On Activities, p. 6
Chapter 2	Chapter Project	The Big Dig!	Ch. 2 Grab & Go File, pp. 22–25
after Chap. 2	Real-World Snapshots	Shifting Gears	Student Edition, pp. 130–131
Chapter 3			
3-1	Hands-On	Too Big and Too Little	Hands-On Activities, p. 7
3-5	Hands-On	Compound Inequalities	Hands-On Activities, p. 8
3-6	Technology	Solving Absolute Value Inequalities Graphically	Technology Activities, pp. 38–39
Chapter 3	Chapter Project	No Sweat!	Ch. 3 Grab & Go File, pp. 20–23
Chapter 4			
4-1	Hands-On	Working with Ratios	Hands-On Activities, p. 9
4-1	Technology	Mrs. Murphy's Algebra Test Scores	Technology Activities, pp. 42–43
4-3	Investigation	Modeling Percents	Student Edition, p. 196
4-5	Investigation	Understanding Probability	Student Edition, p. 210
4-5	Technology	Conducting a Simulation	Student Edition, p. 218
4-5	Hands-On	Examination Simulation	Hands-On Activities, p. 10
Chapter 4	Chapter Project	Checks and Balances	Ch. 4 Grab & Go File, pp. 20–23
after Chap. 4	Real-World Snapshots	A Swing of the Bat	Student Edition, pp. 232–233
Chapter 5			
5-3	Technology	Function Rules, Tables, and Graphs	Student Edition, p. 253
5-3	Hands-On	Direct Measurement	Hands-On Activities, p. 11
5-6	Hands-On	Patterns in Folding	Hands-On Activities, p. 12
Chapter 5	Chapter Project	Fast Talker	Ch. 5 Grab & Go File, pp. 20–23

Use With	Type	Title	Source
Chapter 6			
6-1	CBL2™	Take a Walk, Part 1	Technology Activities, pp. 6–7
6-1	Hands-On	Sloping Binders	Hands-On Activities, p. 13
6-2	Technology	Investigating $y = mx + b$	Student Edition, p. 290
6-2	Hands-On	Hidden Equation	Hands-On Activities, p. 14
6-2	CBL2™	Take a Walk, Part 2	Technology Activities, pp. 8–9
6-4	Technology	Exploring Point-Slope Form	Technology Activities, pp. 44–45
6-4	CBL2™	Race Cars	Technology Activities, pp. 16–17
6-5	CBL2™	Synchronized Strut	Technology Activities, pp. 10–11
6-6	Hands-On	Pages and Weight	Hands-On Activities, p. 15
Chapter 6	Chapter Project	The Choice Is Yours	Ch. 4 Grab & Go File, pp. 22–25
after Chap. 6	Real-World Snapshots	Mathematically Inclined	Student Edition, pp. 336–337
Chapter 7			
7-1	CBL2™	Coming and Going	Technology Activities, pp. 12–13
7-2	Investigation	Solving Systems Using Algebra Tiles	Student Edition, p. 346
7-3	Technology	Fast Food Follies	Technology Activities, pp. 46–47
7-4	Technology	Matrices and Solving Systems	Student Edition, p. 360
7-5	Hands-On	What's the Point?	Hands-On Activities, p. 16
7-6	Technology	Graphing Linear Inequalities	Student Edition, p. 385
7-6	Hands-On	Where's the Intersection?	Hands-On Activities, p. 17
Chapter 7	Chapter Project	Let's Dance	Ch. 7 Grab & Go File, pp. 20–23
Chapter 8			
8-6	Technology	Wheat on a Chessboard	Technology Activities, pp. 48–49
8-6	Hands-On	Geometric Sequences	Hands-On Activities, p. 18
8-8	Technology	Fitting Exponential Curves to Data	Student Edition, p. 436
8-8	CBL2™	Charge It!	Technology Activities, pp. 20–21
8-8	Hands-On	Bouncing Ball	Hands-On Activities, p. 19
Chapter 8	Chapter Project	Moldy Oldies	Ch. 8 Grab & Go File, pp. 26–29
after Chap. 8	Real-World Snapshots	How Fast Can You Run?	Student Edition, pp. 452–453
Chapter 9			
9-1	Technology	Manipulating a Polynomial	Technology Activities, pp. 50–51
9-1	Hands-On	Modeling Polynomial Subtraction	Hands-On Activities, p. 20
9-3	Investigation	Using Models to Multiply	Student Edition, p. 466
9-3	Hands-On	Multiplying Binomials	Hands-On Activities, p. 21
9-5	Investigation	Using Models to Factor	Student Edition, p. 480
9-7	Hands-On	Special Products	Hands-On Activities, p. 22
Chapter 9	Chapter Project	Trees Are Us	Ch.9 Grab & Go File, pp. 26–29

Use With	Type	Title	Source
Chapter 10			
10-2	CBL2™	Keep Your Eye on the Ball	Technology Activities, pp. 14–15
10-4	CBL2™	Back and Forth It Goes	Technology Activities, pp. 18–19
10-4	Technology	Writing a Simple Program	Technology Activities, pp. 52–53
10-5	Technology	Finding Roots	Student Edition, p. 535
10-6	Hands-On	Completing the Square	Hands-On Activities, p. 23
10-8	Hands-On	Quadratic Solutions	Hands-On Activities, p. 24
10-9	CBL2™	Falling Objects	Technology Activities, pp. 22–23
10-9	Hands-On	Latitude and Temperature	Hands-On Activities, p. 25
Chapter 10	Chapter Project	Full Stop Ahead	Ch. 10 Grab & Go File, pp. 28–31
after Chap. 10	Real-World Snapshots	Weight No More	Student Edition, pp. 574–575
Chapter 11			
11-2	Hands-On	The Pythagorean Theorem	Hands-On Activities, p. 26
11-3	Hands-On	Geoboard Challenges	Hands-On Activities, p. 27
11-5	Technology	Repeated Radicals	Technology Activities, pp. 54–55
11-7	Hands-On	Indirect Measurement	Hands-On Activities, p. 28
Chapter 11	Chapter Project	On a Clear Day	Ch. 11 Grab & Go File, pp. 22–25
Chapter 12			
12-2	Technology	Graphing Rational Functions	Student Edition, p. 643
12-2	Technology	Asymptotes and Holes	Technology Activities, pp. 56–57
12-7	Hands-On	Travel Rectangles	Hands-On Activities, p. 29
12-8	Hands-On	Permutations and Combinations	Hands-On Activities, p. 30
Chapter 12	Chapter Project	Good Vibrations	Ch. 12 Grab & Go File, pp. 28–31
after Chap. 12	Real-World Snapshots	Good Vibrations	Student Edition, pp. 700–701

Algebra 1B—Getting Started

The Diagnostic Test on pages 170–171 covers key concepts from Chapters 1–6. Giving the Diagnostic Test before starting Chapter 7 will help you identify concepts that your class or individual students need to review. The chart below correlates each skill tested on the Diagnostic Test for Algebra 1B with the Student Edition lesson you can use for review.

Topic	Diagnostic Test for Algebra 1B	Lesson
Exponents and Order of Operations	3, 9, 10	1-2
Operations with Real Numbers	1, 2, 4, 5, 6	1-4, 1-5, and 1-6
The Distributive Property	7, 8	1-7
Graphing in the Coordinate Plane	11, 12	1-9
Solving Two-Step Equations	13, 14, 20, 21, 22	2-2
Solving Equations with Variables on Both Sides	15, 24	2-4
Solving Inequalities Using Multiplication and Division	16, 23	3-3
Solving Multi-Step Inequalities	17, 18	3-4
Ratios and Proportions	25, 26	4-1
Function Rules, Tables, And Graphs	19	5-3
Slope-Intercept Form of Linear Equations	27, 32	6-2
Standard Form of Linear Equations	30, 31, 33	6-3
Point-Slope Form and Writing Linear Equations	28, 29	6-4

National Assessment of Educational Progress (NAEP 2005)

This chart describes the mathematics that should be assessed at the 12th grade level. Therefore it indicates the mathematics that should be covered in high school mathematics. The NAEP standards are listed in the daily lesson plans. The number N1d in a lesson plan refers to the first objective listed below.

Number Properties and Operations

1. Number sense

N1d	Write, rename, represent, or compare real numbers (e.g., π, $\sqrt{2}$, numerical relationships using number lines, models, or diagrams).
N1f	Represent very large or very small numbers using scientific notation in meaningful contexts.
N1g	Find or model absolute value or apply to problem situations.
N1h	Interpret calculator or computer displays of numbers given in scientific notation.
N1j	Order or compare real numbers, including very large or small real numbers.

2. Estimation

N2a	Establish or apply benchmarks for real numbers in contexts.
N2b	Make estimates of very large or very small numbers appropriate to a given situation by: • identifying when estimation is appropriate or not, • determining the level of accuracy needed, • selecting the appropriate method of estimation, or • analyzing the effect of an estimation method on the accuracy of results.
N2c	Verify solutions or determine the reasonableness of results in a variety of situations including scientific notation, calculator and computer results.
N2d	Estimate square or cube roots of numbers less than 1,000 between two whole numbers.

3. Number operations

N3a	Perform computations with real numbers including common irrational numbers or the absolute value of numbers.
N3d	Describe the effect of multiplying and dividing by numbers including the effect of multiplying or dividing a real number by: • zero, or • a number between zero and one, or • a number less than zero, or • one, or • a number greater than one.
N3g	Solve application problems involving numbers, including rational and common irrationals, using exact answers or estimates as appropriate.

4. Ratios and proportional reasoning

N4b	Use proportions to model problems.
N4c	Use proportional reasoning to solve problems (including rates, scaling, and similarity).
N4d	Solve problems involving percentages (including percent increase and decrease, interest rates, tax, discount, tips, or part/whole relationships).

5. Properties of number and operations

N5b	Solve problems involving factors, multiples, or prime factorization.
N5c	Use prime or composite numbers to solve problems.
N5d	Use divisibility or remainders in problem settings.
N5e	Apply basic properties of operations.
N5f	Provide a mathematical argument about a numerical property or relationship.

Measurement

1. Measuring physical attributes

M1c	Estimate or compare perimeters or areas of two-dimensional geometric figures.
M1d	Estimate or compare volumes or surface area of three-dimensional figures.
M1e	Solve problems involving the coordinate plane such as the distance between two points, the midpoint of a segment, or slopes of perpendicular or parallel lines.

M1f	Solve problems of angle measure, including those involving triangles or other polygons or parallel lines cut by a transversal.
M1h	Solve mathematical or real-world problems involving perimeter or area of plane figures such as polygons, circles, or composite figures.
M1j	Solve problems involving volume or surface area of rectangular solids, cylinders, cones, pyramids, prisms, spheres, or composite shapes.
M1k	Solve problems involving indirect measurement such as finding the height of a building by finding the distance to the base of the building and the angle of elevation to the top.
M1ℓ	Solve problems involving rates such as speed, density, population density, or flow rates.
M1m	Use trigonometric relations in right triangles to solve problems.

2. Systems of measurement

M2a	Select or use appropriate type of unit for the attribute being measured such as volume or surface area.
M2b	Solve problems involving conversions within or between measurement systems, given the relationship between the units.
M2e	Determine appropriate accuracy of measurement in problem situations (e.g., the accuracy of measurement of the dimensions to obtain a specified accuracy of area) and find the measure to that degree of accuracy.
M2f	Construct or solve problems (e.g., number of rolls needed for insulating a house) involving scale drawings.
M2g	Compare lengths, areas, or volumes of similar figures using proportions.

Geometry

1. Dimension and shape

G1b	Use two-dimensional representations of three-dimensional objects to visualize and solve problems involving surface area and volume.
G1c	Give precise mathematical descriptions or definitions of geometric shapes in the plane and in 3-dimensional space.
G1d	Draw or sketch from a written description plane figures (e.g., isosceles triangles, regular polygons, curved figures) and planar images of 3-dimensional figures (e.g., polyhedra, spheres, and hemispheres).
G1e	Describe or analyze properties of spheres and hemispheres.

2. Transformation of shapes and preservation of properties

G2a	Recognize or identify types of symmetries (e.g., point, line, rotational, self-congruences) of two- and three-dimensional figures.
G2b	Give or recognize the precise mathematical relationship (e.g., congruence, similarity, orientation) between a figure and its image under a transformation.
G2c	Perform or describe the effect of a single transformation on two- and three-dimensional geometric shapes (reflections across lines of symmetry, rotations, translations, and dilations).
G2d	Describe the final outcome of successive transformations.
G2e	Justify relationships of congruence and similarity, and apply these relationships using scaling and proportional reasoning.

3. Relationships between geometric figures

G3b	Apply geometric properties and relationships in solving multi-step problems in two and three dimensions (including rigid and non-rigid figures).
G3c	Represent problem situations with geometric models to solve mathematical or real-world problems.
G3d	Use the Pythagorean theorem to solve problems in two- or three-dimensional situations.
G3e	Describe and analyze properties of circles (e.g., perpendicularity of tangent and radius, angle inscribed in a semicircle).
G3f	Analyze properties or relationships of triangles, quadrilaterals, and other polygonal plane figures.
G3g	Describe or analyze properties and relationships of parallel, perpendicular, or intersecting lines including the angle relationships that arise in these cases.

4. Position and direction

| G4b | Describe the intersections of lines in the plane and in space, intersections of a line and a plane or of two planes in space. |
| G4c | Describe or identify conic sections and other cross sections of solids. |

G4d	Represent two-dimensional figures algebraically using coordinates and/or equations.
G4e	Use vectors to represent velocity and direction.
5. Mathematical reasoning	
G5a	Make, test, and validate geometric conjectures using a variety of methods including deductive reasoning and counterexamples.

Data Analysis and Probability

1. Data representation (Histograms, line graphs, scatterplots, box plots, circle graphs, stem and leaf plots, frequency distributions, and tables.)

D1a	Read or interpret data, including interpolating or extrapolating from data.
D1b	Given a set of data, complete a graph and then solve a problem using the data in the graph (histograms, scatterplots, line graphs).
D1c	Solve problems by estimating and computing with univariate or bivariate data (including scatterplots and two-way tables).
D1d	Given a graph or a set of data, determine whether information is represented effectively and appropriately (bar graphs, box plots, histograms, scatterplots, line graphs).
D1e	Compare and contrast the effectiveness of different representations of the same data.

2. Characteristics of data sets

D2a	Calculate, interpret, or use mean, median, mode, range, interquartile range, or standard deviation.
D2b	Recognize how linear transformations of one-variable data affect mean, median, mode, and range (e.g., effect on the mean by adding a constant to each data point).
D2c	Determine the effect of outliers on mean, median, mode, range, interquartile range, or standard deviation.
D2d	Compare two or more data sets using mean, median, mode, range, interquartile range, or standard deviation describing the same characteristic for two different populations or subsets of the same population.
D2e	Given a set of data or a scatterplot, visually choose the line of best fit and explain the meaning of the line. Use the line to make predictions.
D2f	Use or interpret a normal distribution as a mathematical model appropriate for summarizing certain sets of data.
D2g	Given a scatterplot, make decisions or predictions involving a line or curve of best fit.
D2h	Given a scatterplot, estimate the correlation coefficient (e.g., Given a scatterplot, is the correlation closer to 0, .5, or 1.0? Is it a positive or negative correlation?).

3. Experiments and samples

D3a	Identify possible sources of bias in data collection methods and describe how such bias can be controlled and reduced.
D3b	Recognize and describe a method to select a simple random sample.
D3c	Make inferences from sample results.
D3d	Identify or evaluate the characteristics of a good survey or of a well-designed experiment.

4. Probability

D4a	Analyze a situation that involves probability of independent or dependent events.
D4b	Determine the theoretical probability of simple and compound events in familiar or unfamiliar contexts.
D4c	Given the results of an experiment or simulation, estimate the probability of simple or compound events in familiar or unfamiliar contexts.
D4d	Distinguish between experimental and theoretical probability.
D4e	Determine the number of ways an event can occur using tree diagrams, formulas for combinations and permutations, or other counting techniques.
D4f	Determine the probability of the possible outcomes of an event.
D4h	Determine the probability of independent and dependent events.
D4i	Determine conditional probability using two-way tables.
D4j	Interpret probabilities within a given context.

Algebra

1. Patterns, relations, and functions

A1a	Recognize, describe, or extend arithmetic, geometric progressions or patterns using words or symbols.
A1b	Express the function in general terms (either recursively or explicitly), given a table, verbal description, or some terms of a sequence.
A1e	Identify or analyze distinguishing properties of linear, quadratic, inverse ($y = k/x$) or exponential functions from tables, graphs, or equations.
A1g	Determine the domain and range of functions given various contexts.
A1h	Recognize and analyze the general forms of linear, quadratic, inverse, or exponential functions (e.g., in $y = ax + b$, recognize the roles of a and b).
A1i	Express linear and exponential functions in recursive and explicit form given a table or verbal description.

2. Algebraic representations

A2a	Translate between different representations of algebraic expressions using symbols, graphs, tables, diagrams, or written descriptions.
A2b	Analyze or interpret relationships expressed in symbols, graphs, tables, diagrams, or written descriptions.
A2c	Graph or interpret points that are represented by one or more ordered pairs of numbers on a rectangular coordinate system.
A2d	Perform or interpret transformations on the graphs of linear and quadratic functions.
A2e	Use algebraic properties to develop a valid mathematical argument.
A2f	Use an algebraic model of a situation to make inferences or predictions.
A2g	Given a real-world situation, determine if a linear, quadratic, inverse, or exponential function fits the situation (e.g., half-life bacterial growth).
A2h	Solve problems involving exponential growth and decay.

3. Variables, expressions, and operations

A3a	Write algebraic expressions, equations, or inequalities to represent a situation.
A3b	Perform basic operations, using appropriate tools, on algebraic expressions (including grouping and order of multiple operations involving basic operations, exponents, roots, simplifying, and expanding).
A3c	Write equivalent forms of algebraic expressions, equations, or inequalities to represent and explain mathematical relationships.

4. Equations and inequalities

A4a	Solve linear, rational, or quadratic equations or inequalities.
A4c	Analyze situations or solve problems using linear or quadratic equations or inequalities symbolically or graphically.
A4d	Recognize the relationship between the solution of a system of linear equations and its graph.
A4e	Solve problems involving more advanced formulas [e.g., the volumes and surface areas of three dimensional solids; or such formulas as: $A = P(1 + r)^t$, $A = Pe^{rt}$].
A4f	Given a familiar formula, solve for one of the variables.
A4g	Solve or interpret systems of equations or inequalities.

Principles and Standards for School Mathematics (NCTM 2000)

This chart indicates the NCTM standards you will find correlated to the lessons in each daily lesson plan.

1 Number and Operations

2 Algebra

3 Geometry

4 Measurement

5 Data Analysis and Probability

6 Problem Solving

7 Reasoning and Proof

8 Communication

9 Connections

10 Representation

Lesson Plan 1-1, Objective 1
Using Variables

Lesson Objective	NAEP 2005	Local Standards
▼ Model relationships with variables **New Vocabulary:** variable, algebraic expression	A3a **NCTM 2000** 1, 2, 8, 10 **Pacing** Two Year: 0.5 day Two-Year Block: 0.5 day	

1. INTRODUCE

Check Skills You'll Need: Assign these exercises to review the prerequisite skills of understanding and using word phrases.

New Vocabulary: Help students pre-read the lesson by pointing out the new terms introduced in Objective 1.

Targeted Resources

☐ ✎ Transparency: Check Skills You'll Need 1-1

2. TEACH

▼ **Objective:** Teach Examples 1 and 2. Assign Check Understanding questions 1 and 2 after the appropriate example.

Targeted Resources

☐ ✎ Transparency: Additional Examples 1-1
☐ ✎ Transparency: Classroom Aid 10
☐ ✐ Presentation Pro CD-ROM 1-1
☐ ▣ iText 1-1: at **PHSchool.com**

3. PRACTICE

Assignment Guide: Give an assignment based on the ability levels of your students.

▼ **Objective:** Core: 1–16, 25–38
Standardized Test Prep: 48–50
Mixed Review: 54–66

Homework: _____

Targeted Resources

☐ ✎ Transparency: Student Answers 1-1
☐ Grab & Go File: Practice 1-1, Reteaching 1-1, Enrichment 1-1
☐ Practice Workbook 1-1
☐ Spanish Reading and Math Literacy 1A
☐ Reading and Math Literacy 1A
☐ Spanish Practice Workbook 1-1

4. ASSESS

Lesson Quiz: Create a quiz on Objective 1 using the Computer Test Generator.

Targeted Resources

☐ ✐ Computer Test Generator CD-ROM 1-1

Lesson Plan 1-1, Objective 2
Using Variables

Lesson Objective	NAEP 2005	Local Standards
✓ Model relationships with equations and formulas **New Vocabulary:** equation, open sentence	A3a **NCTM 2000** 1, 2, 8, 10 **Pacing** Two Year: 0.5 day Two-Year Block: 0.5 day	

1. INTRODUCE

Check Skills You'll Need: Assign these exercises if not used with Objective 1.

Review: Remind students that a variable represents one or more numbers.

New Vocabulary: Help students pre-read the lesson by pointing out the new terms introduced in Objective 2.

Targeted Resources

☐ ▱ Transparency: Check Skills You'll Need 1-1

2. TEACH

✓ **Objective:** Teach Examples 3 and 4. Assign Check Understanding questions 3 and 4 after the appropriate example.

Targeted Resources

☐ ▱ Transparency: Additional Examples 1-1
☐ ▱ Transparency: Classroom Aid 10
☐ ✆ Presentation Pro CD-ROM 1-1
☐ ▣ iText 1-1: at **PHSchool.com**

3. PRACTICE

Assignment Guide: Give an assignment based on the ability levels of your students.

✓ **Objective:** Core: 17–24, 39–42; Extension: 43–47
Standardized Test Prep: 51–53
Mixed Review: 54–66

Homework: _____

Targeted Resources

☐ ▱ Transparency: Student Answers 1-1
☐ Grab & Go File: Practice 1-1, Reteaching 1-1, Enrichment 1-1
☐ Practice Workbook 1-1
☐ Spanish Reading and Math Literacy 1A
☐ Reading and Math Literacy 1A
☐ Spanish Practice Workbook 1-1
☐ Reasoning and Puzzles 24, 29: at **PHSchool.com**

4. ASSESS

Lesson Quiz: Assign the Lesson Quiz to assess students' mastery of the lesson content.

Targeted Resources

☐ ▱ Transparency: Lesson Quiz 1-1
☐ ▣ Online Lesson Quiz 1-1: at **PHSchool.com**
☐ Grab & Go File: Checkpoint Quiz 1
☐ ✆ Computer Test Generator CD-ROM 1-1

Lesson Plan 1-2, Objective 1
Exponents and Order of Operations

Lesson Objective	NAEP 2005	Local Standards
▼ Simplify and evaluate expressions and formulas **New Vocabulary:** simplify, exponent, base, power, order of operations, evaluate	A3b **NCTM 2000** 2, 3, 8, 9, 10 **Pacing** Two Year: 1 day Two-Year Block: 1 day	

1. INTRODUCE

Check Skills You'll Need: Assign these exercises to review the prerequisite skill of applying the order of operations.

New Vocabulary: Help students pre-read the lesson by pointing out the new terms introduced in Objective 1.

Targeted Resources

☐ ⌨ Transparency: Check Skills You'll Need 1-2

2. TEACH

▼ **Objective:** Have students work the Investigation to explore Order of Operations. Review the summary in the Key Concepts box. Teach Examples 1–3. Assign Check Understanding questions 1–3 after the appropriate example.

Targeted Resources

☐ ⌨ Transparency: Additional Examples 1-2
☐ ⌨ Transparency: Classroom Aid 18, 22
☐ Graphing Calculator Procedure 1:
    at **PHSchool.com**
☐ ✐ Presentation Pro CD-ROM 1-2
☐ ▣ iText 1-2: at **PHSchool.com**

3. PRACTICE

Assignment Guide: Give an assignment based on the ability levels of your students.

▼ **Objective:** Core: 1–14, 42, 45, 47, 50, 54
Standardized Test Prep: 83, 85, 87, 88
Mixed Review: 89–106

Homework: _____

Targeted Resources

☐ ⌨ Transparency: Student Answers 1-2
☐ Grab & Go File: Practice 1-2, Reteaching 1-2, Enrichment 1-2
☐ Practice Workbook 1-2
☐ Spanish Practice Workbook 1-2

4. ASSESS

Lesson Quiz: Create a quiz on Objective 1 using the Computer Test Generator.

Targeted Resources

☐ ✐ Computer Test Generator CD-ROM 1-2

Lesson Plan 1-2, Objective 2
Exponents and Order of Operations

Lesson Objective	NAEP 2005	Local Standards
☑ Simplify and evaluate expressions containing grouping symbols	A3b	
	NCTM 2000	
	2, 3, 8, 9, 10	
	Pacing	
	Two Year: 2 days	
	Two-Year Block: 1 day	

1. INTRODUCE

Check Skills You'll Need: Assign these exercises if not used with Objective 1.

Review: Remind students of the Order of Operations in the Key Concepts box.

Targeted Resources

☐ ⬛ Transparency: Check Skills You'll Need 1-2

2. TEACH

☑ **Objective:** Teach Examples 4–7. Assign Check Understanding 4–7 after the appropriate example.

Targeted Resources

☐ ⬛ Transparency: Additional Examples 1-2
☐ ⬛ Transparency: Classroom Aid 18, 22
☐ Graphing Calculator Procedure 1: at **PHSchool.com**
☐ ⬤ Presentation Pro CD-ROM 1-2
☐ 🖥 iText 1-2: at **PHSchool.com**

3. PRACTICE

Assignment Guide: Give an assignment based on the ability levels of your students.

☑ **Objective:** Core: 15–41, 43–44, 46, 48–49, 51–53, 55–74; Extension: 75–82
Standardized Test Prep: 84, 86
Mixed Review: 89–106

Homework: _____

Targeted Resources

☐ ⬛ Transparency: Student Answers 1-2
☐ Grab & Go File: Practice 1-2, Reteaching 1-2, Enrichment 1-2
☐ Practice Workbook 1-2
☐ Spanish Practice Workbook 1-2
☐ Reasoning and Puzzles 2, 25: at **PHSchool.com**

4. ASSESS

Lesson Quiz: Assign the Lesson Quiz to assess students' mastery of the lesson content.

Targeted Resources

☐ ⬛ Transparency: Lesson Quiz 1-2
☐ 🖥 Online Lesson Quiz 1-2: at **PHSchool.com**
☐ ⬤ Computer Test Generator CD-ROM 1-2

Teacher _____ Class _____ Date _____ M T W Th F

Lesson Plan 1-3, Objective 1
Exploring Real Numbers

Lesson Objective ▼ Classify numbers **New Vocabulary:** natural numbers, whole numbers, integers, rational number, irrational number, real numbers, counterexample	**NAEP 2005** N1d, j **NCTM 2000** 1, 2, 8, 9, 10 **Pacing** Two Year: 1 day Two-Year Block: 0.5 day	**Local Standards**

1. INTRODUCE

Check Skills You'll Need: Assign these exercises to review the prerequisite skills of using fraction and decimal representations of numbers.

New Vocabulary: Help students pre-read the lesson by pointing out the new terms introduced in Objective 1.

Targeted Resources

☐ 🖵 Transparency: Check Skills You'll Need 1-3

2. TEACH

▼ **Objective:** Teach Examples 1–3. Assign Check Understanding 1–3 after the appropriate example. Help students to understand the structure of the diagram in the Key Concepts box.

Targeted Resources

☐ 🖵 Transparency: Additional Examples 1-3
☐ 🖵 Transparency: Classroom Aid 5, 21
☐ ⊘ Presentation Pro CD-ROM 1-3
☐ 🖥 iText 1-3: at **PHSchool.com**

3. PRACTICE

Assignment Guide: Give an assignment based on the ability levels of your students.

▼ **Objective:** Core: 1–23, 42–46, 63, 72
Standardized Test Prep: 82–85
Mixed Review: 86–98

Homework: _____

Targeted Resources

☐ 🖵 Transparency: Student Answers 1-3
☐ Grab & Go File: Practice 1-3, Reteaching 1-3, Enrichment 1-3
☐ Practice Workbook 1-3
☐ Spanish Practice Workbook 1-3

4. ASSESS

Lesson Quiz: Create a quiz on Objective 1 using the Computer Test Generator.

Targeted Resources

☐ ⊘ Computer Test Generator CD-ROM 1-3

Lesson Plan 1-3, Objective 2
Exploring Real Numbers

Lesson Objective ☑ Compare numbers **New Vocabulary:** inequality, opposites, absolute value	**NAEP 2005** N1d, j **NCTM 2000** 1, 2, 8, 9, 10 **Pacing** Two Year: 1 day Two-Year Block: 0.5 day	**Local Standards**

1. INTRODUCE

Check Skills You'll Need: Assign these exercises if not used with Objective 1.

Review: Review real numbers using the Key Concepts box.

New Vocabulary: Help students pre-read the lesson by pointing out the new terms introduced in Objective 2.

Targeted Resources

☐ ▱ Transparency: Check Skills You'll Need 1-3

2. TEACH

☑ **Objective:** Teach Examples 4 and 5. Assign Check Understanding questions after the appropriate example.

Targeted Resources

☐ ▱ Transparency: Additional Examples 1-3
☐ ▱ Transparency: Classroom Aid 5, 21
☐ ⊘ Presentation Pro CD-ROM 1-3
☐ ▤ iText 1-3: at **PHSchool.com**

3. PRACTICE

Assignment Guide: Give an assignment based on the ability levels of your students.

  ☑ **Objective:** Core: 24–41, 47–62, 64–71
  Extension: 73–78
  Standardized Test Prep: 79–81
  Mixed Review: 86–98

Homework: _____

Targeted Resources

☐ ▱ Transparency: Student Answers 1-3
☐ Grab & Go File: Practice 1-3, Reteaching 1-3, Enrichment 1-3
☐ Practice Workbook 1-3
☐ Spanish Practice Workbook 1-3
☐ Reasoning and Puzzles 54: at **PHSchool.com**

4. ASSESS

Lesson Quiz: Assign the Lesson Quiz to assess students' mastery of the lesson content.

Targeted Resources

☐ ▱ Transparency: Lesson Quiz 1-3
☐ ▤ Online Lesson Quiz 1-3: at **PHSchool.com**
☐ ⊘ Computer Test Generator CD-ROM 1-3

Lesson Plan 1-4, Objective 1
Adding Real Numbers

<table>
<tr><td>

Lesson Objective

▼ Add real numbers using models and rules

New Vocabulary: identity property of addition, additive inverse, inverse property of addition

</td><td>

NAEP 2005
N3a, g

NCTM 2000
1, 2, 8, 9, 10

Pacing
Two Year: 1 day
Two-Year Block: 0.5 day

</td><td>

Local Standards

</td></tr>
</table>

1. INTRODUCE

Check Skills You'll Need: Assign these exercises to review the prerequisite skills of adding whole numbers, fractions, and decimals.

New Vocabulary: Help students pre-read the lesson by pointing out the new terms introduced in Objective 1.

Targeted Resources

☐ 📖 Transparency: Check Skills You'll Need 1-4

2. TEACH

▼ **Objective:** Teach Examples 1–3. Assign Check Understanding 1–3 after the appropriate example. Go over the properties and the summary in the Key Concept boxes.

Targeted Resources

☐ 📖 Transparency: Additional Examples 1-4
☐ 📖 Transparency: Classroom Aid 9
☐ Graphing Calculator Procedure 13: at **PHSchool.com**
☐ 🖉 Presentation Pro CD-ROM 1-4
☐ 🖳 iText 1-4: at **PHSchool.com**

3. PRACTICE

Assignment Guide: Give an assignment based on the ability levels of your students.

▼ **Objective:** Core: 1–27, 42–59, 68–69; Extension: 85–92
Standardized Test Prep: 98, 100, 102
Mixed Review: 104–114

Homework: _____

Targeted Resources

☐ 📖 Transparency: Student Answers 1-4
☐ Grab & Go File: Practice 1-4, Reteaching 1-4, Enrichment 1-4
☐ Practice Workbook 1-4
☐ Reading and Math Literacy 1B
☐ Spanish Practice Workbook 1-4
☐ Spanish Reading and Math Literacy 1B
☐ Hands-On Activities 1

4. ASSESS

Lesson Quiz: Create a quiz on Objective 1 using the Computer Test Generator.

Targeted Resources

☐ 🖉 Computer Test Generator CD-ROM 1-4

Lesson Plan 1-4, Objective 2
Adding Real Numbers

Lesson Objective ▼ Apply addition **New Vocabulary:** matrix, element	**NAEP 2005** N3a, g **NCTM 2000** 1, 2, 8, 9, 10 **Pacing** Two Year: 1 day Two-Year Block: 0.5 day	**Local Standards**

1. INTRODUCE

Check Skills You'll Need: Assign these exercises if not used with Objective 1.

Review: Remind students how to add real numbers.

New Vocabulary: Help students pre-read the lesson by pointing out the new terms introduced in Objective 2.

Targeted Resources

☐ ⌨ Transparency: Check Skills You'll Need 1-4

2. TEACH

▼ **Objective:** Teach Examples 4–6. Assign Check Understanding 4–6 after the appropriate example.

Targeted Resources

☐ ⌨ Transparency: Additional Examples 1-4
☐ ⌨ Transparency: Classroom Aid 9
☐ Graphing Calculator Procedure 13:
  at **PHSchool.com**
☐ 💿 Presentation Pro CD-ROM 1-4
☐ 💻 iText 1-4: at **PHSchool.com**

3. PRACTICE

Assignment Guide: Give an assignment based on the ability levels of your students.

▼ **Objective:** Core: 28–41, 60–67, 70–82;
Extension: 83–84, 93–97
Standardized Test Prep: 99, 101, 103
Mixed Review: 104–114

Homework: _____

Targeted Resources

☐ ⌨ Transparency: Student Answers 1-4
☐ Grab & Go File: Practice 1-4, Reteaching 1-4,
  Enrichment 1-4
☐ Practice Workbook 1-4
☐ Reading and Math Literacy 1B
☐ Spanish Practice Workbook 1-4
☐ Spanish Reading and Math Literacy 1B
☐ Hands-On Activities 1
☐ Reasoning and Puzzles 3, 4, 16, 17:
  at **PHSchool.com**

4. ASSESS

Lesson Quiz: Assign the Lesson Quiz to assess students' mastery of the lesson content.

Checkpoint Quiz: Use the Checkpoint Quiz to assess student progress over several lessons.

Targeted Resources

☐ ⌨ Transparency: Lesson Quiz 1-4
☐ 💻 Online Lesson Quiz 1-4: at **PHSchool.com**
☐ Grab & Go File: Checkpoint Quiz 1
☐ 💿 Computer Test Generator CD-ROM 1-4

Lesson Plan 1-5, Objective 1
Subtracting Real Numbers

Lesson Objective ▼ Subtract real numbers	**NAEP 2005** N3a, g **NCTM 2000** 1, 2, 9, 10 **Pacing** Two Year: 1 day Two-Year Block: 0.5 day	Local Standards

1. INTRODUCE

Check Skills You'll Need: Assign these exercises to review the prerequisite skill of adding real numbers.

Targeted Resources
- ☐ 🖳 Transparency: Check Skills You'll Need 1-5

2. TEACH

▼ Objective: Teach Examples 1–3. Assign Check Understanding 1–3 after the appropriate example. Emphasize the rule for subtraction in the Key Concepts box.

Targeted Resources
- ☐ 🖳 Transparency: Additional Examples 1-5
- ☐ 🖉 Presentation Pro CD-ROM 1-5
- ☐ 🖳 iText 1-5: at **PHSchool.com**

3. PRACTICE

Assignment Guide: Give an assignment based on the ability levels of your students.

▼ Objective: Core: 1–20, 52–54, 56–58; Extension: 60–63
Standardized Test Prep: 68
Mixed Review: 72–81

Homework: _____

Targeted Resources
- ☐ 🖳 Transparency: Student Answers 1-5
- ☐ Grab & Go File: Practice 1-5, Reteaching 1-5, Enrichment 1-5
- ☐ Practice Workbook 1-5
- ☐ Spanish Practice Workbook 1-5
- ☐ Hands-On Activities 2

4. ASSESS

Lesson Quiz: Create a quiz on Objective 1 using the Computer Test Generator.

Targeted Resources
- ☐ 🖉 Computer Test Generator CD-ROM 1-5

Lesson Plan 1-5, Objective 2
Subtracting Real Numbers

Lesson Objective	NAEP 2005	Local Standards
▼ Apply subtraction	N3a, g	
	NCTM 2000	
	1, 2, 9, 10	
	Pacing	
	Two Year: 1 day	
	Two-Year Block:	
	0.5 day	

1. INTRODUCE

Check Skills You'll Need: Assign these exercises if not used with Objective 1.

Review: Review subtracting numbers using the Key Concepts box.

Targeted Resources
- ☐ ◰ Transparency: Check Skills You'll Need 1-5

2. TEACH

▼ **Objective:** Teach Examples 4–6. Assign Check Understanding 4–6 after the appropriate example.

Targeted Resources
- ☐ ◰ Transparency: Additional Examples 1-5
- ☐ ◉ Presentation Pro CD-ROM 1-5
- ☐ ▣ iText 1-5: at **PHSchool.com**

3. PRACTICE

Assignment Guide: Give an assignment based on the ability levels of your students.

▼ **Objective:** Core: 21–51, 55, 59; Extension: 64–66
Standardized Test Prep: 67, 69–71
Mixed Review: 72–81

Homework: _____

Targeted Resources
- ☐ ◰ Transparency: Student Answers 1-5
- ☐ Grab & Go File: Practice 1-5, Reteaching 1-5, Enrichment 1-5
- ☐ Practice Workbook 1-5
- ☐ Spanish Practice Workbook 1-5
- ☐ Hands-On Activities 2
- ☐ Reasoning and Puzzles 16, 17: at **PHSchool.com**

4. ASSESS

Lesson Quiz: Assign the Lesson Quiz to assess students' mastery of the lesson content.

Targeted Resources
- ☐ ◰ Transparency: Lesson Quiz 1-5
- ☐ ▣ Online Lesson Quiz 1-5: at **PHSchool.com**
- ☐ ◉ Computer Test Generator CD-ROM 1-5

Teacher _____ Class _____ Date _____ M T W Th F

Lesson Plan 1-6, Objective 1
Multiplying and Dividing Real Numbers

Lesson Objective	NAEP 2005	Local Standards
▼ Multiply real numbers	N3a	
New Vocabulary: Identity Property of Multiplication, Multiplication Property of Zero, Multiplication Property of –1, Inverse Property of Multiplication	**NCTM 2000** 1, 2, 8, 9 **Pacing** Two Year: 1 day Two-Year Block: 0.5 day	

1. INTRODUCE

Check Skills You'll Need: Assign these exercises to review the prerequisite skills of adding integers and finding patterns.

New Vocabulary: Help students pre-read the lesson by pointing out the terms introduced in Objective 1.

Targeted Resources

☐ ▣ Transparency: Check Skills You'll Need 1-6

2. TEACH

▼ Objective: Have students work the Investigation to explore multiplication of integers. Review the properties and the multiplication rules in the Key Concepts boxes. Teach Examples 1–4. Assign Check Understanding 1–4 after the appropriate example.

Targeted Resources

☐ ▣ Transparency: Additional Examples 1-6
☐ ▣ Transparency: Classroom Aid 22
☐ ✐ Presentation Pro CD-ROM 1-6
☐ ▣ iText 1-6: at **PHSchool.com**

3. PRACTICE

Assignment Guide: Give an assignment based on the ability levels of your students.

    ▼ Objective: Core: 1–39, 64–75, 80–87, 89–98;
Extension: 99–104
Standardized Test Prep: 109–110
Mixed Review: 114–127

Homework: _____

Targeted Resources

☐ ▣ Transparency: Student Answers 1-6
☐ Grab & Go File: Practice 1-6, Reteaching 1-6, Enrichment 1-6
☐ Practice Workbook 1-6
☐ Spanish Practice Workbook 1-6
☐ Spanish Reading and Math Literacy 1-6
☐ Technology Activities 15

4. ASSESS

Lesson Quiz: Create a quiz on Objective 1 using the Computer Test Generator.

Targeted Resources

☐ ✐ Computer Test Generator CD-ROM 1-6

Lesson Plan 1-6, Objective 2
Multiplying and Dividing Real Numbers

Lesson Objective ❼ Divide real numbers **New Vocabulary:** multiplicative inverse, reciprocal	**NAEP 2005** N3a **NCTM 2000** 1, 2, 8, 9 **Pacing** Two Year: 1 day Two-Year Block: 0.5 day	**Local Standards**

1. INTRODUCE

Check Skills You'll Need: Assign these exercises if not used with Objective 1.

Review: Remind students how to multiply real numbers.

New Vocabulary: Help students pre-read the lesson by pointing out the terms introduced in Objective 2.

Targeted Resources
- ☐ 📓 Transparency: Check Skills You'll Need 1-6

2. TEACH

❼ Objective: Teach Examples 5–7, pointing out the rules and property in the Key Concepts boxes. Assign Check Understanding 5–7 after the appropriate examples.

Targeted Resources
- ☐ 📓 Transparency: Additional Examples 1-6
- ☐ 📓 Transparency: Classroom Aid 22
- ☐ 🖰 Presentation Pro CD-ROM 1-6
- ☐ 🖳 iText 1-6: at **PHSchool.com**

3. PRACTICE

Assignment Guide: Give an assignment based on the ability levels of your students.

❼ Objective: Core: 40–63, 76–79, 88;
Extension: 105–108
Standardized Test Prep: 111–113
Mixed Review: 114–127

Homework: _____

Targeted Resources
- ☐ 📓 Transparency: Student Answers 1-6
- ☐ Grab & Go File: Practice 1-6, Reteaching 1-6, Enrichment 1-6
- ☐ Practice Workbook 1-6
- ☐ Spanish Practice Workbook 1-6
- ☐ Spanish Reading and Math Literacy 1-6
- ☐ Technology Activities 15
- ☐ Reasoning and Puzzles 18, 19: at **PHSchool.com**

4. ASSESS

Lesson Quiz: Assign the Lesson Quiz to assess students' mastery of the lesson content.

Targeted Resources
- ☐ 📓 Transparency: Lesson Quiz 1-6
- ☐ 🖳 Online Lesson Quiz 1-6: at **PHSchool.com**
- ☐ 🖰 Computer Test Generator CD-ROM 1-6

Lesson Plan 1-7, Objective 1
The Distributive Property

Lesson Objective	NAEP 2005	Local Standards
▼ Use the Distributive Property	A3b	
New Vocabulary: Distributive Property	**NCTM 2000** 1, 2, 9, 10	
	Pacing Two Year: 1 day Two-Year Block: 1 day	

1. INTRODUCE

Check Skills You'll Need: Assign these exercises to review the prerequisite skill of applying order of operations with parentheses.

New Vocabulary: Help students pre-read the lesson by pointing out the new term introduced in Objective 1.

Targeted Resources

☐ ⚏ Transparency: Check Skills You'll Need 1-7

2. TEACH

▼ **Objective:** Review the different forms of the Distributive Property in the Key Concepts box before teaching Examples 1 and 2. Assign Check Understanding 1 and 2 after the appropriate example.

Targeted Resources

☐ ⚏ Transparency: Additional Examples 1-7
☐ ⚏ Transparency: Classroom Aid 16
☐ ❻ Presentation Pro CD-ROM 1-7
☐ 🖥 iText 1-7: at **PHSchool.com**

3. PRACTICE

Assignment Guide: Give an assignment based on the ability levels of your students.

▼ **Objective:** Core: 1–14, 49–54, 85–87
Mixed Review: 105–123

Homework: _____

Targeted Resources

☐ ⚏ Transparency: Student Answers 1-7
☐ Grab & Go File: Practice 1-7, Reteaching 1-7, Enrichment 1-7
☐ Practice Workbook 1-7
☐ Spanish Practice Workbook 1-7
☐ Hands-On Activities 3

4. ASSESS

Lesson Quiz: Create a quiz on Objective 1 using the Computer Test Generator.

Targeted Resources

☐ ❻ Computer Test Generator CD-ROM 1-7

Lesson Plan 1-7, Objective 2
The Distributive Property

Lesson Objective	NAEP 2005	Local Standards
☑ Simplify algebraic expressions **New Vocabulary:** term, constant, coefficient, like terms	A3b **NCTM 2000** 1, 2, 9, 10 **Pacing** Two Year: 2 days Two-Year Block: 1 day	

1. INTRODUCE

Check Skills You'll Need: Assign these exercises if not used with Objective 1.

Review: Review the Distributive Property using the Key Concepts box.

New Vocabulary: Help students pre-read the lesson by pointing out the new terms introduced in Objective 2.

Targeted Resources

☐ ⬛ Transparency: Check Skills You'll Need 1-7

2. TEACH

☑ **Objective:** Teach Examples 3–6. Assign Check Understanding 3–6 after the appropriate example.

Targeted Resources

☐ ⬛ Transparency: Additional Examples 1-7
☐ ⬛ Transparency: Classroom Aid 16
☐ ⬛ Presentation Pro CD-ROM 1-7
☐ ⬛ iText 1-7: at **PHSchool.com**

3. PRACTICE

Assignment Guide: Give an assignment based on the ability levels of your students.

☑ **Objective:** Core: 15–48, 55–84; Extension: 88–96
Standardized Test Prep: 97–104
Mixed Review: 105–123

Homework: _____

Targeted Resources

☐ ⬛ Transparency: Student Answers 1-7
☐ Grab & Go File: Practice 1-7, Reteaching 1-7, Enrichment 1-7
☐ Practice Workbook 1-7
☐ Spanish Practice Workbook 1-7
☐ Hands-On Activities 3
☐ Reasoning and Puzzles 28: at **PHSchool.com**

4. ASSESS

Lesson Quiz: Assign the Lesson Quiz to assess students' mastery of the lesson content.

Targeted Resources

☐ ⬛ Transparency: Lesson Quiz 1-7
☐ ⬛ Online Lesson Quiz 1-7: at **PHSchool.com**
☐ ⬛ Computer Test Generator CD-ROM 1-7

Lesson Plan 1-8, Objective 1
Properties of Real Numbers

Lesson Objective	NAEP 2005	Local Standards
▼ Identify properties	G5a	
	NCTM 2000	
	1, 2, 7, 8, 10	
	Pacing	
	Two Year: 1 day	
	Two-Year Block:	
	0.5 day	

1. INTRODUCE

Check Skills You'll Need: Assign these exercises to review the prerequisite skill of simplifying expressions.

Targeted Resources

☐ 🖳 Transparency: Check Skills You'll Need 1-8

2. TEACH

▼ **Objective:** Review the Properties of Real Numbers in the Key Concepts boxes before teaching Examples 1 and 2. Assign Check Understanding questions 1 and 2 after the appropriate example.

Targeted Resources

☐ 🖳 Transparency: Additional Examples 1-8
☐ Graphing Calculator Procedure 2: at **PHSchool.com**
☐ ✐ Presentation Pro CD-ROM 1-8
☐ 🖳 iText 1-8: at **PHSchool.com**

3. PRACTICE

Assignment Guide: Give an assignment based on the ability levels of your students.

   ▼ **Objective:** Core: 1–16, 31–39
   Standardized Test Prep: 53–58
   Mixed Review: 59–74

Homework: _____

Targeted Resources

☐ 🖳 Transparency: Student Answers 1-8
☐ Grab & Go File: Practice 1-8, Reteaching 1-8, Enrichment 1-8
☐ Practice Workbook 1-8
☐ Reading and Math Literacy 1C
☐ Spanish Practice Workbook 1-8
☐ Spanish Reading and Math Literacy 1C

4. ASSESS

Lesson Quiz: Create a quiz on Objective 1 using the Computer Test Generator.

Targeted Resources

☐ ✐ Computer Test Generator CD-ROM 1-8

Lesson Plan 1-8, Objective 2
Properties of Real Numbers

Lesson Objective	NAEP 2005	Local Standards
▼ Use deductive reasoning	G5a	
New Vocabulary: deductive reasoning	**NCTM 2000** 1, 2, 7, 8, 10	
	Pacing Two Year: 1 day Two-Year Block: 0.5 day	

1. INTRODUCE

Check Skills You'll Need: Assign these exercises if not used with Objective 1.

Review: Review the Properties in the Key Concepts box.

New Vocabulary: Help students pre-read the lesson by pointing out the new term introduced in Objective 2.

Targeted Resources
- ☐ 📧 Transparency: Check Skills You'll Need 1-8

2. TEACH

▼ Objective: Help students to see how the properties justify each step in Example 3. Assign Check Understanding question 3.

Targeted Resources
- ☐ 📧 Transparency: Additional Examples 1-8
- ☐ Graphing Calculator Procedure 2: at **PHSchool.com**
- ☐ 🖋 Presentation Pro CD-ROM 1-8
- ☐ 💻 iText 1-8: at **PHSchool.com**

3. PRACTICE

Assignment Guide: Give an assignment based on the ability levels of your students.

▼ Objective: Core: 17–30, 40–46; Extension: 47–52
Mixed Review: 59–74

Homework: _____

Targeted Resources
- ☐ 📧 Transparency: Student Answers 1-8
- ☐ Grab & Go File: Practice 1-8, Reteaching 1-8, Enrichment 1-8
- ☐ Practice Workbook 1-8
- ☐ Reading and Math Literacy 1C
- ☐ Spanish Practice Workbook 1-8
- ☐ Spanish Reading and Math Literacy 1C
- ☐ Reasoning and Puzzles 28: at **PHSchool.com**

4. ASSESS

Lesson Quiz: Assign the Lesson Quiz to assess students' mastery of the lesson content.

Checkpoint Quiz: Use the Checkpoint Quiz to assess student progress over several lessons.

Targeted Resources
- ☐ 📧 Transparency: Lesson Quiz 1-8
- ☐ 💻 Online Lesson Quiz 1-8: at **PHSchool.com**
- ☐ Grab & Go File: Checkpoint Quiz 2
- ☐ 🖋 Computer Test Generator CD-ROM 1-8

Lesson Plan 1-9, Objective 1
Graphing Data on the Coordinate Plane

Lesson Objective	NAEP 2005	Local Standards
▼ Graph points on the coordinate plane **New Vocabulary:** coordinate plane, *x*-axis, *y*-axis, origin, quadrants, ordered pair, coordinates, *x*-coordinate, *y*-coordinate	A2c; D1a, b, c, d; D2h **NCTM 2000** 2, 5, 10 **Pacing** Two Year: 1 day Two-Year Block: 0.5 day	

1. INTRODUCE

Check Skills You'll Need: Assign these exercises to review the prerequisite skill of graphing numbers on a number line.

New Vocabulary: Help students pre-read the lesson by pointing out the new terms introduced in Objective 1.

Targeted Resources

☐ ⌨ Transparency: Check Skills You'll Need 1-9

2. TEACH

▼ **Objective:** Teach Examples 1–3. Assign Check Understanding 1–3 after the appropriate example.

Targeted Resources

☐ ⌨ Transparency: Additional Examples 1-9
☐ Graphing Calculator Procedure 20: at **PHSchool.com**
☐ ✏ Presentation Pro CD-ROM 1-9
☐ 💻 iText 1-9: at **PHSchool.com**

3. PRACTICE

Assignment Guide: Give an assignment based on the ability levels of your students.

▼ **Objective:** Core: 1–15, 20–28; Extension: 37–38
Standardized Test Prep: 41–44
Mixed Review: 47–57

Homework: _____

Targeted Resources

☐ ⌨ Transparency: Student Answers 1-9
☐ Grab & Go File: Practice 1-9, Reteaching 1-9, Enrichment 1-9
☐ Practice Workbook 1-9
☐ Spanish Practice Workbook 1-9

4. ASSESS

Lesson Quiz: Create a quiz on Objective 1 using the Computer Test Generator.

Targeted Resources

☐ ✏ Computer Test Generator CD-ROM 1-9

Lesson Plan 1-9, Objective 2
Graphing Data on the Coordinate Plane

Lesson Objective	NAEP 2005	Local Standards
☒ Analyze data using scatter plots **New Vocabulary:** scatter plot, positive correlation, negative correlation, no correlation, trend line	A2c; D1a, b, c, d; D2h **NCTM 2000** 2, 5, 10 **Pacing** Two Year: 1 day Two-Year Block: 0.5 day	

1. INTRODUCE

Check Skills You'll Need: Assign these exercises if not used in Objective 1.

Review: Remind students how to graph points on the coordinate plane.

New Vocabulary: Help students pre-read the lesson by pointing out the new terms introduced in Objective 2.

Targeted Resources
- ☐ 🖵 Transparency: Check Skills You'll Need 1-9

2. TEACH

☒ **Objective:** Teach Examples 4 and 5. Assign Check Understanding 4 and 5 after the appropriate example.

Targeted Resources
- ☐ 🖵 Transparency: Additional Examples 1-9
- ☐ Graphing Calculator Procedure 20: at **PHSchool.com**
- ☐ ⊘ Presentation Pro CD-ROM 1-9
- ☐ 🖳 iText 1-9: at **PHSchool.com**

3. PRACTICE

Assignment Guide: Give an assignment based on the ability levels of your students.

☒ **Objective:** Core: 16–19, 29–36; Extension: 39–40
Standardized Test Prep: 45–46
Mixed Review: 45–57

Homework: _____

Targeted Resources
- ☐ 🖵 Transparency: Student Answers 1-9
- ☐ Grab & Go File: Practice 1-9, Reteaching 1-9, Enrichment 1-9
- ☐ Practice Workbook 1-9
- ☐ Spanish Practice Workbook 1-9
- ☐ Reasoning and Puzzles 61, 62: at **PHSchool.com**

4. ASSESS

Lesson Quiz: Assign the Lesson Quiz to assess students' mastery of the lesson content.

Targeted Resources
- ☐ 🖵 Transparency: Lesson Quiz 1-9
- ☐ 🖳 Online Lesson Quiz 1-9: at **PHSchool.com**
- ☐ ⊘ Computer Test Generator CD-ROM 1-9

Teacher _____ Class _____ Date _____ M T W Th F

Lesson Plan 2-1, Objective 1
Solving One-Step Equations

Lesson Objective	NAEP 2005	Local Standards
▼ Solve equations using addition and subtraction	A4a	
New Vocabulary: solution of an equation, equivalent equations, inverse operations	**NCTM 2000** 2, 3, 6, 7, 10	
	Pacing Two Year: 1 day Two-Year Block: 0.5 day	

1. INTRODUCE

Check Skills You'll Need: Assign these exercises to review the prerequisite skills of working with opposites and reciprocals.

New Vocabulary: Help students pre-read the lesson by pointing out the new terms introduced in Objective 1.

Targeted Resources
- ☐ 🖭 Transparency: Check Skills You'll Need 2-1

2. TEACH

▼ **Objective:** Go over the properties in the Key Concepts box. Assign Check Understanding 1–3 after the appropriate example.

Targeted Resources
- ☐ 🖭 Transparency: Additional Examples 2-1
- ☐ 🖭 Transparency: Classroom Aid 9, 10, 16
- ☐ 🖉 Presentation Pro CD-ROM 2-1
- ☐ 🖳 iText 2-1: at **PHSchool.com**

3. PRACTICE

Assignment Guide: Give an assignment based on the ability levels of your students.

▼ **Objective:** Core: 1–20, 55–61, 67–69;
Extension: 81
Standardized Test Prep: 85
Mixed Review: 91–101

Homework: _____

Targeted Resources
- ☐ 🖭 Transparency: Student Answers 2-1
- ☐ Grab & Go File: Practice 2-1, Reteaching 2-1, Enrichment 2-1
- ☐ Practice Workbook 2-1
- ☐ Reading and Math Literacy 2A
- ☐ Spanish Practice Workbook 2-1
- ☐ Spanish Reading and Math Literacy 2A
- ☐ Hands-On Activities 4

4. ASSESS

Lesson Quiz: Create a quiz on Objective 1 using the Computer Test Generator.

Targeted Resources
- ☐ 🖉 Computer Test Generator CD-ROM 2-1

Lesson Plan 2-1, Objective 2
Solving One-Step Equations

Lesson Objective	NAEP 2005	Local Standards
☑ Solve equations using multiplication and division	A4a **NCTM 2000** 2, 3, 6, 7, 10 **Pacing** Two Year: 1 day Two-Year Block: 0.5 day	

1. INTRODUCE

Check Skills You'll Need: Assign these exercises if not used in Objective 1.

Review: Remind students how to solve equations using addition and subtraction.

Targeted Resources

☐ 📖 Transparency: Check Skills You'll Need 2-1

2. TEACH

☑ **Objective:** Go over the properties in the Key Concepts box. Assign Check Understanding questions 4–6 after the appropriate example.

Targeted Resources

☐ 📖 Transparency: Additional Examples 2-1
☐ 📖 Transparency: Classroom Aid 9, 10, 16
☐ 💿 Presentation Pro CD-ROM 2-1
☐ 🖥 iText 2-1: at **PHSchool.com**

3. PRACTICE

Assignment Guide: Give an assignment based on the ability levels of your students.

☑ **Objective:** Core: 21–54, 62–66, 70–80; Extension: 82–84
Standardized Test Prep: 86–90
Mixed Review: 91–101

Homework: _____

Targeted Resources

☐ 📖 Transparency: Student Answers 2-1
☐ Grab & Go File: Practice 2-1, Reteaching 2-1, Enrichment 2-1
☐ Practice Workbook 2-1
☐ Reading and Math Literacy 2A
☐ Spanish Practice Workbook 2-1
☐ Spanish Reading and Math Literacy 2A
☐ Hands-On Activities 4
☐ Reasoning and Puzzles 38-42: at **PHSchool.com**

4. ASSESS

Lesson Quiz: Assign the Lesson Quiz to assess students' mastery of the lesson content.

Targeted Resources

☐ 📖 Transparency: Lesson Quiz 2-1
☐ 🖥 Online Lesson Quiz 2-1: at **PHSchool.com**
☐ 💿 Computer Test Generator CD-ROM 2-1

Lesson Plan 2-2, Objective 1
Solving Two-Step Equations

Lesson Objective	NAEP 2005	Local Standards
▼ Solve two-step equations	A4a, c; G5a	
	NCTM 2000 2, 7, 8, 10	
	Pacing Two Year: 2 days Two-Year Block: 0.5 day	

1. INTRODUCE

Check Skills You'll Need: Assign these exercises to review the prerequisite skill of solving one-step equations.

Targeted Resources

☐ ⛏ Transparency: Check Skills You'll Need 2-2

2. TEACH

▼ **Objective:** Help students see how the tile models go with the algebraic statements beside them. Then go over the algebraic summary in the Key Concepts box. Teach Examples 1–3. Assign Check Understanding 1–3 after the appropriate example.

Targeted Resources

☐ ⛏ Transparency: Additional Examples 2-2
☐ ⛏ Transparency: Classroom Aid 3, 9, 10, 16
☐ ⊘ Presentation Pro CD-ROM 2-2
☐ ▦ iText 2-2: at **PHSchool.com**

3. PRACTICE

Assignment Guide: Give an assignment based on the ability levels of your students.

▼ **Objective:** Core: 1–35, 40–51, 56–69, 74; Extension: 75–77
Standardized Test Prep: 81–83
Mixed Review: 86–97

Homework: _____

Targeted Resources

☐ ⛏ Transparency: Student Answers 2-2
☐ Grab & Go File: Practice 2-2, Reteaching 2-2 Enrichment 2-2
☐ Practice Workbook 2-2
☐ Spanish Practice Workbook 2-2

4. ASSESS

Lesson Quiz: Create a quiz on Objective 1 using the Computer Test Generator.

Targeted Resources

☐ ⊘ Computer Test Generator CD-ROM 2-2

Lesson Plan 2-2, Objective 2
Solving Two-Step Equations

Lesson Objective	NAEP 2005	Local Standards
▼ Use deductive reasoning	A4a, c; G5a	
	NCTM 2000	
	2, 7, 8, 10	
	Pacing	
	Two Year: 1 day	
	Two-Year Block:	
	0.5 day	

1. INTRODUCE

Check Skills You'll Need: Assign these exercises if not used with Objective 1.

Review: Use the Key Concepts box to review solving two-step equations.

Targeted Resources

☐ 📠 Transparency: Check Skills You'll Need 2-2

2. TEACH

▼ **Objective:** Teach Examples 4 and 5. Assign Check Understanding 4 and 5 after the appropriate example.

Targeted Resources

☐ 📠 Transparency: Additional Examples 2-2
☐ 📠 Transparency: Classroom Aid 3, 9, 10, 16
☐ 💿 Presentation Pro CD-ROM 2-2
☐ 💻 iText 2-2: at **PHSchool.com**

3. PRACTICE

Assignment Guide: Give an assignment based on the ability levels of your students.

   ▼ **Objective:** Core: 36–39, 52–55, 70–73;
Extension: 78–80
Standardized Test Prep: 84–85
Mixed Review: 86–97

Homework: _____

Targeted Resources

☐ 📠 Transparency: Student Answers 2-2
☐ Grab & Go File: Practice 2-2, Reteaching 2-2 Enrichment 2-2
☐ Practice Workbook 2-2
☐ Spanish Practice Workbook 2-2
☐ Reasoning and Puzzles 43: at **PHSchool.com**

4. ASSESS

Lesson Quiz: Assign the Lesson Quiz to assess students' mastery of the lesson content.

Targeted Resources

☐ 📠 Transparency: Lesson Quiz 2-2
☐ 💻 Online Lesson Quiz 2-2: at **PHSchool.com**
☐ 💿 Computer Test Generator CD-ROM 2-2

Lesson Plan 2-3, Objective 1
Solving Multi-Step Equations

Lesson Objective	NAEP 2005	Local Standards
▼ Use the Distributive Property when combining like terms	A3a; A4a, c	
	NCTM 2000	
	2, 7, 9, 10	
	Pacing	
	Two Year: 1 day	
	Two-Year Block: 1 day	

1. INTRODUCE

Check Skills You'll Need: Assign these exercises to review the prerequisite skill of solving two-step equations.

Targeted Resources

☐ 🖳 Transparency: Check Skills You'll Need 2-3

2. TEACH

▼ **Objective:** Teach Examples 1 and 2. Assign Check Understanding questions 1 and 2 after the appropriate example.

Targeted Resources

☐ 🖳 Transparency: Additional Examples 2-3
☐ 🖳 Transparency: Classroom Aid 16
☐ 🖉 Presentation Pro CD-ROM 2-3
☐ 🖳 iText 2-3: at **PHSchool.com**

3. PRACTICE

Assignment Guide: Give an assignment based on the ability levels of your students.

▼ **Objective:** Core: 1–11, 52, 54–56, 59–62
Standardized Test Prep: 68–69
Mixed Review: 74–95

Homework: _____

Targeted Resources

☐ 🖳 Transparency: Student Answers 2-3
☐ Grab & Go File: Practice 2-3, Reteaching 2-3, Enrichment 2-3
☐ Practice Workbook 2-3
☐ Spanish Practice Workbook 2-3
☐ Reading and Math Literacy 2B
☐ Spanish Reading and Math Literacy 2B

4. ASSESS

Lesson Quiz: Create a quiz on Objective 1 using the Computer Test Generator.

Targeted Resources

☐ 🖉 Computer Test Generator CD-ROM 2-3

Lesson Plan 2-3, Objective 2
Solving Multi-Step Equations

Lesson Objective	NAEP 2005	Local Standards
▼ Use the Distributive Property when solving equations	A3a; A4a, c **NCTM 2000** 2, 7, 9, 10 **Pacing** Two Year: 1 day Two-Year Block: 1 day	

1. INTRODUCE

Check Skills You'll Need: Assign these exercises if not used with Objective 1.

Review: Remind students how to use the Distributive Property to combine like terms.

Targeted Resources

☐ ✎ Transparency: Check Skills You'll Need 2-3

2. TEACH

▼ **Objective:** Teach Examples 3–5. Assign Check Understanding questions 3–5 after the appropriate example.

Targeted Resources

☐ ✎ Transparency: Additional Examples 2-3
☐ ✎ Transparency: Classroom Aid 16
☐ ⊘ Presentation Pro CD-ROM 2-3
☐ ▨ iText 2-3: at **PHSchool.com**

3. PRACTICE

Assignment Guide: Give an assignment based on the ability levels of your students.

▼ **Objective:** Core: 12–51, 53, 57–58;
Extension: 63–67
Standardized Test Prep: 70–73
Mixed Review: 74–95

Homework: _____

Targeted Resources

☐ ✎ Transparency: Student Answers 2-3
☐ Grab & Go File: Practice 2-3, Reteaching 2-3, Enrichment 2-3
☐ Practice Workbook 2-3
☐ Spanish Practice Workbook 2-3
☐ Reading and Math Literacy 2B
☐ Spanish Reading and Math Literacy 2B

4. ASSESS

Lesson Quiz: Assign the Lesson Quiz to assess students' mastery of the lesson content.

Checkpoint Quiz: Use the Checkpoint Quiz to assess student progress over several lessons.

Targeted Resources

☐ ✎ Transparency: Lesson Quiz 2-3
☐ ▨ Online Lesson Quiz 2-3: at **PHSchool.com**
☐ Grab & Go File: Checkpoint Quiz 1
☐ ⊘ Computer Test Generator CD-ROM 2-3

Teacher _____ Class _____ Date _____ M T W Th F

Lesson Plan 2-4, Objective 1
Equations with Variables on Both Sides

Lesson Objective	NAEP 2005	Local Standards
▼ Solve equations with variables on both sides	A2e; A4a, c	
	NCTM 2000 2, 3, 6, 7, 8	
	Pacing Two Year: 2 days Two-Year Block: 1 day	

1. INTRODUCE

Check Skills You'll Need: Assign these exercises to review the prerequisite skills of combining like terms and solving equations with variables on one side.

Targeted Resources
☐ ⬆ Transparency: Check Skills You'll Need 2-4

2. TEACH

▼ **Objective:** Have students work the Investigation to explore how a table can be used to find or approximate the solution to an equation. Teach Examples 1 and 2. Assign Check Understanding questions 1 and 2 after the appropriate example.

Targeted Resources
☐ ⬆ Transparency: Additional Examples 2-4
☐ Graphing Calculator Procedures 7, 9 at **PHSchool.com**
☐ ✏ Presentation Pro CD-ROM 2-4
☐ ▣ iText 2-4: at **PHSchool.com**

3. PRACTICE

Assignment Guide: Give an assignment based on the ability levels of your students.

▼ **Objective:** Core: 1–20, 38–46; Extension: 55–56
Standardized Test Prep: 57–60, 62
Mixed Review: 64–76

Homework: _____

Targeted Resources
☐ ⬆ Transparency: Student Answers 2-4
☐ Grab & Go File: Practice 2-4, Reteaching 2-4, Enrichment 2-4
☐ Practice Workbook 2-4
☐ Spanish Practice Workbook 2-4
☐ Technology Activities 16
☐ Hands-On Activities 5

4. ASSESS

Lesson Quiz: Create a quiz on Objective 1 using the Computer Test Generator.

Targeted Resources
☐ ✏ Computer Test Generator CD-ROM 2-4

Teacher _____ Class _____ Date _____ M T W Th F

Lesson Plan 2-4, Objective 2
Equations with Variables on Both Sides

Lesson Objective	NAEP 2005	Local Standards
☑ Identify equations that are identities or have no solution	A2e; A4a, c	
New Vocabulary: identity	**NCTM 2000** 2, 3, 6, 7, 8	
	Pacing Two Year: 1 day Two-Year Block: 1 day	

1. INTRODUCE

Check Skills You'll Need: Assign these exercises if not used with Objective 1.

Review: Remind students how to solve equations with variables on both sides.

New Vocabulary: Help students pre-read the lesson by pointing out the new term introduced in Objective 2.

Targeted Resources

☐ 🖭 Transparency: Check Skills You'll Need 2-4

2. TEACH

☑ Objective: Teach Example 3. Then assign Check Understanding question 3.

Targeted Resources

☐ 🖭 Transparency: Additional Examples 2-4
☐ Graphing Calculator Procedures 7, 9 at **PHSchool.com**
☐ 🖉 Presentation Pro CD-ROM 2-4
☐ 🖳 iText 2-4: at **PHSchool.com**

3. PRACTICE

Assignment Guide: Give an assignment based on the ability levels of your students.

   ☑ Objective: Core: 21–37, 47–48; Extension: 49–54
   Standardized Test Prep: 61, 63
   Mixed Review: 64–76

Homework: _____

Targeted Resources

☐ 🖭 Transparency: Student Answers 2-4
☐ Grab & Go File: Practice 2-4, Reteaching 2-4, Enrichment 2-4
☐ Practice Workbook 2-4
☐ Spanish Practice Workbook 2-4
☐ Technology Activities 16
☐ Hands-On Activities 5

4. ASSESS

Lesson Quiz: Assign the Lesson Quiz to assess students' mastery of the lesson content.

Targeted Resources

☐ 🖭 Transparency: Lesson Quiz 2-4
☐ 🖳 Online Lesson Quiz 2-4: at **PHSchool.com**
☐ 🖉 Computer Test Generator CD-ROM 2-4

Algebra 1A and 1B Lesson Plans

Lesson Plan 2-5, Objective 1
Equations and Problem Solving

Lesson Objective	NAEP 2005	Local Standards
▼ Define a variable in terms of another variable **New Vocabulary:** consecutive integers	A4c, f; M1ℓ **NCTM 2000** 2, 3, 4, 6, 9, 10 **Pacing** Two Year: 1 day Two-Year Block: 0.5 day	

1. INTRODUCE

Check Skills You'll Need: Assign these exercises to review the prerequisite skill of writing variable expressions.

New Vocabulary: Help students pre-read the lesson by pointing out the new term introduced in Objective 1.

Targeted Resources
- ☐ Transparency: Check Skills You'll Need 2-5

2. TEACH

▼ **Objective:** Teach Examples 1 and 2. Assign Check Understanding questions 1 and 2 after the appropriate example.

Targeted Resources
- ☐ Transparency: Additional Examples 2-5
- ☐ Presentation Pro CD-ROM 2-5
- ☐ iText 2-5: at **PHSchool.com**

3. PRACTICE

Assignment Guide: Give an assignment based on the ability levels of your students.

▼ **Objective:** Core: 1–9, 16–20, 25, 28–31;
Extension: 32, 34
Standardized Test Prep: 35–37, 39
Mixed Review: 40–50

Homework: _____

Targeted Resources
- ☐ Transparency: Student Answers 2-5
- ☐ Grab & Go File: Practice 2-5, Reteaching 2-5, Enrichment 2-5
- ☐ Practice Workbook 2-5
- ☐ Spanish Practice Workbook 2-5

4. ASSESS

Lesson Quiz: Create a quiz on Objective 1 using the Computer Test Generator.

Targeted Resources
- ☐ Computer Test Generator CD-ROM 2-5

Lesson Plan 2-5, Objective 2
Equations and Problem Solving

Lesson Objective	NAEP 2005	Local Standards
✔ Model distance-rate-time problems	A4c, f; M1ℓ	
New Vocabulary: uniform motion	**NCTM 2000**	
	2, 3, 4, 6, 9, 10	
	Pacing	
	Two Year: 1 day	
	Two-Year Block:	
	0.5 day	

1. INTRODUCE

Check Skills You'll Need: Assign these exercises if not used with Objective 1.

Review: Remind students how to define one variable in terms of another.

New Vocabulary: Help students pre-read the lesson by pointing out the new term introduced in Objective 2.

Targeted Resources
- ☐ ⛭ Transparency: Check Skills You'll Need 2-5

2. TEACH

✔ **Objective:** Teach Examples 3–5. Assign Check Understanding questions 3–5 after the appropriate example.

Targeted Resources
- ☐ ⛭ Transparency: Additional Examples 2-5
- ☐ ✐ Presentation Pro CD-ROM 2-5
- ☐ ▣ iText 2-5: at **PHSchool.com**

3. PRACTICE

Assignment Guide: Give an assignment based on the ability levels of your students.

✔ **Objective:** Core: 10–15, 21–24, 26–27; Extension: 33
Standardized Test Prep: 38
Mixed Review: 40–50

Homework: _____

Targeted Resources
- ☐ ⛭ Transparency: Student Answers 2-5
- ☐ Grab & Go File: Practice 2-5, Reteaching 2-5, Enrichment 2-5
- ☐ Practice Workbook 2-5
- ☐ Spanish Practice Workbook 2-5
- ☐ Reasoning and Puzzles 38, 39, 46: at **PHSchool.com**

4. ASSESS

Lesson Quiz: Assign the Lesson Quiz to assess students' mastery of the lesson content.

Targeted Resources
- ☐ ⛭ Transparency: Lesson Quiz 2-5
- ☐ ▣ Online Lesson Quiz 2-5: at **PHSchool.com**
- ☐ ✐ Computer Test Generator CD-ROM 2-5

Lesson Plan 2-6, Objective 1
Formulas

Lesson Objective	NAEP 2005	Local Standards
▼ Transform literal equations **New Vocabulary:** literal equation	A4f **NCTM 2000** 2, 3, 4, 10 **Pacing** Two Year: 2 days Two-Year Block: 1 day	

1. INTRODUCE

Check Skills You'll Need: Assign these exercises to review the prerequisite skill of evaluating formulas.

New Vocabulary: Help students pre-read the lesson by pointing out the new term introduced in the lesson.

Targeted Resources

☐ ⌂ Transparency: Check Skills You'll Need 2-6

2. TEACH

▼ **Objective:** Have students work the Investigation to see the value of being able to transform a formula. Teach Examples 1–4. Assign Check Understanding questions 1–4 after the appropriate examples.

Targeted Resources

☐ ⌂ Transparency: Additional Examples 2-6
☐ ⊘ Presentation Pro CD-ROM 2-6
☐ ▣ iText 2-6: at **PHSchool.com**

3. PRACTICE

Assignment Guide: Give an assignment based on the ability levels of your students.

▼ **Objective:** Core: 1–43; Extension: 44–46
Standardized Test Prep: 47–50
Mixed Review: 51–55

Homework: _____

Targeted Resources

☐ ⌂ Transparency: Student Answers 2-6
☐ Grab & Go File: Practice 2-6, Reteaching 2-6, Enrichment 2-6
☐ Practice Workbook 2-6
☐ Spanish Practice Workbook 2-6
☐ Reading and Math Literacy 2C
☐ Spanish Reading and Math Literacy 2C
☐ Hands-On Activities 6

4. ASSESS

Lesson Quiz: Assign the Lesson Quiz to assess students' mastery of the lesson content.

Checkpoint Quiz: Use the Checkpoint Quiz to assess student progress over several lessons.

Targeted Resources

☐ ⌂ Transparency: Lesson Quiz 2-6
☐ ▣ Online Lesson Quiz 2-6: at **PHSchool.com**
☐ Grab & Go File: Checkpoint Quiz 2
☐ ⊘ Computer Test Generator CD-ROM 2-6

Lesson Plan 2-7, Objective 1
Using Measures of Central Tendency

Lesson Objective	NAEP 2005	Local Standards
▼ Find mean, median, and mode **New Vocabulary:** Measures of central tendency, mean, outlier, median, mode, range	D1b; D2a **NCTM 2000** 1, 2, 5, 9, 10 **Pacing** Two Year: 1 day Two-Year Block: 0.5 day	

1. INTRODUCE

Check Skills You'll Need: Assign these exercises to review the prerequisite skill of ordering rational numbers.

New Vocabulary: Help students pre-read the lesson by pointing out the new terms introduced in Objective 1.

Targeted Resources

☐ ✎ Transparency: Check Skills You'll Need 2-7

2. TEACH

▼ **Objective:** Review the summary in the Key Concepts box. Teach Examples 1–3. Assign Check Understanding 1–3 after the appropriate examples.

Targeted Resources

☐ ✎ Transparency: Additional Examples 2-7
☐ Graphing Calculator Procedure 21 at **PHSchool.com**
☐ ⊘ Presentation Pro CD-ROM 2-7
☐ ▣ iText 2-7: at **PHSchool.com**

3. PRACTICE

Assignment Guide: Give an assignment based on the ability levels of your students.

▼ **Objective:** Core: 1–13, 20–23, 25–28;
Extension: 30–31
Standardized Test Prep: 32–36
Mixed Review: 37–44

Homework: _____

Targeted Resources

☐ ✎ Transparency: Student Answers 2-7
☐ Grab & Go File: Practice 2-7, Reteaching 2-7, Enrichment 2-7
☐ Practice Workbook 2-7
☐ Spanish Practice Workbook 2-7

4. ASSESS

Lesson Quiz: Create a quiz on Objective 1 using the Computer Test Generator.

Targeted Resources

☐ ⊘ Computer Test Generator CD-ROM 2-7

Lesson Plan 2-7, Objective 2
Using Measures of Central Tendency

Lesson Objective	NAEP 2005	Local Standards
❷ Make and use stem-and-leaf plots **New Vocabulary:** stem-and-leaf plot	D1b; D2a **NCTM 2000** 1, 2, 5, 9, 10 **Pacing** Two Year: 1 day Two-Year Block: 0.5 day	

1. INTRODUCE

Check Skills You'll Need: Assign these exercises if not used with Objective 1.

Review: Use the Key Concepts box to review mean, median, and mode.

New Vocabulary: Help students pre-read the lesson by pointing out the new term introduced in Objective 2.

Targeted Resources

☐ 💻 Transparency: Check Skills You'll Need 2-7

2. TEACH

❷ Objective: Teach Examples 4 and 5. Assign Check Understanding 4 and 5 after the appropriate example.

Targeted Resources

☐ 💻 Transparency: Additional Examples 2-7
☐ Graphing Calculator Procedure 21 at **PHSchool.com**
☐ 💿 Presentation Pro CD-ROM 2-7
☐ 💻 iText 2-7: at **PHSchool.com**

3. PRACTICE

Assignment Guide: Give an assignment based on the ability levels of your students.

❷ Objective: Core: 14–19, 24; Extension: 29
Mixed Review: 37–44

Homework: _____

Targeted Resources

☐ 💻 Transparency: Student Answers 2-7
☐ Grab & Go File: Practice 2-7, Reteaching 2-7, Enrichment 2-7
☐ Practice Workbook 2-7
☐ Spanish Practice Workbook 2-7

4. ASSESS

Lesson Quiz: Assign the Lesson Quiz to assess students' mastery of the lesson content.

Targeted Resources

☐ 💻 Transparency: Lesson Quiz 2-7
☐ 💻 Online Lesson Quiz 2-7: at **PHSchool.com**
☐ 💿 Computer Test Generator CD-ROM 2-7

Lesson Plan 3-1, Objective 1
Inequalities and their Graphs

Lesson Objective	NAEP 2005	Local Standards
▼ Identify solutions of inequalities	A3a; A4a	
New Vocabulary: solution of an inequality	**NCTM 2000** 1, 2, 9, 10	
	Pacing Two Year: 1 day Two-Year Block: 0.5 day	

1. INTRODUCE

Check Skills You'll Need: Assign these exercises to review the prerequisite skills of graphing on a number line and using inequality symbols.

New Vocabulary: Help students pre-read the lesson by pointing out the new term introduced in Objective 1.

Targeted Resources

☐ ⌁ Transparency: Check Skills You'll Need 3-1

2. TEACH

▼ **Objective:** Teach Examples 1 and 2. Assign Check Understanding 1 and 2 after the appropriate example.

Targeted Resources

☐ ⌁ Transparency: Additional Examples 3-1
☐ ⌁ Transparency: Classroom Aid 8
☐ Graphing Calculator Procedure 8 at **PHSchool.com**
☐ ⊘ Presentation Pro CD-ROM 3-1
☐ ▣ iText 3-1: at **PHSchool.com**

3. PRACTICE

Assignment Guide: Give an assignment based on the ability levels of your students.

▼ **Objective:** Core: 1–14, 51, 67; Extension: 69–70 Extension: 68, 71–73
Standardized Test Prep: 74–75, 77
Mixed Review: 80–92

Homework: _____

Targeted Resources

☐ ⌁ Transparency: Student Answers 3-1
☐ Grab & Go File: Practice 3-1, Reteaching 3-1, Enrichment 3-1
☐ Practice Workbook 3-1
☐ Spanish Practice Workbook 3-1
☐ Reading and Math Literacy 3A
☐ Spanish Reading and Math Literacy 3A
☐ Hands-On Activities 7

4. ASSESS

Lesson Quiz: Create a quiz on Objective 1 using the Computer Test Generator.

Targeted Resources

☐ ⊘ Computer Test Generator CD-ROM 3-1

Teacher _____ Class _____ Date _____ M T W Th F

Lesson Plan 3-1, Objective 2
Inequalities and their Graphs

Lesson Objective	NAEP 2005	Local Standards
✔ Graph and write inequalities	A3a; A4a	
	NCTM 2000	
	1, 2, 9, 10	
	Pacing	
	Two Year: 1 day	
	Two-Year Block:	
	0.5 day	

1. INTRODUCE

Check Skills You'll Need: Assign these exercises if not used with Objective 1.

Review: Remind students how to identify the solutions of an inequality.

Targeted Resources

☐ ▱ Transparency: Check Skills You'll Need 3-1

2. TEACH

✔ **Objective:** Teach Examples 3–5. Assign Check Understanding 3–5 after the appropriate example.

Targeted Resources

☐ ▱ Transparency: Additional Examples 3-1
☐ ▱ Transparency: Classroom Aid 8
☐ Graphing Calculator Procedure 8 at **PHSchool.com**
☐ ✆ Presentation Pro CD-ROM 3-1
☐ ▨ iText 3-1: at **PHSchool.com**

3. PRACTICE

Assignment Guide: Give an assignment based on the ability levels of your students.

✔ **Objective:** Core: 15–50, 52–66;
Extension: 68, 71–73
Standardized Test Prep: 76, 78–79
Mixed Review: 80–92

Homework: _____

Targeted Resources

☐ ▱ Transparency: Student Answers 3-1
☐ Grab & Go File: Practice 3-1, Reteaching 3-1, Enrichment 3-1
☐ Practice Workbook 3-1
☐ Spanish Practice Workbook 3-1
☐ Reading and Math Literacy 3A
☐ Spanish Reading and Math Literacy 3A
☐ Hands-On Activities 7
☐ Reasoning and Puzzles 5: at **PHSchool.com**

4. ASSESS

Lesson Quiz: Assign the Lesson Quiz to assess students' mastery of the lesson content.

Targeted Resources

☐ ▱ Transparency: Lesson Quiz 3-1
☐ ▨ Online Lesson Quiz 3-1: at **PHSchool.com**
☐ ✆ Computer Test Generator CD-ROM 3-1

Lesson Plan 3-2, Objective 1
Solving Inequalities Using Addition and Subtraction

Lesson Objective	NAEP 2005	Local Standards
▼ Use addition to solve inequalities **New Vocabulary:** equivalent inequalities	A4a, c **NCTM 2000** 1, 2, 9, 10 **Pacing** Two Year: 1 day Two-Year Block: 0.5 day	

1. INTRODUCE

Check Skills You'll Need: Assign these exercises to review the prerequisite skills of using inequality symbols and solving equations by addition and subtraction.

New Vocabulary: Help students pre-read the lesson by pointing out the new term introduced in Objective 1.

Targeted Resources
- ☐ 🖳 Transparency: Check Skills You'll Need 3-2

2. TEACH

▼ **Objective:** Teach Examples 1 and 2. Assign Check Understanding 1 and 2 after the appropriate example.

Targeted Resources
- ☐ 🖳 Transparency: Additional Examples 3-2
- ☐ 🖉 Presentation Pro CD-ROM 3-2
- ☐ 🖳 iText 3-2: at **PHSchool.com**

3. PRACTICE

Assignment Guide: Give an assignment based on the ability levels of your students.

   ▼ **Objective:** Core: 1–19, 42–54, 75–80;
Extension: 88–89
Standardized Test Prep: 94, 96
Mixed Review: 99–120

Homework: _____

Targeted Resources
- ☐ 🖳 Transparency: Student Answers 3-2
- ☐ Grab & Go File: Practice 3-2, Reteaching 3-2, Enrichment 3-2
- ☐ Practice Workbook 3-2
- ☐ Spanish Practice Workbook 3-2

4. ASSESS

Lesson Quiz: Create a quiz on Objective 1 using the Computer Test Generator.

Targeted Resources
- ☐ 🖉 Computer Test Generator CD-ROM 3-2

Lesson Plan 3-2, Objective 2
Solving Inequalities Using Addition and Subtraction

Lesson Objective	NAEP 2005	Local Standards
❷ Use subtraction to solve inequalities	A4a, c	
	NCTM 2000 1, 2, 9, 10	
	Pacing Two Year: 1 day Two-Year Block: 0.5 day	

1. INTRODUCE

Check Skills You'll Need: Assign these exercises if not used with Objective 1.

Review: Use the Key Concepts box to review the Addition Property of Inequality.

Targeted Resources
- ☐ ⌨ Transparency: Check Skills You'll Need 3-2

2. TEACH

❷ Objective: Teach Examples 3 and 4. Assign Check Understanding 3 and 4 after the appropriate example.

Targeted Resources
- ☐ ⌨ Transparency: Additional Examples 3-2
- ☐ ✐ Presentation Pro CD-ROM 3-2
- ☐ 💻 iText 3-2: at **PHSchool.com**

3. PRACTICE

Assignment Guide: Give an assignment based on the ability levels of your students.

   ❷ Objective: Core: 20–41, 55–74, 81–87;
Extension: 90–92
Standardized Test Prep: 93, 95, 97–98
Mixed Review: 99–120

Homework: _____

Targeted Resources
- ☐ ⌨ Transparency: Student Answers 3-2
- ☐ Grab & Go File: Practice 3-2, Reteaching 3-2, Enrichment 3-2
- ☐ Practice Workbook 3-2
- ☐ Spanish Practice Workbook 3-2
- ☐ Reasoning and Puzzles 55, 56: at **PHSchool.com**

4. ASSESS

Lesson Quiz: Assign the Lesson Quiz to assess students' mastery of the lesson content.

Targeted Resources
- ☐ ⌨ Transparency: Lesson Quiz 3-2
- ☐ 💻 Online Lesson Quiz 3-2: at **PHSchool.com**
- ☐ ✐ Computer Test Generator CD-ROM 3-2

Lesson Plan 3-3, Objective 1
Solving Inequalities Using Multiplication and Division

Lesson Objective	NAEP 2005	Local Standards
▼ Use multiplication to solve inequalities	A4a, c **NCTM 2000** 1, 2, 9, 10 **Pacing** Two Year: 1 day Two-Year Block: 0.5 day	

1. INTRODUCE

Check Skills You'll Need: Assign these exercises to review the prerequisite skills of solving equations by multiplication and division, and writing inequalities for graphs on a number line.

Targeted Resources

☐ 📺 Transparency: Check Skills You'll Need 3-3

2. TEACH

▼ **Objective:** Have students work the Investigation. Go over the summary in the Key Concepts box. Teach Examples 1 and 2. Assign Check Understanding 1 and 2 after the appropriate example.

Targeted Resources

☐ 📺 Transparency: Additional Examples 3-3
☐ 🖉 Presentation Pro CD-ROM 3-3
☐ 🖳 iText 3-3: at **PHSchool.com**

3. PRACTICE

Assignment Guide: Give an assignment based on the ability levels of your students.

▼ **Objective:** Core: 1–16, 31–36, 39–42, 54–55, 67–75; Extension: 78–80
Standardized Test Prep: 84–85
Mixed Review: 90–106

Homework: _____

Targeted Resources

☐ 📺 Transparency: Student Answers 3-3
☐ Grab & Go File: Practice 3-3, Reteaching 3-3, Enrichment 3-3
☐ Practice Workbook 3-3
☐ Spanish Practice Workbook 3-3
☐ Reading and Math Literacy 3B
☐ Spanish Reading and Math Literacy 3B

4. ASSESS

Lesson Quiz: Create a quiz on Objective 1 using the Computer Test Generator.

Targeted Resources

☐ 🖉 Computer Test Generator CD-ROM 3-3

Lesson Plan 3-3, Objective 2
Solving Inequalities Using Multiplication and Division

Lesson Objective	NAEP 2005	Local Standards
✔ Use division to solve inequalities	A4a, c	
	NCTM 2000 1, 2, 9, 10	
	Pacing Two Year: 1 day Two-Year Block: 0.5 day	

1. INTRODUCE

Check Skills You'll Need: Assign these exercises if not used with Objective 1.

Review: Remind students how to solve inequalities using multiplication.

Targeted Resources
- ☐ Transparency: Check Skills You'll Need 3-3

2. TEACH

✔ **Objective:** Review the summary in the Key Concepts box. Teach Examples 3 and 4. Assign Check Understanding 3 and 4 after the appropriate example.

Targeted Resources
- ☐ Transparency: Additional Examples 3-3
- ☐ Presentation Pro CD-ROM 3-3
- ☐ iText 3-3: at **PHSchool.com**

3. PRACTICE

Assignment Guide: Give an assignment based on the ability levels of your students.

✔ **Objective:** Core: 17–30, 37–38, 43–53, 56–66, 76–77; Extension: 81–83
Standardized Test Prep: 86–89
Mixed Review: 90–106

Homework: _____

Targeted Resources
- ☐ Transparency: Student Answers 3-3
- ☐ Grab & Go File: Practice 3-3, Reteaching 3-3, Enrichment 3-3
- ☐ Practice Workbook 3-3
- ☐ Spanish Practice Workbook 3-3
- ☐ Reading and Math Literacy 3B
- ☐ Spanish Reading and Math Literacy 3B
- ☐ Reasoning and Puzzles 58: at **PHSchool.com**

4. ASSESS

Lesson Quiz: Assign the Lesson Quiz to assess students' mastery of the lesson content.

Checkpoint Quiz: Use the Checkpoint Quiz to assess student progress over several lessons.

Targeted Resources
- ☐ Transparency: Lesson Quiz 3-3
- ☐ Online Lesson Quiz 3-3: at **PHSchool.com**
- ☐ Grab & Go File: Checkpoint Quiz 1
- ☐ Computer Test Generator CD-ROM 3-3

Lesson Plan 3-4, Objective 1
Solving Multi-Step Inequalities

Lesson Objective	NAEP 2005	Local Standards
▼ Solve multi-step inequalities with variables on one side	A4a, c	
	NCTM 2000 1, 2, 6, 10	
	Pacing Two Year: 1 day Two-Year Block: 0.5 day	

1. INTRODUCE

Check Skills You'll Need: Assign these exercises to review the prerequisite skill of solving equations with variables on one or both sides.

Targeted Resources
- ☐ 🖳 Transparency: Check Skills You'll Need 3-4

2. TEACH

▼ **Objective:** Teach Examples 1–3. Assign Check Understanding questions 1–3 after the appropriate example.

Targeted Resources
- ☐ 🖳 Transparency: Additional Examples 3-4
- ☐ 🖉 Presentation Pro CD-ROM 3-4
- ☐ 🖳 iText 3-4: at **PHSchool.com**

3. PRACTICE

Assignment Guide: Give an assignment based on the ability levels of your students.

▼ **Objective:** Core: 1–12, 47–49, 52–59, 77–78; Extension: 81–83
Standardized Test Prep: 87
Mixed Review: 92–104

Homework: _____

Targeted Resources
- ☐ 🖳 Transparency: Student Answers 3-4
- ☐ Grab & Go File: Practice 3-4, Reteaching 3-4, Enrichment 3-4
- ☐ Practice Workbook 3-4
- ☐ Spanish Practice Workbook 3-4

4. ASSESS

Lesson Quiz: Create a quiz on Objective 1 using the Computer Test Generator.

Targeted Resources
- ☐ 🖉 Computer Test Generator CD-ROM 3-4

Lesson Plan 3-4, Objective 2
Solving Multi-Step Inequalities

Lesson Objective	NAEP 2005	Local Standards
▼ Solve multi-step inequalities with variables on both sides	A4a, c **NCTM 2000** 1, 2, 6, 10 **Pacing** Two Year: 1 day Two-Year Block: 0.5 day	

1. INTRODUCE

Check Skills You'll Need: Assign these exercises if not used with Objective 1.

Review: Remind students how to solve multi-step inequalities with variables on one side.

Targeted Resources

☐ ⬆ Transparency: Check Skills You'll Need 3-4

2. TEACH

▼ **Objective:** Teach Examples 4 and 5. Assign Check Understanding questions 4 and 5 after the appropriate example.

Targeted Resources

☐ ⬆ Transparency: Additional Examples 3-4
☐ ✆ Presentation Pro CD-ROM 3-4
☐ 💻 iText 3-4: at **PHSchool.com**

3. PRACTICE

Assignment Guide: Give an assignment based on the ability levels of your students.

▼ **Objective:** Core: 13–46, 50–51, 60–76, 79–80; Extension: 84–86
Standardized Test Prep: 88–91
Mixed Review: 92–104

Homework: _____

Targeted Resources

☐ ⬆ Transparency: Student Answers 3-4
☐ Grab & Go File: Practice 3-4, Reteaching 3-4, Enrichment 3-4
☐ Practice Workbook 3-4
☐ Spanish Practice Workbook 3-4

4. ASSESS

Lesson Quiz: Assign the Lesson Quiz to assess students' mastery of the lesson content.

Targeted Resources

☐ ⬆ Transparency: Lesson Quiz 3-4
☐ 💻 Online Lesson Quiz 3-4: at **PHSchool.com**
☐ ✆ Computer Test Generator CD-ROM 3-4

Lesson Plan 3-5, Objective 1
Compound Inequalities

Lesson Objective	NAEP 2005	Local Standards
▼ Solve and graph inequalities containing *and* **New Vocabulary:** compound inequality	A3a; A4a, c **NCTM 2000** 1, 2, 6, 9, 10 **Pacing** Two Year: 1 day Two-Year Block: 0.5 day	

1. INTRODUCE

Check Skills You'll Need: Assign these exercises to review the prerequisite skills of graphing inequalities and evaluating expressions.

New Vocabulary: Help students pre-read the lesson by pointing out the new term introduced in Objective 1.

Targeted Resources

☐ 🖳 Transparency: Check Skills You'll Need 3-5

2. TEACH

▼ **Objective:** Teach Examples 1–3. Assign Check Understanding 1–3 after the appropriate example.

Targeted Resources

☐ 🖳 Transparency: Additional Examples 3-5
☐ 🖉 Presentation Pro CD-ROM 3-5
☐ 🖳 iText 3-5: at **PHSchool.com**

3. PRACTICE

Assignment Guide: Give an assignment based on the ability levels of your students.

▼ **Objective:** Core: 1–19, 40–44, 47–54; Extension: 58–60
Standardized Test Prep: 61, 63
Mixed Review: 64–69

Homework: _____

Targeted Resources

☐ 🖳 Transparency: Student Answers 3-5
☐ Grab & Go File: Practice 3-5, Reteaching 3-5, Enrichment 3-5
☐ Practice Workbook 3-5
☐ Spanish Practice Workbook 3-5
☐ Reading and Math Literacy 3C
☐ Spanish Reading and Math Literacy 3C
☐ Hands-On Activities 8

4. ASSESS

Lesson Quiz: Create a quiz on Objective 1 using the Computer Test Generator.

Targeted Resources

☐ 🖉 Computer Test Generator CD-ROM 3-5

Lesson Plan 3-5, Objective 2
Compound Inequalities

Lesson Objective	NAEP 2005	Local Standards
⊠ Solve and graph inequalities containing *or*	A3a; A4a, c	
	NCTM 2000 1, 2, 6, 9, 10	
	Pacing Two Year: 1 day Two-Year Block: 0.5 day	

1. INTRODUCE

Check Skills You'll Need: Assign these exercises if not used with Objective 1.

Review: Remind students how to solve inequalities containing *and*.

Targeted Resources

☐ ✐ Transparency: Check Skills You'll Need 3-5

2. TEACH

⊠ **Objective:** Teach Examples 4 and 5. Assign Check Understanding 4 and 5 after the appropriate example.

Targeted Resources

☐ ✐ Transparency: Additional Examples 3-5
☐ ⊘ Presentation Pro CD-ROM 3-5
☐ ▣ iText 3-5: at **PHSchool.com**

3. PRACTICE

Assignment Guide: Give an assignment based on the ability levels of your students.

  ⊠ **Objective:** Core: 20–39, 45–46; Extension: 55–57
Standardized Test Prep: 62
Mixed Review: 64–69

Homework: _____

Targeted Resources

☐ ✐ Transparency: Student Answers 3-5
☐ Grab & Go File: Practice 3-5, Reteaching 3-5, Enrichment 3-5
☐ Practice Workbook 3-5
☐ Spanish Practice Workbook 3-5
☐ Reading and Math Literacy 3C
☐ Spanish Reading and Math Literacy 3C
☐ Hands-On Activities 8
☐ Reasoning and Puzzles 59: at **PHSchool.com**

4. ASSESS

Lesson Quiz: Assign the Lesson Quiz to assess students' mastery of the lesson content.

Checkpoint Quiz: Use the Checkpoint Quiz to assess student progress over several lessons.

Targeted Resources

☐ ✐ Transparency: Lesson Quiz 3-5
☐ ▣ Online Lesson Quiz 3-5: at **PHSchool.com**
☐ Grab & Go File: Checkpoint Quiz 2
☐ ⊘ Computer Test Generator CD-ROM 3-5

Lesson Plan 3-6, Objective 1
Absolute Value Equations and Inequalities

Lesson Objective	NAEP 2005	Local Standards
▼ Solve equations that involve absolute value	N1g; A4a, c **NCTM** 1, 2, 6, 9, 10 **Pacing** Two Year: 2 days Two-Year Block: 1 day	

1. INTRODUCE

Check Skills You'll Need: Assign these exercises to review the prerequisite skill of interpreting absolute value expressions.

Targeted Resources
- ☐ ✎ Transparency: Check Skills You'll Need 3-6

2. TEACH

▼ **Objective:** Teach Example 1. Go over the rule in the Key Concepts box. Assign Check Understanding 1. Teach Example 2. Assign Check Understanding 2.

Targeted Resources
- ☐ ✎ Transparency: Additional Examples 3-6
- ☐ ✏ Presentation Pro CD-ROM 3-6
- ☐ 💻 iText 3-6: at **PHSchool.com**

3. PRACTICE

Assignment Guide: Give an assignment based on the ability levels of your students.

▼ **Objective:** Core: 1–21, 37–42, 61–71; Extension: 72–74
Standardized Test Prep: 83
Mixed Review: 87–98

Homework: _____

Targeted Resources
- ☐ ✎ Transparency: Student Answers 3-6
- ☐ Grab & Go File: Practice 3-6, Reteaching 3-6, Enrichment 3-6
- ☐ Practice Workbook 3-6
- ☐ Spanish Practice Workbook 3-6
- ☐ Technology Activities 17

4. ASSESS

Lesson Quiz: Create a quiz on Objective 1 using the Computer Test Generator.

Targeted Resources
- ☐ ✏ Computer Test Generator CD-ROM 3-6

Lesson Plan 3-6, Objective 2
Absolute Value Equations and Inequalities

Lesson Objective	NAEP 2005	Local Standards
❷ Solve inequalities that involve absolute value	N1g; A4a, c **NCTM** 1, 2, 6, 9, 10 **Pacing** Two Year: 1 day Two-Year Block: 1 day	

1. INTRODUCE

Check Skills You'll Need: Assign these exercises if not used with Objective 1.

Review: Remind students how to solve equations that involve absolute-value.

Targeted Resources

☐ 🖹 Transparency: Check Skills You'll Need 3-6

2. TEACH

❷ **Objective:** Go over the rules in the Key Concepts box. Teach Examples 3 and 4. Assign Check Understanding 3 and 4 after the appropriate example.

Targeted Resources

☐ 🖹 Transparency: Additional Examples 3-6
☐ 🖉 Presentation Pro CD-ROM 3-6
☐ 🖳 iText 3-6: at **PHSchool.com**

3. PRACTICE

Assignment Guide: Give an assignment based on the ability levels of your students.

   ❷ **Objective:** Core: 22–36, 43–60; Extension: 75–80
   Standardized Test Prep: 81–82, 84–86
   Mixed Review: 87–98

Homework: _____

Targeted Resources

☐ 🖹 Transparency: Student Answers 3-6
☐ Grab & Go File: Practice 3-6, Reteaching 3-6, Enrichment 3-6
☐ Practice Workbook 3-6
☐ Spanish Practice Workbook 3-6
☐ Technology Activities 17
☐ Reasoning and Puzzles 52, 59: at **PHSchool.com**

4. ASSESS

Lesson Quiz: Assign the Lesson Quiz to assess students' mastery of the lesson content.

Targeted Resources

☐ 🖹 Transparency: Lesson Quiz 3-6
☐ 🖳 Online Lesson Quiz 3-6: at **PHSchool.com**
☐ 🖉 Computer Test Generator CD-ROM 3-6

Lesson Plan 4-1, Objective 1
Ratio and Proportion

Lesson Objective	NAEP 2005	Local Standards
▼ Find ratios and rates	N4b, c; M1ℓ	
New Vocabulary: ratio, rate, unit rate, unit analysis	**NCTM 2000** 1, 2, 4, 9, 10	
	Pacing Two Year: 1 day Two-Year Block: 0.5 day	

1. INTRODUCE

Check Skills You'll Need: Assign these exercises to review the prerequisite skill of simplifying and multiplying fractions.

New Vocabulary: Help students pre-read the lesson by pointing out the new terms introduced in Objective 1.

Targeted Resources

☐ ⌨ Transparency: Check Skills You'll Need 4-1

2. TEACH

▼ **Objective:** Teach Examples 1 and 2. Assign Check Understanding questions 1 and 2 after the appropriate example.

Targeted Resources

☐ ⌨ Transparency: Additional Examples 4-1
☐ ⊘ Presentation Pro CD-ROM 4-1
☐ ▦ iText 4-1: at **PHSchool.com**

3. PRACTICE

Assignment Guide: Give an assignment based on the ability levels of your students.

▼ **Objective:** Core: 1–13, 38–52, 66–68;
Extension: 76
Standardized Test Prep: 77–79
Mixed Review: 82–100

Homework: _____

Targeted Resources

☐ ⌨ Transparency: Student Answers 4-1
☐ Grab & Go File: Practice 4-1, Reteaching 4-1, Enrichment 4-1
☐ Practice Workbook 4-1
☐ Spanish Practice Workbook 4-1
☐ Reading and Math Literacy 4A
☐ Spanish Reading and Math Literacy 4A
☐ Technology Activities 19
☐ Hands-On Activities 9

4. ASSESS

Lesson Quiz: Create a quiz on Objective 1 using the Computer Test Generator.

Targeted Resources

☐ ⊘ Computer Test Generator CD-ROM 4-1

Lesson Plan 4-1, Objective 2
Ratio and Proportion

Lesson Objective	NAEP 2005	Local Standards
▼ Solve proportions	N4b, c; M1ℓ	
New Vocabulary: proportion, extremes of a proportion, means of a proportion, cross products	**NCTM 2000** 1, 2, 4, 9, 10 **Pacing** Two Year: 1 day Two-Year Block: 0.5 day	

1. INTRODUCE

Check Skills You'll Need: Assign these exercises if not used with Objective 1.

Review: Remind students how to find ratios and rates.

New Vocabulary: Help students pre-read the lesson by pointing out the new terms introduced in Objective 2.

Targeted Resources

☐ 🖳 Transparency: Check Skills You'll Need 4-1

2. TEACH

▼ **Objective:** Teach Examples 3–6. Assign Check Understanding questions 3–6 after the appropriate example.

Targeted Resources

☐ 🖳 Transparency: Additional Examples 4-1
☐ 🖉 Presentation Pro CD-ROM 4-1
☐ 🖳 iText 4-1: at **PHSchool.com**

3. PRACTICE

Assignment Guide: Give an assignment based on the ability levels of your students.

> ▼ **Objective:** Core: 14–37, 53–65, 69–71; Extension: 72–75
> **Standardized Test Prep:** 80–81
> **Mixed Review:** 82–100

Homework: _____

Targeted Resources

☐ 🖳 Transparency: Student Answers 4-1
☐ Grab & Go File: Practice 4-1, Reteaching 4-1, Enrichment 4-1
☐ Practice Workbook 4-1
☐ Spanish Practice Workbook 4-1
☐ Reading and Math Literacy 4A
☐ Spanish Reading and Math Literacy 4A
☐ Technology Activities 19
☐ Hands-On Activities 9

4. ASSESS

Lesson Quiz: Assign the Lesson Quiz to assess students' mastery of the lesson content.

Targeted Resources

☐ 🖳 Transparency: Lesson Quiz 4-1
☐ 🖳 Online Lesson Quiz 4-1: at **PHSchool.com**
☐ 🖉 Computer Test Generator CD-ROM 4-1

Lesson Plan 4-2, Objective 1
Proportions and Similar Figures

Lesson Objective	NAEP 2005	Local Standards
▼ Find missing measures of similar figures **New Vocabulary:** similar figures	N4c; G2e; M1k **NCTM 2000** 2, 3, 4, 6 **Pacing** Two Year: 1 day Two-Year Block: 0.5 day	

1. INTRODUCE

Check Skills You'll Need: Assign these exercises to review the prerequisite skills of simplifying ratios and solving proportions.

New Vocabulary: Help students pre-read the lesson by pointing out the new term introduced in Objective 1.

Targeted Resources

☐ ▱ Transparency: Check Skills You'll Need 4-2

2. TEACH

▼ **Objective:** Have students do the Investigation to discover the equality of corresponding ratios. Teach Example 1 and assign Check Understanding question 1.

Targeted Resources

☐ ▱ Transparency: Additional Examples 4-2
☐ ▱ Transparency: Classroom Aid 12, 13
☐ ⊘ Presentation Pro CD-ROM 4-2
☐ ▤ iText 4-2: at **PHSchool.com**

3. PRACTICE

Assignment Guide: Give an assignment based on the ability levels of your students.

▼ **Objective:** Core: 1–8, 21, 23, 29–33; Extension: 36
Standardized Test Prep: 37, 40
Mixed Review: 41–48

Homework: _____

Targeted Resources

☐ ▱ Transparency: Student Answers 4-2
☐ Grab & Go File: Practice 4-2, Reteaching 4-2, Enrichment 4-2
☐ Practice Workbook 4-2
☐ Spanish Practice Workbook 4-2
☐ Reading and Math Literacy 4B
☐ Spanish Reading and Math Literacy 4B

4. ASSESS

Lesson Quiz: Create a quiz on Objective 1 using the Computer Test Generator.

Targeted Resources

☐ ⊘ Computer Test Generator CD-ROM 4-2

Lesson Plan 4-2, Objective 2
Proportions and Similar Figures

Lesson Objective	NAEP 2005	Local Standards
▼ Use similar figures when measuring indirectly **New Vocabulary:** scale drawing, scale	N4c; G2e; M1k **NCTM 2000** 2, 3, 4, 6 **Pacing** Two Year: 1 day Two-Year Block: 0.5 day	

1. INTRODUCE

Check Skills You'll Need: Assign these exercises if not used with Objective 1.

Review: Remind students how to find measures of similar figures.

New Vocabulary: Help students pre-read the lesson by pointing out the new terms introduced in Objective 2.

Targeted Resources

☐ ✐ Transparency: Check Skills You'll Need 4-2

2. TEACH

▼ **Objective:** Teach Examples 2 and 3, and assign Check Understanding questions 2 and 3 after the appropriate examples.

Targeted Resources

☐ ✐ Transparency: Additional Examples 4-2
☐ ✐ Transparency: Classroom Aid 12, 13
☐ ✐ Presentation Pro CD-ROM 4-2
☐ ▪ iText 4-2: at **PHSchool.com**

3. PRACTICE

Assignment Guide: Give an assignment based on the ability levels of your students.

   ▼ **Objective:** Core: 9–20, 22, 24–28;
Extension: 34–35
Standardized Test Prep: 38, 39
Mixed Review: 41–48

Homework: _____

Targeted Resources

☐ ✐ Transparency: Student Answers 4-2
☐ Grab & Go File: Practice 4-2, Reteaching 4-2, Enrichment 4-2
☐ Practice Workbook 4-2
☐ Spanish Practice Workbook 4-2
☐ Reading and Math Literacy 4B
☐ Spanish Reading and Math Literacy 4B

4. ASSESS

Lesson Quiz: Assign the Lesson Quiz to assess students' mastery of the lesson content.

Checkpoint Quiz: Use the Checkpoint Quiz to assess student progress over several lessons.

Targeted Resources

☐ ✐ Transparency: Lesson Quiz 4-2
☐ ▪ Online Lesson Quiz 4-2: at **PHSchool.com**
☐ Grab & Go File: Checkpoint Quiz 1
☐ ✐ Computer Test Generator CD-ROM 4-2

Lesson Plan 4-3, Objective 1
Proportions and Percent Equations

Lesson Objective	NAEP 2005	Local Standards
▼ Use proportions when solving percent problems	N4d **NCTM 2000** 1, 2, 6, 8 **Pacing** Two Year: 1 day Two-Year Block: 0.5 day	

1. INTRODUCE

Check Skills You'll Need: Assign these exercises to review the prerequisite skills of multiplying fractions and decimals, and expressing fractions as decimals and percents.

Targeted Resources
- ☐ 🖵 Transparency: Check Skills You'll Need 4-3

2. TEACH

▼ **Objective:** Teach Examples 1–3. Assign Check Understanding questions 1–3 after the appropriate example. Review the Key Concept box summarizing the use of proportions to solve all three types of percent problems.

Targeted Resources
- ☐ 🖵 Transparency: Additional Examples 4-3
- ☐ 💿 Presentation Pro CD-ROM 4-3
- ☐ 💻 iText 4-3: at **PHSchool.com**

3. PRACTICE

Assignment Guide: Give an assignment based on the ability levels of your students.

▼ **Objective:** Core: 1–19, 39–41; Extension: 59
Standardized Test Prep: 61–63
Mixed Review: 67–74

Homework: _____

Targeted Resources
- ☐ 🖵 Transparency: Student Answers 4-3
- ☐ Grab & Go File: Practice 4-3, Reteaching 4-3, Enrichment 4-3
- ☐ Practice Workbook 4-3
- ☐ Spanish Practice Workbook 4-3
- ☐ Technology Activities 18

4. ASSESS

Lesson Quiz: Create a quiz on Objective 1 using the Computer Test Generator.

Targeted Resources
- ☐ 💿 Computer Test Generator CD-ROM 4-3

Lesson Plan 4-3, Objective 2
Proportions and Percent Equations

Lesson Objective ▼ Write and solve percent equations	NAEP 2005 N4d NCTM 2000 1, 2, 6, 8 Pacing Two Year: 1 day Two-Year Block: 0.5 day	Local Standards

1. INTRODUCE

Check Skills You'll Need: Assign these exercises if not used with Objective 1.

Review: Connect $23\% = \frac{23}{100}$ to $23\% = 0.23$.

Targeted Resources
- ☐ 🖳 Transparency: Check Skills You'll Need 4-3

2. TEACH

▼ Objective: Teach Examples 4–7. Assign Check Understanding questions 4–7 after the appropriate example.

Targeted Resources
- ☐ 🖳 Transparency: Additional Examples 4-3
- ☐ ⊘ Presentation Pro CD-ROM 4-3
- ☐ 🖳 iText 4-3: at **PHSchool.com**

3. PRACTICE

Assignment Guide: Give an assignment based on the ability levels of your students.

   ▼ Objective: Core: 20–38, 42–58; Extension: 60
Standardized Test Prep: 64–66
Mixed Review: 67–74

Homework: _____

Targeted Resources
- ☐ 🖳 Transparency: Student Answers 4-3
- ☐ Grab & Go File: Practice 4-3, Reteaching 4-3, Enrichment 4-3
- ☐ Practice Workbook 4-3
- ☐ Spanish Practice Workbook 4-3
- ☐ Technology Activities 18

4. ASSESS

Lesson Quiz: Assign the Lesson Quiz to assess students' mastery of the lesson content.

Targeted Resources
- ☐ 🖳 Transparency: Lesson Quiz 4-3
- ☐ 🖳 Online Lesson Quiz 4-3: at **PHSchool.com**
- ☐ ⊘ Computer Test Generator CD-ROM 4-3

Lesson Plan 4-4, Objective 1
Percent of Change

Lesson Objective	NAEP 2005	Local Standards
▼ Find percent of change	N4d	
New Vocabulary: percent of change, percent of increase, percent of decrease	**NCTM 2000** 2, 3, 4, 6, 9	
	Pacing Two Year: 1 day Two-Year Block: 0.5 day	

1. INTRODUCE

Check Skills You'll Need: Assign these exercises to review the prerequisite skill of solving percent problems.

New Vocabulary: Help students pre-read the lesson by pointing out the new terms introduced in Objective 1.

Targeted Resources
- ☐ ⌨ Transparency: Check Skills You'll Need 4-4

2. TEACH

▼ **Objective:** Teach Examples 1 and 2. Assign Check Understanding questions 1 and 2 after the appropriate example.

Targeted Resources
- ☐ ⌨ Transparency: Additional Examples 4-4
- ☐ ✺ Presentation Pro CD-ROM 4-4
- ☐ 💻 iText 4-4: at **PHSchool.com**

3. PRACTICE

Assignment Guide: Give an assignment based on the ability levels of your students.

▼ **Objective:** Core: 1–14, 30–40, 42–44, 48; Extension: 54
Standardized Test Prep: 56–57
Mixed Review: 60–68

Homework: _____

Targeted Resources
- ☐ ⌨ Transparency: Student Answers 4-4
- ☐ Grab & Go File: Practice 4-4, Reteaching 4-4, Enrichment 4-4
- ☐ Practice Workbook 4-4
- ☐ Spanish Practice Workbook 4-4

4. ASSESS

Lesson Quiz: Create a quiz on Objective 1 using the Computer Test Generator.

Targeted Resources
- ☐ ✺ Computer Test Generator CD-ROM 4-4

Lesson Plan 4-4, Objective 2
Percent of Change

Lesson Objective ▼ Find percent error **New Vocabulary:** greatest possible error, percent error	**NAEP 2005** N4d **NCTM 2000** 2, 3, 4, 6, 9 **Pacing** Two Year: 1 day Two-Year Block: 0.5 day	**Local Standards**

1. INTRODUCE

Check Skills You'll Need: Assign these exercises if not used with Objective 1.

Review: Remind students how to find percent of change.

New Vocabulary: Help students pre-read the lesson by pointing out the new terms introduced in Objective 2.

Targeted Resources
- ☐ 📖 Transparency: Check Skills You'll Need 4-4

2. TEACH

▼ **Objective:** Teach Examples 3–6. Assign Check Understanding questions 3–6 after the appropriate example.

Targeted Resources
- ☐ 📖 Transparency: Additional Examples 4-4
- ☐ 💿 Presentation Pro CD-ROM 4-4
- ☐ 💻 iText 4-4: at **PHSchool.com**

3. PRACTICE

Assignment Guide: Give an assignment based on the ability levels of your students.

> ▼ **Objective:** Core: 15–29, 41, 45–47, 49–52;
> Extension: 53, 55
> **Standardized Test Prep:** 58–59
> **Mixed Review:** 60–68

Homework: _____

Targeted Resources
- ☐ 📖 Transparency: Student Answers 4-4
- ☐ Grab & Go File: Practice 4-4, Reteaching 4-4, Enrichment 4-4
- ☐ Practice Workbook 4-4
- ☐ Spanish Practice Workbook 4-4

4. ASSESS

Lesson Quiz: Assign the Lesson Quiz to assess students' mastery of the lesson content.

Targeted Resources
- ☐ 📖 Transparency: Lesson Quiz 4-4
- ☐ 💻 Online Lesson Quiz 4-4: at **PHSchool.com**
- ☐ 💿 Computer Test Generator CD-ROM 4-4

Lesson Plan 4-5, Objective 1
Applying Ratios to Probability

Lesson Objective	NAEP 2005	Local Standards
▼ Find theoretical probability **New Vocabulary:** probability, outcome, event, sample space, theoretical probability, complement of an event	D4b, c **NCTM 2000** 2, 5, 6, 7, 10 **Pacing** Two Year: 2 days Two-Year Block: 1 day	

1. INTRODUCE

Check Skills You'll Need: Assign these exercises to review the prerequisite skills of writing decimals or fractions as percents.

New Vocabulary: Help students pre-read the lesson by pointing out the new terms introduced in Objective 1.

Targeted Resources
☐ ⌨ Transparency: Check Skills You'll Need 4-5

2. TEACH

▼ **Objective:** Teach Examples 1 and 2. Assign Check Understanding questions 1 and 2 after the appropriate example.

Targeted Resources
☐ ⌨ Transparency: Additional Examples 4-5
☐ Graphing Calculator Procedure 15: at **PHSchool.com**
☐ ✏ Presentation Pro CD-ROM 4-5
☐ 💻 iText 4-5: at **PHSchool.com**

3. PRACTICE

Assignment Guide: Give an assignment based on the ability levels of your students.

▼ **Objective:** Core: 1–14, 23–32, 37, 39–45
Standardized Test Prep: 50
Mixed Review: 55–70

Homework: _____

Targeted Resources
☐ ⌨ Transparency: Student Answers 4-5
☐ Grab & Go File: Practice 4-5, Reteaching 4-5, Enrichment 4-5
☐ Practice Workbook 4-5
☐ Spanish Practice Workbook 4-5
☐ Reading and Math Literacy 4C
☐ Spanish Reading and Math Literacy 4C
☐ Hands-On Activities 10

4. ASSESS

Lesson Quiz: Create a quiz on Objective 1 using the Computer Test Generator.

Targeted Resources
☐ ✏ Computer Test Generator CD-ROM 4-5

Lesson Plan 4-5, Objective 2
Applying Ratios to Probability

Lesson Objective	NAEP 2005	Local Standards
▼ Find experimental probability	D4b, c	
New Vocabulary: experimental probability	**NCTM 2000** 2, 5, 6, 7, 10	
	Pacing Two Year: 1 day Two-Year Block: 1 day	

1. INTRODUCE

Check Skills You'll Need: Assign these exercises if not used with Objective 1.

Review: Review how to find theoretical probability with students.

New Vocabulary: Help students pre-read the lesson by pointing out the new term introduced in Objective 2.

Targeted Resources

☐ 🖳 Transparency: Check Skills You'll Need 4-5

2. TEACH

▼ **Objective:** Teach Examples 3 and 4. Assign Check Understanding questions 3 and 4 after the appropriate example.

Targeted Resources

☐ 🖳 Transparency: Additional Examples 4-5
☐ Graphing Calculator Procedure 15: at **PHSchool.com**
☐ 🖉 Presentation Pro CD-ROM 4-5
☐ 🖳 iText 4-5: at **PHSchool.com**

3. PRACTICE

Assignment Guide: Give an assignment based on the ability levels of your students.

▼ **Objective:** Core: 15–22, 33–36, 38; Extension: 46–49
Standardized Test Prep: 51–54
Mixed Review: 55–70

Homework: _____

Targeted Resources

☐ 🖳 Transparency: Student Answers 4-5
☐ Grab & Go File: Practice 4-5, Reteaching 4-5, Enrichment 4-5
☐ Practice Workbook 4-5
☐ Spanish Practice Workbook 4-5
☐ Reading and Math Literacy 4C
☐ Spanish Reading and Math Literacy 4C
☐ Hands-On Activities 10

4. ASSESS

Lesson Quiz: Assign the Lesson Quiz to assess students' mastery of the lesson content.

Checkpoint Quiz: Use the Checkpoint Quiz to assess student progress over several lessons.

Targeted Resources

☐ 🖳 Transparency: Lesson Quiz 4-5
☐ 🖳 Online Lesson Quiz 4-5: at **PHSchool.com**
☐ Grab & Go File: Checkpoint Quiz 2
☐ 🖉 Computer Test Generator CD-ROM 4-5

Lesson Plan 4-6, Objective 1
Probability of Compound Events

Lesson Objective	NAEP 2005	Local Standards
▼ Find the probability of independent events	D4h	
New Vocabulary: independent events	**NCTM 2000** 2, 5, 6, 7, 9	
	Pacing Two Year: 2 days Two-Year Block: 1 day	

1. INTRODUCE

Check Skills You'll Need: Assign these exercises to review the prerequisite skills of finding simple probabilities and multiplying ratios.

New Vocabulary: Help students pre-read the lesson by pointing out the new term introduced in Objective 1.

Targeted Resources

☐ 📖 Transparency: Check Skills You'll Need 4-6

2. TEACH

▼ **Objective:** Have students work the Investigation to see that compound events may be independent or dependent. Teach Examples 1 and 2. Review the rule in the Key Concepts box. Assign Check Understanding questions 1 and 2 after the appropriate example.

Targeted Resources

☐ 📖 Transparency: Additional Examples 4-6
☐ 💿 Presentation Pro CD-ROM 4-6
☐ 🖥 iText 4-6: at **PHSchool.com**

3. PRACTICE

Assignment Guide: Give an assignment based on the ability levels of your students.

▼ **Objective:** Core: 1–14, 33; Extension: 43–44
Standardized Test Prep: 46–47
Mixed Review: 50–59

Homework: _____

Targeted Resources

☐ 📖 Transparency: Student Answers 4-6
☐ Grab & Go File: Practice 4-6, Reteaching 4-6, Enrichment 4-6
☐ Practice Workbook 4-6
☐ Spanish Practice Workbook 4-6

4. ASSESS

Lesson Quiz: Create a quiz on Objective 1 using the Computer Test Generator.

Targeted Resources

☐ 💿 Computer Test Generator CD-ROM 4-6

Lesson Plan 4-6, Objective 2
Probability of Compound Events

Lesson Objective ☑ Find the probability of dependent events **New Vocabulary:** independent events, dependent events	**NAEP 2005** D4h **NCTM 2000** 2, 5, 6, 7, 9 **Pacing** Two Year: 1 day Two-Year Block: 1 day	**Local Standards**

1. INTRODUCE

Check Skills You'll Need: Assign these exercises if not used with Objective 1.

Review: Use the Key Concepts box to review the probability of independent events.

New Vocabulary: Help students pre-read the lesson by pointing out the new terms introduced in Objective 2.

Targeted Resources

☐ 🖳 Transparency: Check Skills You'll Need 4-6

2. TEACH

☑ **Objective:** Review the rule in the Key Concepts box. Teach Examples 3 and 4. Assign Check Understanding questions 3 and 4 after the appropriate example.

Targeted Resources

☐ 🖳 Transparency: Additional Examples 4-6
☐ 🖉 Presentation Pro CD-ROM 4-6
☐ 🖳 iText 4-6: at **PHSchool.com**

3. PRACTICE

Assignment Guide: Give an assignment based on the ability levels of your students.

   ☑ **Objective:** Core: 15–32, 34–42; Extension: 45
   Standardized Test Prep: 48–49
   Mixed Review: 50–59

Homework: _____

Targeted Resources

☐ 🖳 Transparency: Student Answers 4-6
☐ Grab & Go File: Practice 4-6, Reteaching 4-6, Enrichment 4-6
☐ Practice Workbook 4-6
☐ Spanish Practice Workbook 4-6

4. ASSESS

Lesson Quiz: Assign the Lesson Quiz to assess students' mastery of the lesson content.

Targeted Resources

☐ 🖳 Transparency: Lesson Quiz 4-6
☐ 🖳 Online Lesson Quiz 4-6: at **PHSchool.com**
☐ 🖉 Computer Test Generator CD-ROM 4-6

Lesson Plan 5-1, Objective 1
Relating Graphs to Events

Lesson Objective	NAEP 2005	Local Standards
▼ Interpret, sketch, and analyze graphs from situations	A2a, c	
	NCTM 2000	
	2, 4, 5, 6, 9, 10	
	Pacing	
	Two Year: 1 day	
	Two-Year Block: 0.5 day	

1. INTRODUCE

Check Skills You'll Need: Assign these exercises to review the prerequisite skill of associating ordered pairs with points in a coordinate plane.

> **Targeted Resources**
> ☐ ⬒ Transparency: Check Skills You'll Need 5-1

2. TEACH

▼ **Objective:** Teach Examples 1–3. Assign Check Understanding questions 1–3 after the appropriate example.

> **Targeted Resources**
> ☐ ⬒ Transparency: Additional Examples 5-1
> ☐ ⊘ Presentation Pro CD-ROM 5-1
> ☐ ▣ iText 5-1: at **PHSchool.com**

3. PRACTICE

Assignment Guide: Give an assignment based on the ability levels of your students.

▼ **Objective:** Core: 1–17; Extension: 18–22
Standardized Test Prep: 23–25
Mixed Review: 26–49

Homework: _____

> **Targeted Resources**
> ☐ ⬒ Transparency: Student Answers 5-1
> ☐ Grab & Go File: Practice 5-1, Reteaching 5-1, Enrichment 5-1
> ☐ Practice Workbook 5-1
> ☐ Spanish Practice Workbook 5-1
> ☐ Reading and Math Literacy 5A
> ☐ Spanish Reading and Math Literacy 5A

4. ASSESS

Lesson Quiz: Assign the Lesson Quiz to assess student's mastery of the lesson content.

> **Targeted Resources**
> ☐ ⬒ Transparency: Lesson Quiz 5-1
> ☐ ▣ Online Lesson Quiz 5-1: at **PHSchool.com**
> ☐ ⊘ Computer Test Generator CD-ROM 5-1

Lesson Plan 5-2, Objective 1
Relations and Functions

Lesson Objective	NAEP 2005	Local Standards
▼ Identify relations and functions **New Vocabulary:** relation, domain, range, function, vertical-line test	A1g **NCTM 2000** 2, 7, 8, 10 **Pacing** Two Year: 1 day Two-Year Block: 0.5 day	

1. INTRODUCE

Check Skills You'll Need: Assign these exercises to review the prerequisite skills of graphing points and evaluating expressions.

New Vocabulary: Help students pre-read the lesson by pointing out the new terms introduced in Objective 1.

Targeted Resources

☐ 🖳 Transparency: Check Skills You'll Need 5-2

2. TEACH

▼ **Objective:** Teach Examples 1–3. Assign Check Understanding questions 1–3 after the appropriate example.

Targeted Resources

☐ 🖳 Transparency: Additional Examples 5-2
☐ ✐ Presentation Pro CD-ROM 5-2
☐ 🖳 iText 5-2: at **PHSchool.com**

3. PRACTICE

Assignment Guide: Give an assignment based on the ability levels of your students.

▼ **Objective:** Core: 1–14, 27–31, 33, 38–40; Extension: 47
Standardized Test Prep: 53
Mixed Review: 54–66

Homework: _____

Targeted Resources

☐ 🖳 Transparency: Student Answers 5-2
☐ Grab & Go File: Practice 5-2, Reteaching 5-2, Enrichment 5-2
☐ Practice Workbook 5-2
☐ Spanish Practice Workbook 5-2
☐ Reading and Math Literacy 5B
☐ Spanish Reading and Math Literacy 5B

4. ASSESS

Lesson Quiz: Create a quiz on Objective 1 using the Computer Test Generator.

Targeted Resources

☐ ✐ Computer Test Generator CD-ROM 5-2

Lesson Plan 5-2, Objective 2
Relations and Functions

Lesson Objective ☑ Evaluate functions **New Vocabulary:** function rule, function notation	**NAEP 2005** A1g **NCTM 2000** 2, 7, 8, 10 **Pacing** Two Year: 1 day Two-Year Block: 0.5 day	**Local Standards**

1. INTRODUCE

Check Skills You'll Need: Assign these exercises if not used with Objective 1.

Review: Use the Key Concepts box to review functions.

New Vocabulary: Help students pre-read the lesson by pointing out the new terms introduced in Objective 2.

Targeted Resources

☐ ⬐ Transparency: Check Skills You'll Need 5-2

2. TEACH

☑ **Objective:** Teach Examples 4 and 5. Assign Check Understanding questions 4 and 5 after the appropriate example.

Targeted Resources

☐ ⬐ Transparency: Additional Examples 5-2
☐ ✎ Presentation Pro CD-ROM 5-2
☐ 🖳 iText 5-2: at **PHSchool.com**

3. PRACTICE

Assignment Guide: Give an assignment based on the ability levels of your students.

　☑ **Objective:** Core: 15–26, 32, 34–37, 41–42;
　Extension: 43–46; 48
　Standardized Test Prep: 49–52
　Mixed Review: 54–66

Homework: _____

Targeted Resources

☐ ⬐ Transparency: Student Answers 5-2
☐ Grab & Go File: Practice 5-2, Reteaching 5-2, Enrichment 5-2
☐ Practice Workbook 5-2
☐ Spanish Practice Workbook 5-2
☐ Reading and Math Literacy 5B
☐ Spanish Reading and Math Literacy 5B

4. ASSESS

Lesson Quiz: Assign the Lesson Quiz to assess students' mastery of the lesson content.

Checkpoint Quiz: Use the Checkpoint Quiz to assess student progress over several lessons.

Targeted Resources

☐ ✎ Computer Test Generator CD-ROM 5-2
☐ 🖳 Online Lesson Quiz 5-2: at **PHSchool.com**
☐ Grab & Go File: Checkpoint Quiz 1
☐ ✎ Computer Test Generator CD-ROM 5-2

Lesson Plan 5-3, Objective 1
Function Rules, Tables, and Graphs

Lesson Objective	NAEP 2005	Local Standards
▼ Model functions using rules, tables, and graphs **New Vocabulary:** independent variable, dependent variable	A2a, f, g **NCTM 2000** 2, 7, 8, 10 **Pacing** Two Year: 2 days Two-Year Block: 1 day	

1. INTRODUCE

Check Skills You'll Need: Assign these exercises to review the prerequisite skill of making a graph from a table.

New Vocabulary: Help students pre-read the lesson by pointing out the new terms introduced in the lesson.

Targeted Resources

☐ ⛭ Transparency: Check Skills You'll Need 5-3

2. TEACH

▼ **Objective:** Have students do the Investigation to see that a function can be represented by a table, a rule, or a graph. Teach Examples 1–3. Assign Check Understanding questions 1–3 after the appropriate examples.

Targeted Resources

☐ ⛭ Transparency: Additional Examples 5-3
☐ Graphing Calculator Procedures 4, 6:
  at **PHSchool.com**
☐ ✐ Presentation Pro CD-ROM 5-3
☐ ▣ iText 5-3: at **PHSchool.com**

3. PRACTICE

Assignment Guide: Give an assignment based on the ability levels of your students.

▼ **Objective:** Core: 1–43; Extension: 44–46
Standardized Test Prep: 47–52
Mixed Review: 53–76

Homework: _____

Targeted Resources

☐ ⛭ Transparency: Student Answers 5-3
☐ Grab & Go File: Practice 5-3, Reteaching 5-3, Enrichment 5-3
☐ Practice Workbook 5-3
☐ Spanish Practice Workbook 5-3
☐ Hands-On Activities 11
☐ Reasoning and Puzzles 86, 88: at **PHSchool.com**

4. ASSESS

Lesson Quiz: Assign the Lesson Quiz to assess students' mastery of the lesson content.

Targeted Resources

☐ ⛭ Transparency: Lesson Quiz 5-3
☐ ▣ Online Lesson Quiz 5-3: at **PHSchool.com**
☐ ✐ Computer Test Generator CD-ROM 5-3

Lesson Plan 5-4, Objective 1
Writing a Function Rule

Lesson Objective	NAEP 2005	Local Standards
▼ Write a function rule given a table or a real-world situation	A1b; A2a; A3a **NCTM 2000** 2, 6, 8, 9, 10 **Pacing** Two Year: 2 days Two-Year Block: 1 day	

1. INTRODUCE

Check Skills You'll Need: Assign these exercises to review the prerequisite skills of modeling a function rule with a table and evaluating functions.

Targeted Resources
☐ 🖳 Transparency: Check Skills You'll Need 5-4

2. TEACH

▼ **Objective:** Teach Examples 1–3. Assign Check Understanding questions 1–3 after the appropriate examples.

Targeted Resources
☐ 🖳 Transparency: Additional Examples 5-4
☐ 🖉 Presentation Pro CD-ROM 5-4
☐ 🖳 iText 5-4: at **PHSchool.com**

3. PRACTICE

Assignment Guide: Give an assignment based on the ability levels of your students.

▼ **Objective:** Core: 1–30; Extension: 31–35
Standardized Test Prep: 36–41
Mixed Review: 42–54

Homework: _____

Targeted Resources
☐ 🖳 Transparency: Student Answers 5-4
☐ Grab & Go File: Practice 5-4, Reteaching 5-4, Enrichment 5-4
☐ Practice Workbook 5-4
☐ Spanish Practice Workbook 5-4

4. ASSESS

Lesson Quiz: Assign the Lesson Quiz to assess students' mastery of the lesson content.

Targeted Resources
☐ 🖳 Transparency: Lesson Quiz 5-4
☐ 🖳 Online Lesson Quiz 5-4: at **PHSchool.com**
☐ 🖉 Computer Test Generator CD-ROM 5-4

Lesson Plan 5-5, Objective 1
Direct Variation

Lesson Objective	NAEP 2005	Local Standards
▼ Write an equation of a direct variation	A1b; A2a, b	
New Vocabulary: direct variation, constant of variation	**NCTM 2000** 2, 5, 6, 8, 10	
	Pacing Two Year: 1 day Two-Year Block: 0.5 day	

1. INTRODUCE

Check Skills You'll Need: Assign these exercises to review the prerequisite skills of solving literal equations and proportions.

New Vocabulary: Help students pre-read the lesson by pointing out the new terms introduced in Objective 1.

Targeted Resources

☐ 🖳 Transparency: Check Skills You'll Need 5-5

2. TEACH

▼ **Objective:** Have students do the Investigation to discover that in this function the rate of change is constant and the graph passes through the origin. Review the summary in the Key Concepts box. Teach Examples 1–3. Assign Check Understanding 1–3 after the appropriate examples.

Targeted Resources

☐ 🖳 Transparency: Additional Examples 5-5
☐ 🖉 Presentation Pro CD-ROM 5-5
☐ 🖳 iText 5-5: at **PHSchool.com**

3. PRACTICE

Assignment Guide: Give an assignment based on the ability levels of your students.

 ▼ **Objective:** Core: 1–23, 29–44; Extension: 53
 Standardized Test Prep: 54–55
 Mixed Review: 60–72

Homework: _____

Targeted Resources

☐ 🖳 Transparency: Student Answers 5-5
☐ Grab & Go File: Practice 5-5, Reteaching 5-5, Enrichment 5-5
☐ Practice Workbook 5-5
☐ Reading and Math Literacy 5C
☐ Spanish Practice Workbook 5-5
☐ Spanish Reading and Math Literacy 5C

4. ASSESS

Lesson Quiz: Create a quiz on Objective 1 using the Computer Test Generator.

Targeted Resources

☐ 🖉 Computer Test Generator CD-ROM 5-5

Lesson Plan 5-5, Objective 2
Direct Variation

Lesson Objective	NAEP 2005	Local Standards
☑ Use ratios and proportions with direct variations	A1b; A2a, b	
	NCTM 2000 2, 5, 6, 8, 10	
	Pacing Two Year: 1 day Two-Year Block: 0.5 day	

1. INTRODUCE

Check Skills You'll Need: Assign these exercises if not used with Objective 1.

Review: Use the Key Concepts box to review Direct Variation.

Targeted Resources

☐ ⌨ Transparency: Check Skills You'll Need 5-5

2. TEACH

☑ **Objective:** Teach Examples 4–5. Assign Check Understanding 4–5 after the appropriate examples.

Targeted Resources

☐ ⌨ Transparency: Additional Examples 5-5
☐ ✐ Presentation Pro CD-ROM 5-5
☐ 💻 iText 5-5: at **PHSchool.com**

3. PRACTICE

Assignment Guide: Give an assignment based on the ability levels of your students.

  ☑ **Objective:** Core: 24–28, 45–46; Extension: 47–52
  Standardized Test Prep: 56–59
  Mixed Review: 60–72

Homework: _____

Targeted Resources

☐ ⌨ Transparency: Student Answers 5-5
☐ Grab & Go File: Practice 5-5, Reteaching 5-5, Enrichment 5-5
☐ Practice Workbook 5-5
☐ Reading and Math Literacy 5C
☐ Spanish Practice Workbook 5-5
☐ Spanish Reading and Math Literacy 5C
☐ Reasoning and Puzzles 87: at **PHSchool.com**

4. ASSESS

Lesson Quiz: Assign the Lesson Quiz to assess students' mastery of the lesson content.

Checkpoint Quiz: Use the Checkpoint Quiz to assess student progress over several lessons.

Targeted Resources

☐ ⌨ Transparency: Lesson Quiz 5-5
☐ 💻 Online Lesson Quiz 5-5: at **PHSchool.com**
☐ Grab & Go File: Checkpoint Quiz 2
☐ ✐ Computer Test Generator CD-ROM 5-5

Lesson Plan 5-6, Objective 1
Describing Number Patterns

Lesson Objective	NAEP 2005	Local Standards
▼ Use inductive reasoning in continuing number patterns	A1a, b	
New Vocabulary: inductive reasoning, conjecture	**NCTM 2000** 2, 5, 6, 7	
	Pacing Two Year: 1 day Two-Year Block: 0.5 day	

1. INTRODUCE

Check Skills You'll Need: Assign these exercises to review the prerequisite skills of evaluating expressions and subtracting real numbers.

New Vocabulary: Help students pre-read the lesson by pointing out the new terms introduced in Objective 1.

Targeted Resources
- ☐ ◸ Transparency: Check Skills You'll Need 5-6

2. TEACH

▼ **Objective:** Teach Example 1. Assign Check Understanding question 1.

Targeted Resources
- ☐ ◸ Transparency: Additional Examples 5-6
- ☐ ◸ Transparency: Classroom Aid 30
- ☐ ✇ Presentation Pro CD-ROM 5-6
- ☐ ▨ iText 5-6: at **PHSchool.com**

3. PRACTICE

Assignment Guide: Give an assignment based on the ability levels of your students.

▼ **Objective:** Core: 1–12, 34–44, 49–55; Extension: 69–70, 72
Standardized Test Prep: 79
Mixed Review: 82–96

Homework: _____

Targeted Resources
- ☐ ◸ Transparency: Student Answers 5-6
- ☐ Grab & Go File: Practice 5-6, Reteaching 5-6, Enrichment 5-6
- ☐ Practice Workbook 5-6
- ☐ Spanish Practice Workbook 5-6
- ☐ Hands-On Activities 12

4. ASSESS

Lesson Quiz: Create a quiz on Objective 1 using the Computer Test Generator.

Targeted Resources
- ☐ ✇ Computer Test Generator CD-ROM 5-6

Lesson Plan 5-6, Objective 2
Describing Number Patterns

Lesson Objective	NAEP 2005	Local Standards
☑ Write rules for arithmetic sequences **New Vocabulary:** sequence, term, arithmetic sequence, common difference	A1a, b **NCTM 2000** 2, 5, 6, 7 **Pacing** Two Year: 1 day Two-Year Block: 0.5 day	

1. INTRODUCE

Check Skills You'll Need: Assign these exercises if not used with Objective 1.

Review: Remind students how to extend number patterns.

New Vocabulary: Help students pre-read the lesson by pointing out the new terms introduced in Objective 2.

Targeted Resources

☐ ✎ Transparency: Check Skills You'll Need 5-6

2. TEACH

☑ **Objective:** Teach Example 2. Assign Check Understanding question 2. Go over the formula in the Key Concepts box. Teach Example 3. Assign Check Understanding question 3.

Targeted Resources

☐ ✎ Transparency: Additional Examples 5-6
☐ ✎ Transparency: Classroom Aid 30
☐ ✐ Presentation Pro CD-ROM 5-6
☐ 🖳 iText 5-6: at **PHSchool.com**

3. PRACTICE

Assignment Guide: Give an assignment based on the ability levels of your students.

    ☑ **Objective:** Core: 13–33, 45–48, 56–68;
Extension: 71, 73
Standardized Test Prep: 74–78, 80–81
Mixed Review: 82–96

Homework: _____

Targeted Resources

☐ ✎ Transparency: Student Answers 5-6
☐ Grab & Go File: Practice 5-6, Reteaching 5-6, Enrichment 5-6
☐ Practice Workbook 5-6
☐ Spanish Practice Workbook 5-6
☐ Hands-On Activities 12

4. ASSESS

Lesson Quiz: Assign the Lesson Quiz to assess students' mastery of the lesson content.

Targeted Resources

☐ ✎ Transparency: Lesson Quiz 5-6
☐ 🖳 Online Lesson Quiz 5-6: at **PHSchool.com**
☐ ✐ Computer Test Generator CD-ROM 5-6

Lesson Plan 6-1, Objective 1
Rate of Change and Slope

Lesson Objective	NAEP 2005	Local Standards
▼ Find rates of change from tables and graphs	A2a, b	
New Vocabulary: rate of change	**NCTM 2000** 2, 3, 4, 9, 10	
	Pacing Two Year: 1 day Two-Year Block: 0.5 day	

1. INTRODUCE

Check Skills You'll Need: Assign these exercises to review the prerequisite skills of evaluating function rules and simplifying ratios of differences.

New Vocabulary: Help students pre-read the lesson by pointing out the new term introduced in Objective 1.

Targeted Resources
- ☐ ⬚ Transparency: Check Skills You'll Need 6-1

2. TEACH

▼ **Objective:** Have students work the Investigation to explore Rate of Change. Review the formula in the Key Concepts box. Teach Examples 1 and 2. Assign Check Understanding questions 1 and 2 after the appropriate example.

Targeted Resources
- ☐ ⬚ Transparency: Additional Examples 6-1
- ☐ ⬚ Transparency: Classroom Aid 23
- ☐ Graphing Calculator Procedure 5: at **PHSchool.com**
- ☐ ✐ Presentation Pro CD-ROM 6-1
- ☐ ▣ iText 6-1: at **PHSchool.com**

3. PRACTICE

Assignment Guide: Give an assignment based on the ability levels of your students.

▼ **Objective:** Core: 1–6, 27–29, 40, 54
Standardized Test Prep: 74
Mixed Review: 76–87

Homework: _____

Targeted Resources
- ☐ ⬚ Transparency: Student Answers 6-1
- ☐ Grab & Go File: Practice 6-1, Reteaching 6-1, Enrichment 6-1
- ☐ Practice Workbook 6-1
- ☐ Spanish Practice Workbook 6-1
- ☐ Reading and Math Literacy 6A
- ☐ Spanish Reading and Math Literacy 6A
- ☐ Hands-On Activities 13

4. ASSESS

Lesson Quiz: Create a quiz on Objective 1 using the Computer Test Generator.

Targeted Resources
- ☐ ✐ Computer Test Generator CD-ROM 6-1

Lesson Plan 6-1, Objective 2
Rate of Change and Slope

Lesson Objective	NAEP 2005	Local Standards
⍰ Find slope **New Vocabulary:** slope	A2a, b **NCTM 2000** 2, 3, 4, 9, 10 **Pacing** Two Year: 1 day Two-Year Block: 0.5 day	

1. INTRODUCE

Check Skills You'll Need: Assign these exercises if not used with Objective 1.

Review: Review rate of change with students.

New Vocabulary: Help students pre-read the lesson by pointing out the new terms introduced in Objective 2.

Targeted Resources

☐ ⌨ Transparency: Check Skills You'll Need 6-1

2. TEACH

⍰ **Objective:** Teach Examples 3–5. Review the summary in the Key Concepts box. Assign Check Understanding questions 3–5 after the appropriate example.

Targeted Resources

☐ ⌨ Transparency: Additional Examples 6-1
☐ ⌨ Transparency: Classroom Aid 23
☐ Graphing Calculator Procedure 5:
    at **PHSchool.com**
☐ ✐ Presentation Pro CD-ROM 6-1
☐ 🖥 iText 6-1: at **PHSchool.com**

3. PRACTICE

Assignment Guide: Give an assignment based on the ability levels of your students.

⍰ **Objective:** Core: 7–26, 30–39, 41–53, 55–62;
Extension: 63–71
Standardized Test Prep: 72–73, 75
Mixed Review: 76–87

Homework: _____

Targeted Resources

☐ ⌨ Transparency: Student Answers 6-1
☐ Grab & Go File: Practice 6-1, Reteaching 6-1,
    Enrichment 6-1
☐ Practice Workbook 6-1
☐ Spanish Practice Workbook 6-1
☐ Reading and Math Literacy 6A
☐ Spanish Reading and Math Literacy 6A
☐ Hands-On Activities 13
☐ Reasoning and Puzzles 63, 64, 108:
    at **PHSchool.com**

4. ASSESS

Lesson Quiz: Assign the Lesson Quiz to assess students' mastery of the lesson content.

Targeted Resources

☐ ⌨ Transparency: Lesson Quiz 6-1
☐ 🖥 Online Lesson Quiz 6-1: at **PHSchool.com**
☐ ✐ Computer Test Generator CD-ROM 6-1

Lesson Plan 6-2, Objective 1
Slope-Intercept Form

Lesson Objective	NAEP 2005	Local Standards
▼ Write equations in slope-intercept form **New Vocabulary:** linear equation, *y*-intercept, slope-intercept form	A1h; A4c, d **NCTM 2000** 2, 4, 9, 10 **Pacing** Two Year: 1 day Two-Year Block: 0.5 day	

1. INTRODUCE

Check Skills You'll Need: Assign these exercises to review the prerequisite skills of evaluating expressions and solving linear equations for *y*.

New Vocabulary: Help students pre-read the lesson by pointing out the new terms introduced in Objective 1.

Targeted Resources
- ☐ ⛃ Transparency: Check Skills You'll Need 6-2

2. TEACH

▼ **Objective:** Go over the statement in the Key Concepts box. Teach Examples 1–3. Assign Check Understanding questions 1–3 after the appropriate examples.

Targeted Resources
- ☐ ⛃ Transparency: Additional Examples 6-2
- ☐ ⛃ Transparency: Classroom Aid 24
- ☐ ✐ Presentation Pro CD-ROM 6-2
- ☐ ▦ iText 6-2: at **PHSchool.com**

3. PRACTICE

Assignment Guide: Give an assignment based on the ability levels of your students.

▼ **Objective:** Core: 1–27, 41–49, 56–65, 68–74; Extension: 78–80
Standardized Test Prep: 83–85
Mixed Review: 87–91

Homework: _____

Targeted Resources
- ☐ ⛃ Transparency: Student Answers 6-2
- ☐ Grab & Go File: Practice 6-2, Reteaching 6-2, Enrichment 6-2
- ☐ Practice Workbook 6-2
- ☐ Spanish Practice Workbook 6-2
- ☐ Hands-On Activities 14

4. ASSESS

Lesson Quiz: Create a quiz on Objective 1 using the Computer Test Generator.

Targeted Resources
- ☐ ✐ Computer Test Generator CD-ROM 6-2

Lesson Plan 6-2, Objective 2
Slope-Intercept Form

Lesson Objective	NAEP 2005	Local Standards
⍦ Graph linear equations	A1h; A4c, d	
	NCTM 2000 2, 4, 9, 10	
	Pacing Two Year: 1 day Two-Year Block: 0.5 day	

1. INTRODUCE

Check Skills You'll Need: Assign these exercises if not used with Objective 1.

Review: Use the Key Concepts box to review slope-intercept form.

Targeted Resources

☐ ⌂ Transparency: Check Skills You'll Need 6-2

2. TEACH

⍦ **Objective:** Teach Examples 4 and 5. Assign Check Understanding questions 4 and 5 after the appropriate examples.

Targeted Resources

☐ ⌂ Transparency: Additional Examples 6-2
☐ ⌂ Transparency: Classroom Aid 24
☐ ✆ Presentation Pro CD-ROM 6-2
☐ ▦ iText 6-2: at **PHSchool.com**

3. PRACTICE

Assignment Guide: Give an assignment based on the ability levels of your students.

⍦ **Objective:** Core: 28–40, 50–55, 66–67, 75–77; Extension: 81–82
Standardized Test Prep: 86
Mixed Review: 87–91

Homework: _____

Targeted Resources

☐ ⌂ Transparency: Student Answers 6-2
☐ Grab & Go File: Practice 6-2, Reteaching 6-2, Enrichment 6-2
☐ Practice Workbook 6-2
☐ Spanish Practice Workbook 6-2
☐ Hands-On Activities 14
☐ Reasoning and Puzzles 64: at **PHSchool.com**

4. ASSESS

Lesson Quiz: Assign the Lesson Quiz to assess students' mastery of the lesson content.

Targeted Resources

☐ ⌂ Transparency: Lesson Quiz 6-2
☐ ▦ Online Lesson Quiz 6-2: at **PHSchool.com**
☐ ✆ Computer Test Generator CD-ROM 6-2

Lesson Plan 6-3, Objective 1
Standard Form

Lesson Objective	NAEP 2005	Local Standards
▼ Graph equations using intercepts **New Vocabulary:** standard form of a linear equation, *x*-intercept	A1h **NCTM 2000** 2, 6, 8, 9, 10 **Pacing** Two Year: 1 day Two-Year Block: 0.5 day	

1. INTRODUCE

Check Skills You'll Need: Assign these exercises to review the prerequisite skills of solving linear equations for *y* and clearing equations of decimals.

New Vocabulary: Help students pre-read the lesson by pointing out the new terms introduced in Objective 1.

Targeted Resources

☐ 💻 Transparency: Check Skills You'll Need 6-3

2. TEACH

▼ **Objective:** Have students work the Investigation to see how to find and use the *x*- and *y*- intercepts to graph a linear equation. Go over the standard form shown in the Key Concepts box. Teach examples 1–3. Assign Check Understanding 1–3 after the appropriate examples.

Targeted Resources

☐ 💻 Transparency: Additional Examples 6-3
☐ 💻 Transparency: Classroom Aid 24
☐ Graphing Calculator Procedure 5:
  at **PHSchool.com**
☐ 💿 Presentation Pro CD-ROM 6-3
☐ 🖥 iText 6-3: at **PHSchool.com**

3. PRACTICE

Assignment Guide: Give an assignment based on the ability levels of your students.

▼ **Objective:** Core: 1–26, 38–46, 49–57;
Extension: 64–65
Standardized Test Prep: 69
Mixed Review: 70–78

Homework: _____

Targeted Resources

☐ 💻 Transparency: Student Answers 6-3
☐ Grab & Go File: Practice 6-3, Reteaching 6-3,
  Enrichment 6-3
☐ Practice Workbook 6-3
☐ Spanish Practice Workbook 6-3
☐ Reading and Math Literacy 6B
☐ Spanish Reading and Math Literacy 6B

4. ASSESS

Lesson Quiz: Create a quiz on Objective 1 using the Computer Test Generator.

Targeted Resources

☐ 💿 Computer Test Generator CD-ROM 6-3

Lesson Plan 6-3, Objective 2
Standard Form

Lesson Objective ▼ Write equations in standard form	NAEP 2005 A1h **NCTM 2000** 2, 6, 8, 9, 10 **Pacing** Two Year: 1 day Two-Year Block: 0.5 day	Local Standards

1. INTRODUCE

Check Skills You'll Need: Assign these exercises if not used with Objective 1.

Review: Use the Key Concepts box to review the standard form of a linear equation.

Targeted Resources
- ☐ 🖴 Transparency: Check Skills You'll Need 6-3

2. TEACH

▼ **Objective:** Teach Examples 4 and 5. Assign Check Understanding 4 and 5 after the appropriate examples.

Targeted Resources
- ☐ 🖴 Transparency: Additional Examples 6-3
- ☐ 🖴 Transparency: Classroom Aid 24
- ☐ Graphing Calculator Procedure 5: at **PHSchool.com**
- ☐ 🖉 Presentation Pro CD-ROM 6-3
- ☐ 🖥 iText 6-3: at **PHSchool.com**

3. PRACTICE

Assignment Guide: Give an assignment based on the ability levels of your students.

▼ **Objective:** Core: 27–37, 47–48, 58–62; Extension: 63
Standardized Test Prep: 66–68
Mixed Review: 70–78

Homework: _____

Targeted Resources
- ☐ 🖴 Transparency: Student Answers 6-3
- ☐ Grab & Go File: Practice 6-3, Reteaching 6-3, Enrichment 6-3
- ☐ Practice Workbook 6-3
- ☐ Spanish Practice Workbook 6-3
- ☐ Reading and Math Literacy 6B
- ☐ Spanish Reading and Math Literacy 6B

4. ASSESS

Lesson Quiz: Assign the Lesson Quiz to assess students' mastery of the lesson content.

Checkpoint Quiz: Use the Checkpoint Quiz to assess student progress over several lessons.

Targeted Resources
- ☐ 🖴 Transparency: Lesson Quiz 6-3
- ☐ 🖥 Online Lesson Quiz 6-3: at **PHSchool.com**
- ☐ Grab & Go File: Checkpoint Quiz 1
- ☐ 🖉 Computer Test Generator CD-ROM 6-3

Lesson Plan 6-4, Objective 1
Point-Slope Form and Writing Linear Equations

Lesson Objective	NAEP 2005	Local Standards
▼ Graph and write linear equations using point-slope form **New Vocabulary:** point-slope form	A1h; A3a **NCTM 2000** 2, 6, 8, 9, 10 **Pacing** Two Year: 1 day Two-Year Block: 0.5 day	

1. INTRODUCE

Check Skills You'll Need: Assign these exercises to review the prerequisite skills of finding rate of change from a table and simplifying expressions.

New Vocabulary: Help students pre-read the lesson by pointing out the new term introduced in Objective 1.

Targeted Resources

☐ 🖳 Transparency: Check Skills You'll Need 6-4

2. TEACH

▼ **Objective:** Go over the formula in the Key Concepts box. Teach Examples 1–3. Assign Check Understanding 1–3 after the appropriate examples.

Targeted Resources

☐ 🖳 Transparency: Additional Examples 6-4
☐ 🖳 Transparency: Classroom Aid 24
☐ 🖉 Presentation Pro CD-ROM 6-4
☐ 🖳 iText 6-4: at **PHSchool.com**

3. PRACTICE

Assignment Guide: Give an assignment based on the ability levels of your students.

▼ **Objective:** Core: 1–30, 36–53, 56–59;
Extension: 61–63
Standardized Test Prep: 65–69
Mixed Review: 70–81

Homework: _____

Targeted Resources

☐ 🖳 Transparency: Student Answers 6-4
☐ Grab & Go File: Practice 6-4, Reteaching 6-4, Enrichment 6-4
☐ Practice Workbook 6-4
☐ Spanish Practice Workbook 6-4
☐ Technology Activities pp. 44–45

4. ASSESS

Lesson Quiz: Create a quiz on Objective 1 using the Computer Test Generator.

Targeted Resources

☐ 🖉 Computer Test Generator CD-ROM 6-4

Lesson Plan 6-4, Objective 2
Point-Slope Form and Writing Linear Equations

Lesson Objective ▼ Write a linear equation using data	NAEP 2005 A1h; A3a NCTM 2000 2, 6, 8, 9, 10 Pacing Two Year: 1 day Two-Year Block: 0.5 day	Local Standards

1. INTRODUCE

Check Skills You'll Need: Assign these exercises if not used with Objective 1.

Review: Use the Key Concepts box to review point-slope form.

Targeted Resources
☐ ⛏ Transparency: Check Skills You'll Need 6-4

2. TEACH

▼ **Objective:** Teach Examples 4 and 5. Assign Check Understanding 4 and 5 after the appropriate examples. Review the three forms of linear equations shown in the Key Concepts box.

Targeted Resources
☐ ⛏ Transparency: Additional Examples 6-4
☐ ⛏ Transparency: Classroom Aid 24
☐ ✎ Presentation Pro CD-ROM 6-4
☐ ▣ iText 6-4: at **PHSchool.com**

3. PRACTICE

Assignment Guide: Give an assignment based on the ability levels of your students.

▼ **Objective:** Core: 31–35, 54–55, 60; Extension: 64
Mixed Review: 70–81

Homework: _____

Targeted Resources
☐ ⛏ Transparency: Student Answers 6-4
☐ Grab & Go File: Practice 6-4, Reteaching 6-4, Enrichment 6-4
☐ Practice Workbook 6-4
☐ Spanish Practice Workbook 6-4
☐ Technology Activities 6, 20

4. ASSESS

Lesson Quiz: Assign the Lesson Quiz to assess students' mastery of the lesson content.

Targeted Resources
☐ ⛏ Transparency: Lesson Quiz 6-4
☐ ▣ Online Lesson Quiz 6-4: at **PHSchool.com**
☐ ✎ Computer Test Generator CD-ROM 6-4

Lesson Plan 6-5, Objective 1
Parallel and Perpendicular Lines

Lesson Objective	NAEP 2005	Local Standards
▼ Determine whether lines are parallel **New Vocabulary:** parallel lines	A2e; G3g **NCTM 2000** 2, 3, 4, 6, 9, 10 **Pacing** Two Year: 1 day Two-Year Block: 0.5 day	

1. INTRODUCE

Check Skills You'll Need: Assign these exercises to review the prerequisite skills of finding reciprocals and finding slope and *y*-intercept from a linear equation.

New Vocabulary: Help students pre-read the lesson by pointing out the new term introduced in Objective 1.

Targeted Resources
- ☐ ⬒ Transparency: Check Skills You'll Need 6-5

2. TEACH

▼ **Objective:** Go over the property in the Key Concepts box. Teach Examples 1 and 2. Assign Check Understanding 1 and 2 after the appropriate examples.

Targeted Resources
- ☐ ⬒ Transparency: Additional Examples 6-5
- ☐ ⬒ Transparency: Classroom Aid 25
- ☐ ✐ Presentation Pro CD-ROM 6-5
- ☐ ▣ iText 6-5: at **PHSchool.com**

3. PRACTICE

Assignment Guide: Give an assignment based on the ability levels of your students.

▼ **Objective:** Core: 1–18, 42–43, 46–47, 53–62; Extension: 68
Standardized Test Prep: 74–79
Mixed Review: 80–91

Homework: _____

Targeted Resources
- ☐ ⬒ Transparency: Student Answers 6-5
- ☐ Grab & Go File: Practice 6-5, Reteaching 6-5, Enrichment 6-5
- ☐ Practice Workbook 6-5
- ☐ Spanish Practice Workbook 6-5

4. ASSESS

Lesson Quiz: Create a quiz on Objective 1 using the Computer Test Generator.

Targeted Resources
- ☐ ✐ Computer Test Generator CD-ROM 6-5

Teacher _____ Class _____ Date _____ M T W Th F

Lesson Plan 6-5, Objective 2
Parallel and Perpendicular Lines

Lesson Objective	NAEP 2005	Local Standards
☑ Determine whether lines are perpendicular **New Vocabulary:** perpendicular lines, negative reciprocal	A2e; G3g **NCTM 2000** 2, 3, 4, 6, 9, 10 **Pacing** Two Year: 1 day Two-Year Block: 0.5 day	

1. INTRODUCE

Check Skills You'll Need: Assign these exercises if not used with Objective 1.

Review: Use the Key Concepts box to review the slopes of parallel lines.

New Vocabulary: Help students pre-read the lesson by pointing out the new terms introduced in Objective 2.

Targeted Resources
- ☐ 📖 Transparency: Check Skills You'll Need 6-5

2. TEACH

☑ **Objective:** Go over the property in the Key Concepts box. Teach Examples 3 and 4. Assign Check Understanding 3 and 4 after the appropriate examples.

Targeted Resources
- ☐ 📖 Transparency: Additional Examples 6-5
- ☐ 📖 Transparency: Classroom Aid 25
- ☐ 💿 Presentation Pro CD-ROM 6-5
- ☐ 💻 iText 6-5: at **PHSchool.com**

3. PRACTICE

Assignment Guide: Give an assignment based on the ability levels of your students.

☑ **Objective:** Core: 19–41, 44–45, 48–52, 63–65; Extension: 66–67, 69–72
Standardized Test Prep: 73
Mixed Review: 80–91

Homework: _____

Targeted Resources
- ☐ 📖 Transparency: Student Answers 6-5
- ☐ Grab & Go File: Practice 6-5, Reteaching 6-5, Enrichment 6-5
- ☐ Practice Workbook 6-5
- ☐ Spanish Practice Workbook 6-5

4. ASSESS

Lesson Quiz: Assign the Lesson Quiz to assess students' mastery of the lesson content.

Targeted Resources
- ☐ 📖 Transparency: Lesson Quiz 6-5
- ☐ 💻 Online Lesson Quiz 6-5: at **PHSchool.com**
- ☐ 💿 Computer Test Generator CD-ROM 6-5

Lesson Plan 6-6, Objective 1
Scatter Plots and Equations of Lines

Lesson Objective	NAEP 2005	Local Standards
▼ Write an equation for a trend line and use it to make predications	A2f; D2e, g	
	NCTM 2000	
	2, 3, 4, 5, 6	
	Pacing	
	Two Year: 1 day	
	Two-Year Block: 0.5 day	

1. INTRODUCE

Check Skills You'll Need: Assign these exercises to review the prerequisite skills of drawing a scatter plot.

Targeted Resources
- ☐ 🔲 Transparency: Check Skills You'll Need 6-6

2. TEACH

▼ **Objective:** Teach Example 1. Assign Check Understanding question 1.

Targeted Resources
- ☐ 🔲 Transparency: Additional Examples 6-6
- ☐ Graphing Calculator Procedure 22: at **PHSchool.com**
- ☐ 🖉 Presentation Pro CD-ROM 6-6
- ☐ 🖥 iText 6-6: at **PHSchool.com**

3. PRACTICE

Assignment Guide: Give an assignment based on the ability levels of your students.

▼ **Objective:** Core: 1–6, 12–13, 15, 19
Standardized Test Prep: 21–23
Mixed Review: 24–35

Homework: _____

Targeted Resources
- ☐ 🔲 Transparency: Student Answers 6-6
- ☐ Grab & Go File: Practice 6-6, Reteaching 6-6, Enrichment 6-6
- ☐ Practice Workbook 6-6
- ☐ Spanish Practice Workbook 6-6
- ☐ Reading and Math Literacy 6C
- ☐ Spanish Reading and Math Literacy 6C
- ☐ Hands-On Activities 19

4. ASSESS

Lesson Quiz: Create a quiz on Objective 1 using the Computer Test Generator.

Targeted Resources
- ☐ 🖉 Computer Test Generator CD-ROM 6-6

Lesson Plan 6-6, Objective 2
Scatter Plots and Equations of Lines

Lesson Objective	NAEP 2005	Local Standards
▼ Write an equation for a line of best fit and use it to make predications **New Vocabulary:** line of best fit, correlation coefficient	A2f; D2e, g **NCTM 2000** 2, 3, 4, 5, 6 **Pacing** Two Year: 1 day Two-Year Block: 0.5 day	

1. INTRODUCE

Check Skills You'll Need: Assign these exercises if not used with Objective 1.

Review: Remind the students how to write an equation for a trend line.

New Vocabulary: Help students pre-read the lesson by pointing out the new terms introduced in Objective 2.

Targeted Resources

☐ ⌨ Transparency: Check Skills You'll Need 6-6

2. TEACH

▼ **Objective:** Teach Example 2. Assign Check Understanding question 2.

Targeted Resources

☐ ⌨ Transparency: Additional Examples 6-6
☐ Graphing Calculator Procedure 22: at **PHSchool.com**
☐ ✐ Presentation Pro CD-ROM 6-6
☐ 💻 iText 6-6: at **PHSchool.com**

3. PRACTICE

Assignment Guide: Give an assignment based on the ability levels of your students.

▼ **Objective:** Core: 7–11, 14, 16–18; Extension: 20
Mixed Review: 24–35

Homework: _____

Targeted Resources

☐ ⌨ Transparency: Student Answers 6-6
☐ Grab & Go File: Practice 6-6, Reteaching 6-6, Enrichment 6-6
☐ Practice Workbook 6-6
☐ Spanish Practice Workbook 6-6
☐ Reading and Math Literacy 6C
☐ Spanish Reading and Math Literacy 6C
☐ Hands-On Activities 19

4. ASSESS

Lesson Quiz: Assign the Lesson Quiz to assess students' mastery of the lesson content.

Checkpoint Quiz: Use the Checkpoint Quiz to assess student progress over several lessons.

Targeted Resources

☐ ⌨ Transparency: Lesson Quiz 6-6
☐ 💻 Online Lesson Quiz 6-6: at **PHSchool.com**
☐ Grab & Go File: Checkpoint Quiz 2
☐ ✐ Computer Test Generator CD-ROM 6-6

Teacher _____   Class _____   Date _____   M T W Th F

Lesson Plan 6-7, Objective 1
Graphing Absolute Value Equations

Lesson Objective	NAEP 2005	Local Standards
▼ Translate the graph of an absolute value equation **New Vocabulary:** absolute value equation, translation	A2d **NCTM 2000** 1, 2, 3, 7, 10 **Pacing** Two Year: 2 days Two-Year Block: 1 day	

1. INTRODUCE

Check Skills You'll Need: Assign these exercises to review the prerequisite skills of interpreting absolute value expressions and making a table from an equation.

New Vocabulary: Help students pre-read the lesson by pointing out the new terms introduced in the lesson.

Targeted Resources

☐ 📧 Transparency: Check Skills You'll Need 6-7

2. TEACH

▼ **Objective:** Teach Examples 1–5. Assign Check Understanding questions 1–5 after the appropriate examples.

Targeted Resources

☐ 📧 Transparency: Additional Examples 6-7
☐ 📧 Transparency: Classroom Aid 27
☐ ✐ Presentation Pro CD-ROM 6-7
☐ 💻 iText 6-7: at **PHSchool.com**

3. PRACTICE

Assignment Guide: Give an assignment based on the ability levels of your students.

▼ **Objective:** Core: 1–41; Extension: 42–43
Standardized Test Prep: 44–48
Mixed Review: 49–53

Homework: _____

Targeted Resources

☐ 📧 Transparency: Student Answers 6-7
☐ Grab & Go File: Practice 6-7, Reteaching 6-7, Enrichment 6-7
☐ Practice Workbook 6-7
☐ Spanish Practice Workbook 6-7

4. ASSESS

Lesson Quiz: Assign the Lesson Quiz to assess students' mastery of the lesson content.

Targeted Resources

☐ 📧 Transparency: Lesson Quiz 6-7
☐ 💻 Online Lesson Quiz 6-7: at **PHSchool.com**
☐ ✐ Computer Test Generator CD-ROM 6-7

Lesson Plan 7-1, Objective 1
Solving Systems by Graphing

Lesson Objective	NAEP 2005	Local Standards
▼ Solve systems by graphing	A4d, g	
New Vocabulary: system of linear equations, solution of a system of linear equations	**NCTM 2000** 2, 8, 10	
	Pacing Two Year: 1 day Two-Year Block: 0.5 day	

1. INTRODUCE

Check Skills You'll Need: Assign these exercises to review the prerequisite skills of solving linear equations and graphing pairs of linear equations.

New Vocabulary: Help students pre-read the lesson by pointing out the new terms introduced in Objective 1.

Targeted Resources

☐ ✑ Transparency: Check Skills You'll Need 7-1

2. TEACH

▼ **Objective:** Teach Examples 1 and 2. Assign Check Understanding questions 1 and 2 after the appropriate examples.

Targeted Resources

☐ ✑ Transparency: Additional Examples 7-1
☐ ✑ Transparency: Classroom Aid 3
☐ ✐ Presentation Pro CD-ROM 7-1
☐ ▦ iText 7-1: at **PHSchool.com**

3. PRACTICE

Assignment Guide: Give an assignment based on the ability levels of your students.

▼ **Objective:** Core: 1–14, 23–26, 29–39;
Extension: 42
Standardized Test Prep: 43–44, 46
Mixed Review: 47–57

Homework: _____

Targeted Resources

☐ ✑ Transparency: Student Answers 7-1
☐ Grab & Go File: Practice 7-1, Reteaching 7-1, Enrichment 7-1
☐ Practice Workbook 7-1
☐ Spanish Practice Workbook 7-1
☐ Reading and Math Literacy 7A
☐ Spanish Reading and Math Literacy 7A

4. ASSESS

Lesson Quiz: Create a quiz on Objective 1 using the Computer Test Generator.

Targeted Resources

☐ ✐ Computer Test Generator CD-ROM 7-1

Lesson Plan 7-1, Objective 2
Solving Systems by Graphing

Lesson Objective ▼ Analyze special types of systems **New Vocabulary:** no solution, infinitely many solutions	**NAEP 2005** A4d, g **NCTM 2000** 2, 8, 10 **Pacing** Two Year: 1 day Two-Year Block: 0.5 day	**Local Standards**

1. INTRODUCE

Check Skills You'll Need: Assign these exercises if not used with Objective 1.

Review: Review solving systems by graphing with the students.

New Vocabulary: Help students pre-read the lesson by pointing out the new terms introduced in Objective 2.

Targeted Resources
- ☐ 🖮 Transparency: Check Skills You'll Need 7-1

2. TEACH

▼ Objective: Teach Examples 3 and 4. Assign Check Understanding questions 3 and 4 after the appropriate examples. Review the three possible situations in the Key Concepts box.

Targeted Resources
- ☐ 🖮 Transparency: Additional Examples 7-1
- ☐ 🖮 Transparency: Classroom Aid 3
- ☐ 🖉 Presentation Pro CD-ROM 7-1
- ☐ 🖳 iText 7-1: at **PHSchool.com**

3. PRACTICE

Assignment Guide: Give an assignment based on the ability levels of your students.

▼ Objective: Core: 15–22, 27–28; Extension: 40–41
Standardized Test Prep: 45
Mixed Review: 47–57

Homework: _____

Targeted Resources
- ☐ 🖮 Transparency: Student Answers 7-1
- ☐ Grab & Go File: Practice 7-1, Reteaching 7-1, Enrichment 7-1
- ☐ Practice Workbook 7-1
- ☐ Spanish Practice Workbook 7-1
- ☐ Reading and Math Literacy 7A
- ☐ Spanish Reading and Math Literacy 7A
- ☐ Reasoning and Puzzles 68: at **PHSchool.com**

4. ASSESS

Lesson Quiz: Assign the Lesson Quiz to assess students' mastery of the lesson content.

Targeted Resources
- ☐ 🖮 Transparency: Lesson Quiz 7-1
- ☐ 🖳 Online Lesson Quiz 7-1: at **PHSchool.com**
- ☐ 🖉 Computer Test Generator CD-ROM 7-1

Lesson Plan 7-2, Objective 1
Solving Systems Using Substitution

Lesson Objective	NAEP 2005	Local Standards
▼ Solve systems using substitution	A4g	
New Vocabulary: substitution method	**NCTM 2000** 2, 3, 8, 9, 10	
	Pacing Two Year: 2 days Two-Year Block: 1 day	

1. INTRODUCE

Check Skills You'll Need: Assign these exercises to review the prerequisite skills of solving linear equations and checking solutions of a pair of equations.

New Vocabulary: Help students pre-read the lesson by pointing out the new term introduced in the lesson.

Targeted Resources

☐ 🖳 Transparency: Check Skills You'll Need 7-2

2. TEACH

▼ **Objective:** Have students work the Investigation to see that the graphing method provides only an approximate solution to a system of linear equations. Teach Examples 1–3. Assign Check Understanding questions 1–3 after the appropriate examples.

Targeted Resources

☐ 🖳 Transparency: Additional Examples 7-2
☐ 🖉 Presentation Pro CD-ROM 7-2
☐ 🖳 iText 7-2: at **PHSchool.com**

3. PRACTICE

Assignment Guide: Give an assignment based on the ability levels of your students.

   ▼ **Objective:** Core: 1–40; Extension: 41–46
Standardized Test Prep: 47–50
Mixed Review: 51–59

Homework: _____

Targeted Resources

☐ 🖳 Transparency: Student Answers 7-2
☐ Grab & Go File: Practice 7-2, Reteaching 7-2, Enrichment 7-2
☐ Practice Workbook 7-2
☐ Spanish Practice Workbook 7-2
☐ Reading and Math Literacy 7B
☐ Spanish Reading and Math Literacy 7B
☐ Reasoning and Puzzles 71, 72: at **PHSchool.com**

4. ASSESS

Lesson Quiz: Assign the Lesson Quiz to assess students' mastery of the lesson content.

Checkpoint Quiz: Use the Checkpoint Quiz to assess student progress over several lessons.

Targeted Resources

☐ 🖳 Transparency: Lesson Quiz 7-2
☐ 🖳 Online Lesson Quiz 7-2: at **PHSchool.com**
☐ Grab & Go File: Checkpoint Quiz 1
☐ 🖉 Computer Test Generator CD-ROM 7-2

Lesson Plan 7-3, Objective 1
Solving Systems Using Elimination

Lesson Objective	NAEP 2005	Local Standards
▼ Solve systems by adding or subtracting	A4g	
New Vocabulary: elimination method	**NCTM 2000** 1, 2, 8, 9, 10	
	Pacing Two Year: 1 day Two-Year Block: 0.5 day	

1. INTRODUCE

Check Skills You'll Need: Assign these exercises to review the prerequisite skills of solving systems by substitution.

New Vocabulary: Help students pre-read the lesson by pointing out the new term introduced in Objective 1.

Targeted Resources

☐ ◣ Transparency: Check Skills You'll Need 7-3

2. TEACH

▼ **Objective:** Teach Examples 1 and 2. Assign Check Understanding questions 1 and 2 after the appropriate example.

Targeted Resources

☐ ◣ Transparency: Additional Examples 7-3
☐ ✐ Presentation Pro CD-ROM 7-3
☐ ▣ iText 7-3: at **PHSchool.com**

3. PRACTICE

Assignment Guide: Give an assignment based on the ability levels of your students.

▼ **Objective:** Core: 1–8, 32, 39–41; Extension: 43
Standardized Test Prep: 47–48
Mixed Review: 51–62

Homework: _____

Targeted Resources

☐ ◣ Transparency: Student Answers 7-3
☐ Grab & Go File: Practice 7-3, Reteaching 7-3, Enrichment 7-3
☐ Practice Workbook 7-3
☐ Spanish Practice Workbook 7-3
☐ Technology Activities 21

4. ASSESS

Lesson Quiz: Create a quiz on Objective 1 using the Computer Test Generator.

Targeted Resources

☐ ✐ Computer Test Generator CD-ROM 7-3

Lesson Plan 7-3, Objective 2
Solving Systems Using Elimination

Lesson Objective	NAEP 2005	Local Standards
▼ Multiply first when solving systems	A4g	
	NCTM 2000	
	1, 2, 8, 9, 10	
	Pacing	
	Two Year: 1 day	
	Two-Year Block:	
	0.5 day	

1. INTRODUCE

Check Skills You'll Need: Assign these exercises if not used with Objective 1.

Review: Review adding or subtracting to solve systems.

Targeted Resources
☐ ⬓ Transparency: Check Skills You'll Need 7-3

2. TEACH

▼ **Objective:** Teach Examples 3–5. Assign Check Understanding questions 3–5 after the appropriate example. Review the flowchart to help students determine the best way to eliminate a variable.

Targeted Resources
☐ ⬓ Transparency: Additional Examples 7-3
☐ ✎ Presentation Pro CD-ROM 7-3
☐ ▣ iText 7-3: at **PHSchool.com**

3. PRACTICE

Assignment Guide: Give an assignment based on the ability levels of your students.

    ▼ **Objective:** Core: 9–31, 33–38; Extension: 42, 44–46
    Standardized Test Prep: 49–50
    Mixed Review: 51–62

Homework: _____

Targeted Resources
☐ ⬓ Transparency: Student Answers 7-3
☐ Grab & Go File: Practice 7-3, Reteaching 7-3, Enrichment 7-3
☐ Practice Workbook 7-3
☐ Spanish Practice Workbook 7-3
☐ Technology Activities 21
☐ Reasoning and Puzzles 69: at **PHSchool.com**

4. ASSESS

Lesson Quiz: Assign the Lesson Quiz to assess students' mastery of the lesson content.

Targeted Resources
☐ ⬓ Transparency: Lesson Quiz 7-3
☐ ▣ Online Lesson Quiz 7-3: at **PHSchool.com**
☐ ✎ Computer Test Generator CD-ROM 7-3

Lesson Plan 7-4, Objective 1
Applications of Linear Systems

Lesson Objective	NAEP 2005	Local Standards
▼ Write systems of linear equations	A4a, g	
	NCTM 2000 1, 2, 8, 9, 10	
	Pacing Two Year: 4 days Two-Year Block: 2 days	

1. INTRODUCE

Check Skills You'll Need: Assign these exercises to review the prerequisite skills of solving distance-time-rate problems.

Targeted Resources
- ☐ ⌁ Transparency: Check Skills You'll Need 7-4

2. TEACH

▼ **Objective:** Review the summary of system solution methods in the Key Concepts box. Teach Examples 1–3. Assign Check Understanding questions 1–3 after the appropriate examples.

Targeted Resources
- ☐ ⌁ Transparency: Additional Examples 7-4
- ☐ ⊘ Presentation Pro CD-ROM 7-4
- ☐ ▣ iText 7-4: at **PHSchool.com**

3. PRACTICE

Assignment Guide: Give an assignment based on the ability levels of your students.

▼ **Objective:** Core: 1–22; Extension: 23–24
Standardized Test Prep: 25–28
Mixed Review: 29–43

Homework: _____

Targeted Resources
- ☐ ⌁ Transparency: Student Answers 7-4
- ☐ Grab & Go File: Practice 7-4, Reteaching 7-4, Enrichment 7-4
- ☐ Practice Workbook 7-4
- ☐ Spanish Practice Workbook 7-4

4. ASSESS

Lesson Quiz: Assign the Lesson Quiz to assess students' mastery of the lesson content.

Targeted Resources
- ☐ ⌁ Transparency: Lesson Quiz 7-4
- ☐ ▣ Online Lesson Quiz 7-4: at **PHSchool.com**
- ☐ ⊘ Computer Test Generator CD-ROM 7-4

Lesson Plan 7-5, Objective 1
Linear Inequalities

Lesson Objective	NAEP 2005	Local Standards
▼ Graph linear inequalities **New Vocabulary:** linear inequality, solutions of an inequality	A3a; A4a, c **NCTM 2000** 1, 2, 6, 9, 10 **Pacing** Two Year: 1 day Two-Year Block: 0.5 day	

1. INTRODUCE

Check Skills You'll Need: Assign these exercises to review the prerequisite skills of interpreting inequality symbols and using slope-intercept form.

New Vocabulary: Help students pre-read the lesson by pointing out the new terms introduced in Objective 1.

Targeted Resources

☐ ⌐ Transparency: Check Skills You'll Need 7-5

2. TEACH

▼ **Objective:** Have students work the Investigation to see the relationship between the graph of a linear inequality and the graph of the associated linear equation. Teach Examples 1 and 2. Assign Check Understanding 1 and 2 after the appropriate example.

Targeted Resources

☐ ⌐ Transparency: Additional Examples 7-5
☐ ✺ Presentation Pro CD-ROM 7-5
☐ ▣ iText 7-5: at **PHSchool.com**

3. PRACTICE

Assignment Guide: Give an assignment based on the ability levels of your students.

▼ **Objective:** Core: 1–22, 25–36, 38–43;
Extension: 46–47
Standardized Test Prep: 50–52, 54
Mixed Review: 55–70

Homework: _____

Targeted Resources

☐ ⌐ Transparency: Student Answers 7-5
☐ Grab & Go File: Practice 7-5, Reteaching 7-5, Enrichment 7-5
☐ Practice Workbook 7-5
☐ Spanish Practice Workbook 7-5
☐ Reading and Math Literacy 7C
☐ Spanish Reading and Math Literacy 7C
☐ Hands-On Activities 16

4. ASSESS

Lesson Quiz: Create a quiz on Objective 1 using the Computer Test Generator.

Targeted Resources

☐ ✺ Computer Test Generator CD-ROM 7-5

Lesson Plan 7-5, Objective 2
Linear Inequalities

Lesson Objective	NAEP 2005	Local Standards
✒ Write and use linear inequalities when modeling real-worl situations	A3a; A4a, c	
	NCTM 2000 1, 2, 6, 9, 10	
	Pacing Two Year: 1 day Two-Year Block: 0.5 day	

1. INTRODUCE

Check Skills You'll Need: Assign these exercises if not used with Objective 1.

Review: Review graphing linear inequalities.

Targeted Resources
- ☐ Transparency: Check Skills You'll Need 7-5

2. TEACH

✒ **Objective:** Teach Example 3. Assign Check Understanding question 3.

Targeted Resources
- ☐ Transparency: Additional Examples 7-5
- ☐ Presentation Pro CD-ROM 7-5
- ☐ iText 7-5: at **PHSchool.com**

3. PRACTICE

Assignment Guide: Give an assignment based on the ability levels of your students.

✒ **Objective:** Core: 23–24, 37, 44–45; Extension: 48–49
Standardized Test Prep: 53
Mixed Review: 55–70

Homework: _____

Targeted Resources
- ☐ Transparency: Student Answers 7-5
- ☐ Grab & Go File: Practice 7-5, Reteaching 7-5, Enrichment 7-5
- ☐ Practice Workbook 7-5
- ☐ Spanish Practice Workbook 7-5
- ☐ Reading and Math Literacy 7C
- ☐ Spanish Reading and Math Literacy 7C
- ☐ Hands-On Activities 16

4. ASSESS

Lesson Quiz: Assign the Lesson Quiz to assess students' mastery of the lesson content.

Checkpoint Quiz: Use the Checkpoint Quiz to assess student progress over several lessons.

Targeted Resources
- ☐ Transparency: Lesson Quiz 7-5
- ☐ Online Lesson Quiz 7-5: at **PHSchool.com**
- ☐ Grab & Go File: Checkpoint Quiz 2
- ☐ Computer Test Generator CD-ROM 7-5

Lesson Plan 7-6, Objective 1
Systems of Linear Inequalities

Lesson Objective	NAEP 2005	Local Standards
▼ Solve systems of linear inequalities by graphing **New Vocabulary:** system of linear inequalities, solution of a system of linear inequalities	A4c, g **NCTM 2000** 1, 2, 6, 8, 10 **Pacing** Two Year: 2 days Two-Year Block: 1 day	

1. INTRODUCE

Check Skills You'll Need: Assign these exercises to review the prerequisite skills of solving systems of equations by graphing and graphing linear inequalities.

New Vocabulary: Help students pre-read the lesson by pointing out the new terms introduced in Objective 1.

Targeted Resources

☐ ⌐ Transparency: Check Skills You'll Need 7-6

2. TEACH

▼ **Objective:** Teach Examples 1 and 2. Assign Check Understanding questions 1 and 2 after the appropriate examples.

Targeted Resources

☐ ⌐ Transparency: Additional Examples 7-6
☐ ⊘ Presentation Pro CD-ROM 7-6
☐ ▣ iText 7-6: at **PHSchool.com**

3. PRACTICE

Assignment Guide: Give an assignment based on the ability levels of your students.

▼ **Objective:** Core: 1–19, 25–34, 36–42;
Extension: 44–46
Standardized Test Prep: 49, 51
Mixed Review: 53–70

Homework: _____

Targeted Resources

☐ ⌐ Transparency: Student Answers 7-6
☐ Grab & Go File: Practice 7-6, Reteaching 7-6, Enrichment 7-6
☐ Practice Workbook 7-6
☐ Spanish Practice Workbook 7-6
☐ Hands-On Activities 17

4. ASSESS

Lesson Quiz: Create a quiz on Objective 1 using the Computer Test Generator.

Targeted Resources

☐ ⊘ Computer Test Generator CD-ROM 7-6

Lesson Plan 7-6, Objective 2
Systems of Linear Inequalities

Lesson Objective	NAEP 2005	Local Standards
❷ Model real-world situations using systems of linear inequalities	A4c, g **NCTM 2000** 1, 2, 6, 8, 10 **Pacing** Two Year: 1 day Two-Year Block: 1 day	

1. INTRODUCE

Check Skills You'll Need: Assign these exercises if not used with Objective 1.

Review: Review solving systems of linear inequalities by graphing.

Targeted Resources
- ☐ ⌁ Transparency: Check Skills You'll Need 7-6

2. TEACH

❷ **Objective:** Teach Examples 3 and 4. Assign Check Understanding questions 3 and 4 after the appropriate examples.

Targeted Resources
- ☐ ⌁ Transparency: Additional Examples 7-6
- ☐ ✺ Presentation Pro CD-ROM 7-6
- ☐ ▣ iText 7-6: at **PHSchool.com**

3. PRACTICE

Assignment Guide: Give an assignment based on the ability levels of your students.

❷ **Objective:** Core: 20–24, 35; Extension: 43, 47–48
Standardized Test Prep: 50, 52
Mixed Review: 53–70

Homework: _____

Targeted Resources
- ☐ ⌁ Transparency: Student Answers 7-6
- ☐ Grab & Go File: Practice 7-6, Reteaching 7-6, Enrichment 7-6
- ☐ Practice Workbook 7-6
- ☐ Spanish Practice Workbook 7-6
- ☐ Hands-On Activities 17

4. ASSESS

Lesson Quiz: Assign the Lesson Quiz to assess students' mastery of the lesson content.

Targeted Resources
- ☐ ⌁ Transparency: Lesson Quiz 7-6
- ☐ ▣ Online Lesson Quiz 7-6: at **PHSchool.com**
- ☐ ✺ Computer Test Generator CD-ROM 7-6

Lesson Plan 8-1, Objective 1
Zero and Negative Exponents

Lesson Objective	NAEP 2005	Local Standards
▼ Simplify expressions with zero and negative exponents	N1d; N5e	
	NCTM 2000 2, 4, 8, 1	
	Pacing Two Year: 1 day Two-Year Block: 0.5 day	

1. INTRODUCE

Check Skills You'll Need: Assign these exercises to review the prerequisite skills of simplifying expressions with natural number exponents and evaluating expressions.

Targeted Resources

☐ 🖳 Transparency: Check Skills You'll Need 8-1

2. TEACH

▼ **Objective:** Have students work the Investigation to see the logic in the definitions of zero and negative exponents. Discuss the properties in the Key Concept boxes. Teach Examples 1 and 2. Assign Check Understanding 1 and 2 after the appropriate example.

Targeted Resources

☐ 🖳 Transparency: Additional Examples 8-1
☐ Graphing Calculator Procedure 17:
  at **PHSchool.com**
☐ 🖉 Presentation Pro CD-ROM 8-1
☐ 🖳 iText 8-1: at **PHSchool.com**

3. PRACTICE

Assignment Guide: Give an assignment based on the ability levels of your students.

  ▼ **Objective:** Core: 1–32, 46–67, 73–78; Extension: 81–84
Standardized Test Prep: 89, 91–93
Mixed Review: 94–103

Homework: _____

Targeted Resources

☐ 🖳 Transparency: Student Answers 8-1
☐ Grab & Go File: Practice 8-1, Reteaching 8-1, Enrichment 8-1
☐ Practice Workbook 8-1
☐ Spanish Practice Workbook 8-1
☐ Reading and Math Literacy 8A
☐ Spanish Reading and Math Literacy 8A

4. ASSESS

Lesson Quiz: Create a quiz on Objective 1 using the Computer Test Generator.

Targeted Resources

☐ 🖉 Computer Test Generator CD-ROM 8-1

Lesson Plan 8-1, Objective 2
Zero and Negative Exponents

Lesson Objective	NAEP 2005	Local Standards
❷ Evaluate exponential expressions	N1d; N5e	
	NCTM 2000	
	2, 4, 8, 1	
	Pacing	
	Two Year: 1 day	
	Two-Year Block:	
	0.5 day	

1. INTRODUCE

Check Skills You'll Need: Assign these exercises if not used with Objective 1.

Review: Review the properties in the Key Concepts box.

Targeted Resources

☐ 📥 Transparency: Check Skills You'll Need 8-1

2. TEACH

❷ **Objective:** Teach Examples 3 and 4. Assign Check Understanding 3 and 4 after the appropriate example.

Targeted Resources

☐ 📥 Transparency: Additional Examples 8-1
☐ Graphing Calculator Procedure 17: at **PHSchool.com**
☐ ✐ Presentation Pro CD-ROM 8-1
☐ 💻 iText 8-1: at **PHSchool.com**

3. PRACTICE

Assignment Guide: Give an assignment based on the ability levels of your students.

❷ **Objective:** Core: 33–45, 68–72, 79–80; Extension: 85–87
Standardized Test Prep: 88, 90
Mixed Review: 94–103

Homework: _____

Targeted Resources

☐ 📥 Transparency: Student Answers 8-1
☐ Grab & Go File: Practice 8-1, Reteaching 8-1, Enrichment 8-1
☐ Practice Workbook 8-1
☐ Spanish Practice Workbook 8-1
☐ Reading and Math Literacy 8A
☐ Spanish Reading and Math Literacy 8A
☐ Reasoning & Puzzles 10, 30: at **PHSchool.com**

4. ASSESS

Lesson Quiz: Assign the Lesson Quiz to assess students' mastery of the lesson content.

Targeted Resources

☐ 📥 Transparency: Lesson Quiz 8-1
☐ 💻 Online Lesson Quiz 8-1: at **PHSchool.com**
☐ ✐ Computer Test Generator CD-ROM 8-1

Lesson Plan 8-2, Objective 1
Scientific Notation

Lesson Objective ▼ Write numbers in scientific and standard notation **New Vocabulary:** scientific notation	**NAEP 2005** N1f; N2c **NCTM 2000** 1, 4, 8, 9, 10 **Pacing** Two Year: 1 day Two-Year Block: 0.5 day	**Local Standards**

1. INTRODUCE

Check Skills You'll Need: Assign these exercises to review the prerequisite skill of simplifying expressions involving powers of ten.

New Vocabulary: Help students pre-read the lesson by pointing out the new term introduced in Objective 1.

Targeted Resources
- ☐ 🖳 Transparency: Check Skills You'll Need 8-2

2. TEACH

▼ **Objective:** Review the definition in the key Concepts box. Teach Examples 1–3. Assign Check Understanding questions 1–3 after the appropriate example.

Targeted Resources
- ☐ 🖳 Transparency: Additional Examples 8-2
- ☐ Graphing Calculator Procedure 18: at **PHSchool.com**
- ☐ 🖉 Presentation Pro CD-ROM 8-2
- ☐ 🖳 iText 8-2: at **PHSchool.com**

3. PRACTICE

Assignment Guide: Give an assignment based on the ability levels of your students.

▼ **Objective:** Core: 1–22, 34–41; Extension: 48
Standardized Test Prep: 49, 51
Mixed Review: 53–60

Homework: _____

Targeted Resources
- ☐ 🖳 Transparency: Student Answers 8-2
- ☐ Grab & Go File: Practice 8-2, Reteaching 8-2, Enrichment 8-2
- ☐ Practice Workbook 8-2
- ☐ Spanish Practice Workbook 8-2

4. ASSESS

Lesson Quiz: Create a quiz on Objective 1 using the Computer Test Generator.

Targeted Resources
- ☐ 🖉 Computer Test Generator CD-ROM 8-2

Lesson Plan 8-2, Objective 2
Scientific Notation

Lesson Objective	NAEP 2005	Local Standards
☑ Use scientific notation	N1f; N2c	
	NCTM 2000	
	1, 4, 8, 9, 10	
	Pacing	
	Two Year: 1 day	
	Two-Year Block:	
	0.5 day	

1. INTRODUCE

Check Skills You'll Need: Assign these exercises if not used with Objective 1.

Review: Use the Key Concepts box to review scientific notation.

Targeted Resources
- ☐ 💻 Transparency: Check Skills You'll Need 8-2

2. TEACH

☑ **Objective:** Teach Examples 4–6. Assign Check Understanding questions 4–6 after the appropriate example.

Targeted Resources
- ☐ 💻 Transparency: Additional Examples 8-2
- ☐ Graphing Calculator Procedure 18: at **PHSchool.com**
- ☐ ✎ Presentation Pro CD-ROM 8-2
- ☐ 🖥 iText 8-2: at **PHSchool.com**

3. PRACTICE

Assignment Guide: Give an assignment based on the ability levels of your students.

☑ **Objective:** Core: 23–33, 42–45; Extension: 46–47
Standardized Test Prep: 50, 52
Mixed Review: 53–60

Homework: _____

Targeted Resources
- ☐ 💻 Transparency: Student Answers 8-2
- ☐ Grab & Go File: Practice 8-2, Reteaching 8-2, Enrichment 8-2
- ☐ Practice Workbook 8-2
- ☐ Spanish Practice Workbook 8-2
- ☐ Reasoning & Puzzles 13: at **PHSchool.com**

4. ASSESS

Lesson Quiz: Assign the Lesson Quiz to assess students' mastery of the lesson content.

Targeted Resources
- ☐ 💻 Transparency: Lesson Quiz 8-2
- ☐ 🖥 Online Lesson Quiz 8-2: at **PHSchool.com**
- ☐ ✎ Computer Test Generator CD-ROM 8-2

Lesson Plan 8-3, Objective 1
Multiplication Properties of Exponents

Lesson Objective ▼ Multiply powers	NAEP 2005 N1f; N2c, e NCTM 2000 1, 4, 8, 9, 10 Pacing Two Year: 2 days Two-Year Block: 1 day	Local Standards

1. INTRODUCE

Check Skills You'll Need: Assign these exercises to review the prerequisite skills of applying negative, zero, and positive exponents.

Targeted Resources
☐ ✎ Transparency: Check Skills You'll Need 8-3

2. TEACH

▼ **Objective:** Review the property in the Key Concepts box. Teach Examples 1–3. Assign Check Understanding questions 1–3 after the appropriate example.

Targeted Resources
☐ ✎ Transparency: Additional Examples 8-3
☐ ✐ Presentation Pro CD-ROM 8-3
☐ ▤ iText 8-3: at **PHSchool.com**

3. PRACTICE

Assignment Guide: Give an assignment based on the ability levels of your students.

▼ **Objective:** Core: 1–21, 31–47, 55–57, 65–70; Extension: 71–76
Standardized Test Prep: 79, 82, 84
Mixed Review: 85–99

Homework: _____

Targeted Resources
☐ ✎ Transparency: Student Answers 8-3
☐ Grab & Go File: Practice 8-3, Reteaching 8-3, Enrichment 8-3
☐ Practice Workbook 8-3
☐ Spanish Practice Workbook 8-3

4. ASSESS

Lesson Quiz: Create a quiz on Objective 1 using the Computer Test Generator.

Targeted Resources
☐ ✐ Computer Test Generator CD-ROM 8-3

Lesson Plan 8-3, Objective 2
Multiplication Properties of Exponents

Lesson Objective ▼ Work with scientific notation	NAEP 2005 N1f; N2c, e NCTM 2000 1, 4, 8, 9, 10 Pacing Two Year: 1 day Two-Year Block: 1 day	Local Standards

1. INTRODUCE

Check Skills You'll Need: Assign these exercises if not used with Objective 1.

Review: Use the Key Concepts box to review multiplying powers.

Targeted Resources
- ☐ ✎ Transparency: Check Skills You'll Need 8-3

2. TEACH

▼ **Objective:** Teach Examples 4 and 5. Assign Check Understanding questions 4 and 5 after the appropriate example.

Targeted Resources
- ☐ ✎ Transparency: Additional Examples 8-3
- ☐ ∅ Presentation Pro CD-ROM 8-3
- ☐ 💻 iText 8-3: at **PHSchool.com**

3. PRACTICE

Assignment Guide: Give an assignment based on the ability levels of your students.

　▼ **Objective:** Core: 22–30, 48–54, 58–64; Extension: 77–78
　Standardized Test Prep: 80, 81, 83
　Mixed Review: 85–99

Homework: _____

Targeted Resources
- ☐ ✎ Transparency: Student Answers 8-3
- ☐ Grab & Go File: Practice 8-3, Reteaching 8-3, Enrichment 8-3
- ☐ Practice Workbook 8-3
- ☐ Spanish Practice Workbook 8-3

4. ASSESS

Lesson Quiz: Assign the Lesson Quiz to assess students' mastery of the lesson content.

Targeted Resources
- ☐ ✎ Transparency: Lesson Quiz 8-3
- ☐ 💻 Online Lesson Quiz 8-3: at **PHSchool.com**
- ☐ ∅ Computer Test Generator CD-ROM 8-3

Lesson Plan 8-4, Objective 1
More Multiplication Properties of Exponents

Lesson Objective	NAEP 2005	Local Standards
▼ Raise a power to a power	N5e **NCTM 2000** 1, 2, 4, 6, 10 **Pacing** Two Year: 2 days Two-Year Block: 1 day	

1. INTRODUCE

Check Skills You'll Need: Assign these exercises to review the prerequisite skill of multiplying powers of the same base.

Targeted Resources

☐ 🖳 Transparency: Check Skills You'll Need 8-4

2. TEACH

▼ Objective: Have students work the Investigation to explore Powers of Powers. Review the property in the Key Concepts box. Teach Examples 1 and 2. Assign Check Understanding questions 1 and 2 after the appropriate example.

Targeted Resources

☐ 🖳 Transparency: Additional Examples 8-4
☐ ⊘ Presentation Pro CD-ROM 8-4
☐ 🖳 iText 8-4: at **PHSchool.com**

3. PRACTICE

Assignment Guide: Give an assignment based on the ability levels of your students.

▼ Objective: Core: 1–8, 32–37, 52–56, 60–62;
Extension: 63–65
Standardized Test Prep: 69–71
Mixed Review: 74–85

Homework: _____

Targeted Resources

☐ 🖳 Transparency: Student Answers 8-4
☐ Grab & Go File: Practice 8-4, Reteaching 8-4, Enrichment 8-4
☐ Practice Workbook 8-4
☐ Spanish Practice Workbook 8-4
☐ Reading and Math Literacy 8B
☐ Spanish Reading and Math Literacy 8B

4. ASSESS

Lesson Quiz: Create a quiz on Objective 1 using the Computer Test Generator.

Targeted Resources

☐ ⊘ Computer Test Generator CD-ROM 8-4

Lesson Plan 8-4, Objective 2
More Multiplication Properties of Exponents

Lesson Objective	NAEP 2005	Local Standards
✔ Raise a product to a power	N5e	
	NCTM 2000	
	1, 2, 4, 6, 10	
	Pacing	
	Two Year: 1 day	
	Two-Year Block:	
	1 day	

1. INTRODUCE

Check Skills You'll Need: Assign these exercises if not used with Objective 1.

Review: Use the Key Concepts box to review raising a power to a power.

Targeted Resources

☐ 🖿 Transparency: Check Skills You'll Need 8-4

2. TEACH

✔ **Objective:** Review the property in the Key Concepts box. Teach Examples 3–5. Assign Check Understanding questions 3–5 after the appropriate example.

Targeted Resources

☐ 🖿 Transparency: Additional Examples 8-4
☐ 🖉 Presentation Pro CD-ROM 8-4
☐ 🖳 iText 8-4: at **PHSchool.com**

3. PRACTICE

Assignment Guide: Give an assignment based on the ability levels of your students.

✔ **Objective:** Core: 9–31, 38–51, 57–59;
Extension: 66–68
Standardized Test Prep: 72–73
Mixed Review: 74–85

Homework: _____

Targeted Resources

☐ 🖿 Transparency: Student Answers 8-4
☐ Grab & Go File: Practice 8-4, Reteaching 8-4, Enrichment 8-4
☐ Practice Workbook 8-4
☐ Spanish Practice Workbook 8-4
☐ Reading and Math Literacy 8B
☐ Spanish Reading and Math Literacy 8B
☐ Reasoning & Puzzles 78: at **PHSchool.com**

4. ASSESS

Lesson Quiz: Assign the Lesson Quiz to assess students' mastery of the lesson content.

Checkpoint Quiz: Use the Checkpoint Quiz to assess student progress over several lessons.

Targeted Resources

☐ 🖿 Transparency: Lesson Quiz 8-4
☐ 🖳 Online Lesson Quiz 8-4: at **PHSchool.com**
☐ Grab & Go File: Checkpoint Quiz 1
☐ 🖉 Computer Test Generator CD-ROM 8-4

Lesson Plan 8-5, Objective 1
Division Properties of Exponents

Lesson Objective ▼ Divide powers with the same base	NAEP 2005 N5e NCTM 2000 1, 2, 4, 6, 10 Pacing Two Year: 1 day Two-Year Block: 0.5 day	Local Standards

1. INTRODUCE

Check Skills You'll Need: Assign these exercises to review the prerequisite skills of simplifying fractions.

Targeted Resources
- ☐ 🖳 Transparency: Check Skills You'll Need 8-5

2. TEACH

▼ **Objective:** Review the property in the Key Concepts box. Teach Examples 1 and 2. Assign Check Understanding questions 1 and 2 after the appropriate example.

Targeted Resources
- ☐ 🖳 Transparency: Additional Examples 8-5
- ☐ ⊘ Presentation Pro CD-ROM 8-5
- ☐ 🖳 iText 8-5: at **PHSchool.com**

3. PRACTICE

Assignment Guide: Give an assignment based on the ability levels of your students.

▼ **Objective:** Core: 1–20, 37–45; Extension: 79–80
Standardized Test Prep: 84–85
Mixed Review: 91–103

Homework: _____

Targeted Resources
- ☐ 🖳 Transparency: Student Answers 8-5
- ☐ Grab & Go File: Practice 8-5, Reteaching 8-5, Enrichment 8-5
- ☐ Practice Workbook 8-5
- ☐ Spanish Practice Workbook 8-5

4. ASSESS

Lesson Quiz: Create a quiz on Objective 1 using the Computer Test Generator.

Targeted Resources
- ☐ ⊘ Computer Test Generator CD-ROM 8-5

Lesson Plan 8-5, Objective 2
Division Properties of Exponents

Lesson Objective	NAEP 2005	Local Standards
⬙ Raise a quotient to a power	N5e	
	NCTM 2000	
	1, 2, 4, 6, 10	
	Pacing	
	Two Year: 1 day	
	Two-Year Block:	
	0.5 day	

1. INTRODUCE

Check Skills You'll Need: Assign these exercises if not used with Objective 1.

Review: Use the Key Concepts box to review dividing powers.

Targeted Resources

☐ 🖳 Transparency: Check Skills You'll Need 8-5

2. TEACH

⬙ **Objective:** Review the property in the Key Concepts box. Teach Examples 3 and 4. Assign Check Understanding questions 3 and 4 after the appropriate example.

Targeted Resources

☐ 🖳 Transparency: Additional Examples 8-5
☐ 🖉 Presentation Pro CD-ROM 8-5
☐ 🖳 iText 8-5: at **PHSchool.com**

3. PRACTICE

Assignment Guide: Give an assignment based on the ability levels of your students.

⬙ **Objective:** Core: 21–36, 46–78; Extension: 81–83
Standardized Test Prep: 86–90
Mixed Review: 91–103

Homework: _____

Targeted Resources

☐ 🖳 Transparency: Student Answers 8-5
☐ Grab & Go File: Practice 8-5, Reteaching 8-5, Enrichment 8-5
☐ Practice Workbook 8-5
☐ Spanish Practice Workbook 8-5

4. ASSESS

Lesson Quiz: Assign the Lesson Quiz to assess students' mastery of the lesson content.

Targeted Resources

☐ 🖳 Transparency: Lesson Quiz 8-5
☐ 🖳 Online Lesson Quiz 8-5: at **PHSchool.com**
☐ 🖉 Computer Test Generator CD-ROM 8-5

Lesson Plan 8-6, Objective 1
Geometric Sequences

Lesson Objective ▼ Form geometric sequences **New Vocabulary:** geometric sequence, common ratio	**NAEP 2005** A1a; A1i **NCTM 2000** 2, 3, 6, 9, 10 **Pacing** Two Year: 1 day Two-Year Block: 0.5 day	**Local Standards**

1. INTRODUCE

Check Skills You'll Need: Assign these exercises to review the prerequisite skills of finding common differences of arithmetic sequences and extending geometric sequences.

New Vocabulary: Help students pre-read the lesson by pointing out the new terms introduced in Objective 1.

Targeted Resources
- ☐ ✎ Transparency: Check Skills You'll Need 8-6

2. TEACH

▼ **Objective:** Teach Examples 1–3. Assign Check Understanding 1–3 after the appropriate example.

Targeted Resources
- ☐ ✎ Transparency: Additional Examples 8-6
- ☐ ✐ Presentation Pro CD-ROM 8-6
- ☐ ▣ iText 8-6: at **PHSchool.com**

3. PRACTICE

Assignment Guide: Give an assignment based on the ability levels of your students.

▼ **Objective:** Core: 1–18, 30–35, 37–40;
Extension: 45–47
Standardized Test Prep: 51
Mixed Review: 55–72

Homework: _____

Targeted Resources
- ☐ ✎ Transparency: Student Answers 8-6
- ☐ Grab & Go File: Practice 8-6, Reteaching 8-6, Enrichment 8-6
- ☐ Practice Workbook 8-6
- ☐ Spanish Practice Workbook 8-6
- ☐ Technology Activities 22
- ☐ Hands-On Activities 18

4. ASSESS

Lesson Quiz: Create a quiz on Objective 1 using the Computer Test Generator.

Targeted Resources
- ☐ ✐ Computer Test Generator CD-ROM 8-6

Algebra 1A and 1B Lesson Plans

Lesson Plan 8-6, Objective 2
Geometric Sequences

Lesson Objective	NAEP 2005	Local Standards
▼ Use formulas when describing geometric sequences	A1a; A1i	
	NCTM 2000 2, 3, 6, 9, 10	
	Pacing Two Year: 1 day Two-Year Block: 0.5 day	

1. INTRODUCE

Check Skills You'll Need: Assign these exercises if not used with Objective 1.

Review: Review geometric sequences.

Targeted Resources

☐ 🖳 Transparency: Check Skills You'll Need 8-6

2. TEACH

▼ **Objective:** Go over the formula in the Key Concepts box. Teach Examples 4 and 5. Assign Check Understanding 4 and 5 after the appropriate example.

Targeted Resources

☐ 🖳 Transparency: Additional Examples 8-6
☐ ✇ Presentation Pro CD-ROM 8-6
☐ 🖥 iText 8-6: at **PHSchool.com**

3. PRACTICE

Assignment Guide: Give an assignment based on the ability levels of your students.

   ▼ **Objective:** Core: 19–29, 36, 41–43;
Extension: 44, 48–50
Standardized Test Prep: 52–54
Mixed Review: 55–72

Homework: _____

Targeted Resources

☐ 🖳 Transparency: Student Answers 8-6
☐ Grab & Go File: Practice 8-6, Reteaching 8-6, Enrichment 8-6
☐ Practice Workbook 8-6
☐ Spanish Practice Workbook 8-6
☐ Technology Activities 22
☐ Hands-On Activities 18

4. ASSESS

Lesson Quiz: Assign the Lesson Quiz to assess students' mastery of the lesson content.

Targeted Resources

☐ 🖳 Transparency: Lesson Quiz 8-6
☐ 🖥 Online Lesson Quiz 8-6: at **PHSchool.com**
☐ ✇ Computer Test Generator CD-ROM 8-6

Lesson Plan 8-7, Objective 1
Exponential Functions

Lesson Objective ▼ Evaluate exponential functions **New Vocabulary:** exponential function	**NAEP 2005** A1e, h **NCTM 2000** 2, 4, 5, 8, 10 **Pacing** Two Year: 1 day Two-Year Block: 0.5 day	**Local Standards**

1. INTRODUCE

Check Skills You'll Need: Assign these exercises to review the prerequisite skills of graphing direct variations and simplifying exponential expressions.

New Vocabulary: Help students pre-read the lesson by pointing out the new term introduced in Objective 1.

Targeted Resources
- ☐ 🖳 Transparency: Check Skills You'll Need 8-7

2. TEACH

▼ Objective: Go over the definition in the Key Concepts box. Teach Examples 1 and 2. Assign Check Understanding questions 1 and 2 after the appropriate example.

Targeted Resources
- ☐ 🖳 Transparency: Additional Examples 8-7
- ☐ 🖳 Transparency: Classroom Aid 27
- ☐ 🖸 Presentation Pro CD-ROM 8-7
- ☐ 🖳 iText 8-7: at **PHSchool.com**

3. PRACTICE

Assignment Guide: Give an assignment based on the ability levels of your students.

▼ Objective: Core: 1–11, 25–34, 36–42;
Extension: 44–47
Standardized Test Prep: 51–54
Mixed Review: 56–65

Homework: _____

Targeted Resources
- ☐ 🖳 Transparency: Student Answers 8-7
- ☐ Grab & Go File: Practice 8-7, Reteaching 8-7, Enrichment 8-7
- ☐ Practice Workbook 8-7
- ☐ Spanish Practice Workbook 8-7
- ☐ Reading and Math Literacy 8C
- ☐ Spanish Reading and Math Literacy 8C

4. ASSESS

Lesson Quiz: Create a quiz on Objective 1 using the Computer Test Generator.

Targeted Resources
- ☐ 🖸 Computer Test Generator CD-ROM 8-7

Lesson Plan 8-7, Objective 2
Exponential Functions

Lesson Objective	NAEP 2005	Local Standards
☑ Graph exponential functions	A1e, h	
	NCTM 2000 2, 4, 5, 8, 10	
	Pacing Two Year: 1 day Two-Year Block: 0.5 day	

1. INTRODUCE

Check Skills You'll Need: Assign these exercises if not used with Objective 1.

Review: Use the Key Concepts box to review exponential functions.

Targeted Resources

☐ 📖 Transparency: Check Skills You'll Need 8-7

2. TEACH

☑ **Objective:** Teach Examples 3 and 4. Assign Check Understanding questions 3 and 4 after the appropriate example.

Targeted Resources

☐ 📖 Transparency: Additional Examples 8-7
☐ 📖 Transparency: Classroom Aid 27
☐ 🖉 Presentation Pro CD-ROM 8-7
☐ 💻 iText 8-7: at **PHSchool.com**

3. PRACTICE

Assignment Guide: Give an assignment based on the ability levels of your students.

    ☑ **Objective:** Core: 12–24, 35, 43; Extension: 48–50
Standardized Test Prep: 55
Mixed Review: 56–65

Homework: _____

Targeted Resources

☐ 📖 Transparency: Student Answers 8-7
☐ Grab & Go File: Practice 8-7, Reteaching 8-7, Enrichment 8-7
☐ Practice Workbook 8-7
☐ Spanish Practice Workbook 8-7
☐ Reading and Math Literacy 8C
☐ Spanish Reading and Math Literacy 8C

4. ASSESS

Lesson Quiz: Assign the Lesson Quiz to assess students' mastery of the lesson content.

Checkpoint Quiz: Use the Checkpoint Quiz to assess student progress over several lessons.

Targeted Resources

☐ 📖 Transparency: Lesson Quiz 8-7
☐ 💻 Online Lesson Quiz 8-7: at **PHSchool.com**
☐ Grab & Go File: Checkpoint Quiz 2
☐ 🖉 Computer Test Generator CD-ROM 8-7

Lesson Plan 8-8, Objective 1
Exponential Growth and Decay

Lesson Objective	NAEP 2005	Local Standards
▼ Model exponential growth **New Vocabulary:** exponential growth, growth factor, compound interest, interest period, exponential decay, decay factor	A2g, h **NCTM 2000** 2, 4, 5, 6, 8, 10 **Pacing** Two Year: 2 days Two-Year Block: 1 day	

1. INTRODUCE

Check Skills You'll Need: Assign these exercises to review the prerequisite skill of calculating simple interest.

New Vocabulary: Help students pre-read the lesson by pointing out the new terms introduced in Objective 1.

Targeted Resources

☐ ⬅ Transparency: Check Skills You'll Need 8-8

2. TEACH

▼ **Objective:** Go over the formula in the Key Concepts box. Teach Examples 1–3. Assign Check Understanding questions 1–3 after the appropriate example.

Targeted Resources

☐ ⬅ Transparency: Additional Examples 8-8
☐ ✎ Presentation Pro CD-ROM 8-8
☐ 💻 iText 8-8: at **PHSchool.com**

3. PRACTICE

Assignment Guide: Give an assignment based on the ability levels of your students.

▼ **Objective:** Core: 1–19, 31–43; Extension: 54
Standardized Test Prep: 57–59
Mixed Review: 60–63

Homework: _____

Targeted Resources

☐ ⬅ Transparency: Student Answers 8-8
☐ Grab & Go File: Practice 8-8, Reteaching 8-8, Enrichment 8-8
☐ Practice Workbook 8-8
☐ Spanish Practice Workbook 8-8
☐ Technology Activities 8
☐ Hands-On Activities 19

4. ASSESS

Lesson Quiz: Create a quiz on Objective 1 using the Computer Test Generator.

Targeted Resources

☐ ✎ Computer Test Generator CD-ROM 8-8

Lesson Plan 8-8, Objective 2
Exponential Growth and Decay

Lesson Objective	NAEP 2005	Local Standards
▼ Model exponential decay **New Vocabulary:** exponential growth, growth factor, compound interest, interest period, exponential decay, decay factor	A2g, h **NCTM 2000** 2, 4, 5, 6, 8, 10 **Pacing** Two Year: 1 day Two-Year Block: 1 day	

1. INTRODUCE

Check Skills You'll Need: Assign these exercises if not used in Objective 1.

Review: Use the Key Concepts box to review exponential growth.

New Vocabulary: Help students pre-read the lesson by pointing out the new terms introduced in Objective 2.

Targeted Resources
☐ ☞ Transparency: Check Skills You'll Need 8-8

2. TEACH

▼ **Objective:** Teach Examples 4 and 5. Assign Check Understanding questions 4 and 5 after the appropriate example.

Targeted Resources
☐ ☞ Transparency: Additional Examples 8-8
☐ ✐ Presentation Pro CD-ROM 8-8
☐ 💻 iText 8-8: at **PHSchool.com**

3. PRACTICE

Assignment Guide: Give an assignment based on the ability levels of your students.

   ▼ **Objective:** Core: 20–30, 44–52; Extension: 53, 55
Standardized Test Prep: 56
Mixed Review: 60–63

Homework: _____

Targeted Resources
☐ ☞ Transparency: Student Answers 8-8
☐ Grab & Go File: Practice 8-8, Reteaching 8-8, Enrichment 8-8
☐ Practice Workbook 8-8
☐ Spanish Practice Workbook 8-8
☐ Technology Activities 8
☐ Hands-On Activities 19

4. ASSESS

Lesson Quiz: Assign the Lesson Quiz to assess students' mastery of the lesson content.

Targeted Resources
☐ ☞ Transparency: Lesson Quiz 8-8
☐ 💻 Online Lesson Quiz 8-8: at **PHSchool.com**
☐ ✐ Computer Test Generator CD-ROM 8-8

Lesson Plan 9-1, Objective 1
Adding and Subtracting Polynomials

Lesson Objective	NAEP 2005	Local Standards
▼ Describe polynomials	A3b	
New Vocabulary: monomial, degree of a monomial, polynomial, standard form of a polynomial, degree of a polynomial, binomial, trinomial	**NCTM 2000** 2, 3, 8, 10	
	Pacing Two Year: 1 day Two-Year Block: 0.5 day	

1. INTRODUCE

Check Skills You'll Need: Assign these exercises to review the prerequisite skill of simplifying expressions.

New Vocabulary: Help students pre-read the lesson by pointing out the new terms introduced in Objective 1.

Targeted Resources

☐ ⛫ Transparency: Check Skills You'll Need 9-1

2. TEACH

▼ **Objective:** Have students work the Investigation to explore Using Polynomials. Teach Examples 1 and 2. Assign Check Understanding questions 1 and 2 after the appropriate example.

Targeted Resources

☐ ⛫ Transparency: Additional Examples 9-1
☐ ⛫ Transparency: Classroom Aid 3
☐ ⊘ Presentation Pro CD-ROM 9-1
☐ ▦ iText 9-1: at **PHSchool.com**

3. PRACTICE

Assignment Guide: Give an assignment based on the ability levels of your students.

▼ **Objective:** Core: 1–20, 42, 51
Standardized Test Prep: 56
Mixed Review: 63–86

Homework: _____

Targeted Resources

☐ ⛫ Transparency: Student Answers 9-1
☐ Grab & Go File: Practice 9-1, Reteaching 9-1, Enrichment 9-1
☐ Practice Workbook 9-1
☐ Spanish Practice Workbook 9-1
☐ Reading and Math Literacy 9A
☐ Spanish Reading and Math Literacy 9A
☐ Technology Activities 23
☐ Hands-On Activities 20

4. ASSESS

Lesson Quiz: Create a quiz on Objective 1 using the Computer Test Generator.

Targeted Resources

☐ ⊘ Computer Test Generator CD-ROM 9-1

Teacher _____ Class _____ Date _____ M T W Th F

Lesson Plan 9-1, Objective 2
Adding and Subtracting Polynomials

Lesson Objective	NAEP 2005	Local Standards
▼ Add and subtract polynomials	A3b	
	NCTM 2000 2, 3, 8, 10	
	Pacing Two Year: 1 day Two-Year Block: 0.5 day	

1. INTRODUCE

Check Skills You'll Need: Assign these exercises if not used with Objective 1.

Review: Remind students how to describe polynomials.

Targeted Resources

☐ 🖳 Transparency: Check Skills You'll Need 9-1

2. TEACH

▼ **Objective:** Teach Examples 3 and 4. Assign Check Understanding questions 3 and 4 after the appropriate example.

Targeted Resources

☐ 🖳 Transparency: Additional Examples 9-1
☐ 🖳 Transparency: Classroom Aid 3
☐ ✐ Presentation Pro CD-ROM 9-1
☐ 🖳 iText 9-1: at **PHSchool.com**

3. PRACTICE

Assignment Guide: Give an assignment based on the ability levels of your students.

  ▼ **Objective:** Core: 21–41, 43–50; Extension: 52–55
  Standardized Test Prep: 57–62
  Mixed Review: 63–86

Homework: _____

Targeted Resources

☐ 🖳 Transparency: Student Answers 9-1
☐ Grab & Go File: Practice 9-1, Reteaching 9-1, Enrichment 9-1
☐ Practice Workbook 9-1
☐ Spanish Practice Workbook 9-1
☐ Reading and Math Literacy 9A
☐ Spanish Reading and Math Literacy 9A
☐ Technology Activities 23
☐ Hands-On Activities 20
☐ Reasoning & Puzzles 73, 74: at **PHSchool.com**

4. ASSESS

Lesson Quiz: Assign the Lesson Quiz to assess students' mastery of the lesson content.

Targeted Resources

☐ 🖳 Transparency: Lesson Quiz 9-1
☐ 🖳 Online Lesson Quiz 9-1: at **PHSchool.com**
☐ ✐ Computer Test Generator CD-ROM 9-1

Lesson Plan 9-2, Objective 1
Multiplying and Factoring

Lesson Objective	NAEP 2005	Local Standards
▼ Multiply a polynomial by a monomial	A3b, c	
	NCTM 2000 2, 3, 8, 10	
	Pacing Two Year: 1 day Two-Year Block: 0.5 day	

1. INTRODUCE

Check Skills You'll Need: Assign these exercises to review the prerequisite skills of multiplying natural numbers and applying the Distributive Property.

Targeted Resources
- ☐ 🖳 Transparency: Check Skills You'll Need 9-2

2. TEACH

▼ **Objective:** Teach Example 1. Assign Check Understanding question 1.

Targeted Resources
- ☐ 🖳 Transparency: Additional Examples 9-2
- ☐ ✐ Presentation Pro CD-ROM 9-2
- ☐ 🖳 iText 9-2: at **PHSchool.com**

3. PRACTICE

Assignment Guide: Give an assignment based on the ability levels of your students.

▼ **Objective:** Core: 1–12, 25–32; Extension: 43
Standardized Test Prep: 45–49
Mixed Review: 51–67

Homework: _____

Targeted Resources
- ☐ 🖳 Transparency: Student Answers 9-2
- ☐ Grab & Go File: Practice 9-2, Reteaching 9-2, Enrichment 9-2
- ☐ Spanish Practice Workbook 9-2
- ☐ Practice Workbook 9-2

4. ASSESS

Lesson Quiz: Create a quiz on Objective 1 using the Computer Test Generator.

Targeted Resources
- ☐ ✐ Computer Test Generator CD-ROM 9-2

Teacher _____ Class _____ Date _____ M T W Th F

Lesson Plan 9-2, Objective 2
Multiplying and Factoring

Lesson Objective	NAEP 2005	Local Standards
❷ Factor a monomial from a polynomial	A3b, c	
	NCTM 2000 2, 3, 8, 10	
	Pacing Two Year: 1 day Two-Year Block: 0.5 day	

1. INTRODUCE

Check Skills You'll Need: Assign these exercises if not used with Objective 1.

Review: Remind students how to distribute a monomial.

Targeted Resources
- ☐ 🖵 Transparency: Check Skills You'll Need 9-2

2. TEACH

❷ **Objective:** Teach Examples 2 and 3. Assign Check Understanding questions 2 and 3 after the appropriate example.

Targeted Resources
- ☐ 🖵 Transparency: Additional Examples 9-2
- ☐ ✐ Presentation Pro CD-ROM 9-2
- ☐ 🖳 iText 9-2: at **PHSchool.com**

3. PRACTICE

Assignment Guide: Give an assignment based on the ability levels of your students.

❷ **Objective:** Core: 13–24, 33–42; Extension: 44
Standardized Test Prep: 50
Mixed Review: 51–67

Homework: _____

Targeted Resources
- ☐ 🖵 Transparency: Student Answers 9-2
- ☐ Grab & Go File: Practice 9-2, Reteaching 9-2, Enrichment 9-2
- ☐ Spanish Practice Workbook 9-2
- ☐ Practice Workbook 9-2
- ☐ Reasoning & Puzzles 75: at **PHSchool.com**

4. ASSESS

Lesson Quiz: Assign the Lesson Quiz to assess students' mastery of the lesson content.

Targeted Resources
- ☐ 🖵 Transparency: Lesson Quiz 9-2
- ☐ 🖳 Online Lesson Quiz 9-2: at **PHSchool.com**
- ☐ ✐ Computer Test Generator CD-ROM 9-2

Lesson Plan 9-3, Objective 1
Multiplying Binomials

Lesson Objective	NAEP 2005	Local Standards
▼ Multiply binomials using FOIL	A3b, c	
	NCTM 2000	
	2, 3, 8, 10	
	Pacing	
	Two Year: 1 day	
	Two-Year Block:	
	0.5 day	

1. INTRODUCE

Check Skills You'll Need: Assign these exercises to review the prerequisite skills of multiplying a polynomial by a monomial and adding and subtracting polynomials.

Targeted Resources
☐ 📖 Transparency: Check Skills You'll Need 9-3

2. TEACH

▼ **Objective:** Teach Examples 1–3. Assign Check Understanding questions 1–3 after the appropriate example.

Targeted Resources
☐ 📖 Transparency: Additional Examples 9-3
☐ 💿 Presentation Pro CD-ROM 9-3
☐ 💻 iText 9-3: at **PHSchool.com**

3. PRACTICE

Assignment Guide: Give an assignment based on the ability levels of your students.

▼ **Objective:** Core: 1–21, 30–35, 42–46;
Extension: 47–51
Standardized Test Prep: 59, 61, 63
Mixed Review: 64–89

Homework: _____

Targeted Resources
☐ 📖 Transparency: Student Answers 9-3
☐ Grab & Go File: Practice 9-3, Reteaching 9-3, Enrichment 9-3
☐ Practice Workbook 9-3
☐ Spanish Practice Workbook 9-3
☐ Reading and Math Literacy 9B
☐ Spanish Reading and Math Literacy 9B
☐ Hands-On Activities 21

4. ASSESS

Lesson Quiz: Create a quiz on Objective 1 using the Computer Test Generator.

Targeted Resources
☐ 💿 Computer Test Generator CD-ROM 9-3

Lesson Plan 9-3, Objective 2
Multiplying Binomials

Lesson Objective	NAEP 2005	Local Standards
▼ Multiply trinomials by binomials	A3b, c	
	NCTM 2000	
	2, 3, 8, 10	
	Pacing	
	Two Year: 1 day	
	Two-Year Block:	
	0.5 day	

1. INTRODUCE

Check Skills You'll Need: Assign these exercises if not used with Objective 1.

Review: Review FOIL with the students.

Targeted Resources
- ☐ 🖳 Transparency: Check Skills You'll Need 9-3

2. TEACH

▼ **Objective:** Teach Example 4. Assign the Check Understanding question 4.

Targeted Resources
- ☐ 🖳 Transparency: Additional Examples 9-3
- ☐ 🖉 Presentation Pro CD-ROM 9-3
- ☐ 🖥 iText 9-3: at **PHSchool.com**

3. PRACTICE

Assignment Guide: Give an assignment based on the ability levels of your students.

▼ **Objective:** Core: 22–29, 36–41; Extension: 52–58
Standardized Test Prep: 60, 62
Mixed Review: 64–89

Homework: _____

Targeted Resources
- ☐ 🖳 Transparency: Student Answers 9-3
- ☐ Grab & Go File: Practice 9-3, Reteaching 9-3, Enrichment 9-3
- ☐ Practice Workbook 9-3
- ☐ Spanish Practice Workbook 9-3
- ☐ Reading and Math Literacy 9B
- ☐ Spanish Reading and Math Literacy 9B
- ☐ Hands-On Activities 21
- ☐ Reasoning & Puzzles 76, 78, 95: at **PHSchool.com**

4. ASSESS

Lesson Quiz: Assign the Lesson Quiz to assess students' mastery of the lesson content.

Checkpoint Quiz: Use the Checkpoint Quiz to assess student progress over several lessons.

Targeted Resources
- ☐ 🖳 Transparency: Lesson Quiz 9-3
- ☐ 🖥 Online Lesson Quiz 9-3: at **PHSchool.com**
- ☐ Grab & Go File: Checkpoint Quiz 1
- ☐ 🖉 Computer Test Generator CD-ROM 9-3

Lesson Plan 9-4, Objective 1
Multiplying Special Cases

Lesson Objective	NAEP 2005	Local Standards
▼ Find the square of a binomial	A3b, c	
	NCTM 2000	
	2, 7, 8, 9, 10	
	Pacing	
	Two Year: 2 days	
	Two-Year Block: 1 day	

1. INTRODUCE

Check Skills You'll Need: Assign these exercises to review the prerequisite skills of squaring monomials and multiplying binomials.

Targeted Resources
- ☐ ⬚ Transparency: Check Skills You'll Need 9-4

2. TEACH

▼ Objective: Have students work the Investigation to Explore Special Products. Discuss the rule in the Key Concepts box. Teach Examples 1–3. Assign Check Understanding questions 1–3 after the appropriate example.

Targeted Resources
- ☐ ⬚ Transparency: Additional Examples 9-4
- ☐ ⬚ Presentation Pro CD-ROM 9-4
- ☐ ⬚ iText 9-4: at **PHSchool.com**

3. PRACTICE

Assignment Guide: Give an assignment based on the ability levels of your students.

▼ Objective: Core: 1–14, 26–40, 42–43; Extension: 53–54
Standardized Test Prep: 59
Mixed Review: 64–80

Targeted Resources
- ☐ ⬚ Transparency: Student Answers 9-4
- ☐ Grab & Go File: Practice 9-4, Reteaching 9-4, Enrichment 9-4
- ☐ Practice Workbook 9-4
- ☐ Spanish Practice Workbook 9-4

Homework: _____

4. ASSESS

Lesson Quiz: Create a quiz on Objective 1 using the Computer Test Generator.

Targeted Resources
- ☐ ⬚ Computer Test Generator CD-ROM 9-4

Lesson Plan 9-4, Objective 2
Multiplying Special Cases

Lesson Objective	NAEP 2005	Local Standards
▼ Find the difference of squares	A3b, c	
	NCTM 2000	
	2, 7, 8, 9, 10	
	Pacing	
	Two Year: 1 day	
	Two-Year Block:	
	1 day	

1. INTRODUCE

Check Skills You'll Need: Assign these exercises if not used with Objective 1.

Review: Use the Key Concepts box to review the square of a binomial.

Targeted Resources
- ☐ 🖳 Transparency: Check Skills You'll Need 9-4

2. TEACH

▼ **Objective:** Teach Examples 4 and 5. Assign Check Understanding questions 4 and 5 after the appropriate example.

Targeted Resources
- ☐ 🖳 Transparency: Additional Examples 9-4
- ☐ 🖉 Presentation Pro CD-ROM 9-4
- ☐ 🖥 iText 9-4: at **PHSchool.com**

3. PRACTICE

Assignment Guide: Give an assignment based on the ability levels of your students.

▼ **Objective:** Core: 15–25, 41, 44–52; Extension: 55–57
Standardized Test Prep: 58, 60–63
Mixed Review: 64–80

Homework: _____

Targeted Resources
- ☐ 🖳 Transparency: Student Answers 9-4
- ☐ Grab & Go File: Practice 9-4, Reteaching 9-4, Enrichment 9-4
- ☐ Practice Workbook 9-4
- ☐ Spanish Practice Workbook 9-4
- ☐ Reasoning & Puzzles 78, 80, 81: at **PHSchool.com**

4. ASSESS

Lesson Quiz: Assign the Lesson Quiz to assess students' mastery of the lesson content.

Targeted Resources
- ☐ 🖳 Transparency: Lesson Quiz 9-4
- ☐ 🖥 Online Lesson Quiz 9-4: at **PHSchool.com**
- ☐ 🖉 Computer Test Generator CD-ROM 9-4

Lesson Plan 9-5, Objective 1
Factoring Trinomials of the Type
$x^2 + bx + c$

Lesson Objective	NAEP 2005	Local Standards
▼ Factor trinomials	A3b, c	
	NCTM 2000	
	2, 6, 8, 10	
	Pacing	
	Two Year: 3 days	
	Two-Year Block: 2 days	

1. INTRODUCE

Check Skills You'll Need: Assign these exercises to review the prerequisite skill of factoring natural numbers.

Targeted Resources

☐ ✎ Transparency: Check Skills You'll Need 9-5

2. TEACH

▼ **Objective:** Teach Examples 1–4. Assign Check Understanding questions 1–4 after the appropriate example.

Targeted Resources

☐ ✎ Transparency: Additional Examples 9-5
☐ ✐ Presentation Pro CD-ROM 9-5
☐ 💻 iText 9-5: at **PHSchool.com**

3. PRACTICE

Assignment Guide: Give an assignment based on the ability levels of your students.

▼ **Objective:** Core: 1–58; Extension: 59–64
Standardized Test Prep: 65–71
Mixed Review: 72–86

Homework: _____

Targeted Resources

☐ ✎ Transparency: Student Answers 9-5
☐ Grab & Go File: Practice 9-5, Reteaching 9-5, Enrichment 9-5
☐ Practice Workbook 9-5
☐ Spanish Practice Workbook 9-5
☐ Reasoning & Puzzles 82: at **PHSchool.com**

4. ASSESS

Lesson Quiz: Assign the Lesson Quiz to assess students' mastery of the lesson content.

Targeted Resources

☐ ✎ Transparency: Lesson Quiz 9-5
☐ 💻 Online Lesson Quiz 9-5: at **PHSchool.com**
☐ ✐ Computer Test Generator CD-ROM 9-5

Teacher _____ Class _____ Date _____ M T W Th F

Lesson Plan 9-6, Objective 1
Factoring Trinomials of the Type
$ax^2 + bx + c$

Lesson Objective	NCTM 2000	Local Standards
▼ Factor trinomials of the type $ax^2 + bx + c$	2, 6, 8, 10 **Pacing** Two Year: 3 days Two-Year Block: 2 days	

1. INTRODUCE

Check Skills You'll Need: Assign these exercises to review the prerequisite skill of factoring trinomials.

Targeted Resources
☐ 🖾 Transparency: Check Skills You'll Need 9-6

2. TEACH

▼ **Objective:** Teach Examples 1–3. Assign Check Understanding questions 1–3 after the appropriate example.

Targeted Resources
☐ 🖾 Transparency: Additional Examples 9-6
☐ ✐ Presentation Pro CD-ROM 9-6
☐ 🖳 iText 9-6: at **PHSchool.com**

3. PRACTICE

Assignment Guide: Give an assignment based on the ability levels of your students.

  ▼ **Objective:** Core: 1–41; Extension: 42–47
Standardized Test Prep: 48–53
Mixed Review: 54–80

Homework: _____

Targeted Resources
☐ 🖾 Transparency: Student Answers 9-6
☐ Grab & Go File: Practice 9-6, Reteaching 9-6, Enrichment 9-6
☐ Practice Workbook 9-6
☐ Spanish Practice Workbook 9-6

4. ASSESS

Lesson Quiz: Assign the Lesson Quiz to assess students' mastery of the lesson content.

Targeted Resources
☐ 🖾 Transparency: Lesson Quiz 9-6
☐ 🖳 Online Lesson Quiz 9-6: at **PHSchool.com**
☐ ✐ Computer Test Generator CD-ROM 9-6

Lesson Plan 9-7, Objective 1
Factoring Special Cases

Lesson Objective	NAEP 2005	Local Standards
▼ Factor perfect-square trinomials **New Vocabulary:** perfect square trinomial	A3b, c **NCTM 2000** 2, 6, 8, 10 **Pacing** Two Year: 2 days Two-Year Block: 1 day	

1. INTRODUCE

Check Skills You'll Need: Assign these exercises to review the prerequisite skills of squaring monomials and binomials.

New Vocabulary: Help students pre-read the lesson by pointing out the new term introduced in Objective 1.

Targeted Resources

☐ ✍ Transparency: Check Skills You'll Need 9-7

2. TEACH

▼ **Objective:** Have students work the Investigation to explore Perfect-Square Trinomials. Discuss the rules in the Key Concepts box. Teach Examples 1 and 2. Assign Check Understanding 1 and 2 after the appropriate example.

Targeted Resources

☐ ✍ Transparency: Additional Examples 9-7
☐ ✐ Presentation Pro CD-ROM 9-7
☐ ▣ iText 9-7: at **PHSchool.com**

3. PRACTICE

Assignment Guide: Give an assignment based on the ability levels of your students.

▼ **Objective:** Core: 1–12, 37, 46–54
Standardized Test Prep: 67–70
Mixed Review: 73–91

Homework: _____

Targeted Resources

☐ ✍ Transparency: Student Answers 9-7
☐ Grab & Go File: Practice 9-7, Reteaching 9-7, Enrichment 9-7
☐ Practice Workbook 9-7
☐ Spanish Practice Workbook 9-7
☐ Reading and Math Literacy 9C
☐ Spanish Reading and Math Literacy 9C
☐ Hands-On Activities 22

4. ASSESS

Lesson Quiz: Create a quiz on Objective 1 using the Computer Test Generator.

Targeted Resources

☐ ✐ Computer Test Generator CD-ROM 9-7

Lesson Plan 9-7, Objective 2
Factoring Special Cases

Lesson Objective	NAEP 2005	Local Standards
▼ Factor the difference of squares	A3b, c	
	NCTM 2000	
	2, 6, 8, 10	
	Pacing	
	Two Year: 1 day	
	Two-Year Block:	
	1 day	

1. INTRODUCE

Check Skills You'll Need: Assign these exercises if not used with Objective 1.

Review: Use the Key Concepts box to review perfect square trinomials.

Targeted Resources
- ☐ 📖 Transparency: Check Skills You'll Need 9-7

2. TEACH

▼ **Objective:** Teach Examples 3–5. Assign Check Understanding 3–5 after the appropriate example.

Targeted Resources
- ☐ 📖 Transparency: Additional Examples 9-7
- ☐ ✒ Presentation Pro CD-ROM 9-7
- ☐ 💻 iText 9-7: at **PHSchool.com**

3. PRACTICE

Assignment Guide: Give an assignment based on the ability levels of your students.

    ▼ **Objective:** Core: 13–36, 38–45, 55–64;
Extension: 65–66
Standardized Test Prep: 71–72
Mixed Review: 73–91

Homework: _____

Targeted Resources
- ☐ 📖 Transparency: Student Answers 9-7
- ☐ Grab & Go File: Practice 9-7, Reteaching 9-7, Enrichment 9-7
- ☐ Practice Workbook 9-7
- ☐ Spanish Practice Workbook 9-7
- ☐ Reading and Math Literacy 9C
- ☐ Spanish Reading and Math Literacy 9C
- ☐ Hands-On Activities 22

4. ASSESS

Lesson Quiz: Assign the Lesson Quiz to assess students' mastery of the lesson content.

Checkpoint Quiz: Use the Checkpoint Quiz to assess student progress over several lessons.

Targeted Resources
- ☐ 📖 Transparency: Lesson Quiz 9-7
- ☐ 💻 Online Lesson Quiz 9-7: at **PHSchool.com**
- ☐ Grab & Go File: Checkpoint Quiz 2
- ☐ ✒ Computer Test Generator CD-ROM 9-7

Lesson Plan 9-8, Objective 1
Factoring by Grouping

Lesson Objective	NAEP 2005	Local Standards
▼ Factor polynomials with four terms	A3b, c	
New Vocabulary: factor by grouping	**NCTM 2000** 2, 3, 6, 8, 10	
	Pacing Two Year: 1 day Two-Year Block: 0.5 day	

1. INTRODUCE

Check Skills You'll Need: Assign these exercises to review the prerequisite skills of finding greatest common factors and multiplying polynomials.

New Vocabulary: Help students pre-read the lesson by pointing out the new term introduced in Objective 1.

Targeted Resources
- ☐ 💻 Transparency: Check Skills You'll Need 9-8

2. TEACH

▼ **Objective:** Teach Examples 1 and 2. Assign Check Understanding questions 1 and 2 after the appropriate example.

Targeted Resources
- ☐ 💻 Transparency: Additional Examples 9-8
- ☐ 🖸 Presentation Pro CD-ROM 9-8
- ☐ 🖥 iText 9-8: at **PHSchool.com**

3. PRACTICE

Assignment Guide: Give an assignment based on the ability levels of your students.

   ▼ **Objective:** Core: 1–16, 33–38, 40–41; Extension: 42–45
Standardized Test Prep: 50–51
Mixed Review: 54–84

Homework: _____

Targeted Resources
- ☐ 💻 Transparency: Student Answers 9-8
- ☐ Grab & Go File: Practice 9-8, Reteaching 9-8, Enrichment 9-8
- ☐ Practice Workbook 9-8
- ☐ Spanish Practice Workbook 9-8

4. ASSESS

Lesson Quiz: Create a quiz on Objective 1 using the Computer Test Generator.

Targeted Resources
- ☐ 🖸 Computer Test Generator CD-ROM 9-8

Teacher _____ Class _____ Date _____ M T W Th F

Lesson Plan 9-8, Objective 2
Factoring by Grouping

Lesson Objective	NAEP 2005	Local Standards
✓2 Factor trinomials by grouping	A3b, c	
	NCTM 2000 2, 3, 6, 8, 10	
	Pacing Two Year: 1 day Two-Year Block: 0.5 day	

1. INTRODUCE

Check Skills You'll Need: Assign these exercises if not used with Objective 1.

Review: Remind students how to factor polynomials with four terms.

Targeted Resources
- ☐ 🖳 Transparency: Check Skills You'll Need 9-8

2. TEACH

✓ Objective: Teach Examples 3 and 4. Assign Check Understanding questions 3 and 4 after the appropriate example. Review the summary in the Key Concepts box.

Targeted Resources
- ☐ 🖳 Transparency: Additional Examples 9-8
- ☐ 🖉 Presentation Pro CD-ROM 9-8
- ☐ 🖳 iText 9-8: at **PHSchool.com**

3. PRACTICE

Assignment Guide: Give an assignment based on the ability levels of your students.

> **✓ Objective:** Core: 17–32, 39; Extension: 46–49
> **Standardized Test Prep:** 52–53
> **Mixed Review:** 54–84

Homework: _____

Targeted Resources
- ☐ 🖳 Transparency: Student Answers 9-8
- ☐ Grab & Go File: Practice 9-8, Reteaching 9-8, Enrichment 9-8
- ☐ Practice Workbook 9-8
- ☐ Spanish Practice Workbook 9-8
- ☐ Reasoning & Puzzles 83: at **PHSchool.com**

4. ASSESS

Lesson Quiz: Assign the Lesson Quiz to assess students' mastery of the lesson content.

Targeted Resources
- ☐ 🖳 Transparency: Lesson Quiz 9-8
- ☐ 🖳 Online Lesson Quiz 9-8: at **PHSchool.com**
- ☐ 🖉 Computer Test Generator CD-ROM 9-8

Lesson Plan 10-1, Objective 1
Exploring Quadratic Graphs

Lesson Objective	NAEP 2005	Local Standards
▼ Graph quadratic functions of the form $y = ax^2$ **New Vocabulary:** quadratic function, standard form of a quadratic function, parabola, axis of symmetry, vertex, minimum, maximum	A1e, h; A2d **NCTM 2000** 2, 8, 9, 10 **Pacing** Two Year: 1 day Two-Year Block: 0.5 day	

1. INTRODUCE

Check Skills You'll Need: Assign these exercises to review the prerequisite skills of evaluating expressions and graphing equations.

New Vocabulary: Help students pre-read the lesson by pointing out the new terms introduced in Objective 1.

Targeted Resources

☐ 🔌 Transparency: Check Skills You'll Need 10-1

2. TEACH

▼ **Objective:** Have students work the Investigation to explore the influence the coefficient of x^2 has on quadratic curves. Discuss the definition in the Key Concepts box. Teach Examples 1–3. Assign Check Understanding 1–3 after the appropriate example.

Targeted Resources

☐ 🔌 Transparency: Additional Examples 10-1
☐ 🖉 Presentation Pro CD-ROM 10-1
☐ 💻 iText 10-1: at **PHSchool.com**

3. PRACTICE

Assignment Guide: Give an assignment based on the ability levels of your students.

  ▼ **Objective:** Core: 1–13, 27–30, 34–37, 40–44; Extension: 48
  Mixed Review: 54–66

Homework: _____

Targeted Resources

☐ 🔌 Transparency: Student Answers 10-1
☐ Grab & Go File: Practice 10-1, Reteaching 10-1, Enrichment 10-1
☐ Practice Workbook 10-1
☐ Spanish Practice Workbook 10-1
☐ Reading and Math Literacy 10A
☐ Spanish Reading and Math Literacy 10A

4. ASSESS

Lesson Quiz: Create a quiz on Objective 1 using the Computer Test Generator.

Targeted Resources

☐ 🖉 Computer Test Generator CD-ROM 10-1

Teacher _____ Class _____ Date _____ M T W Th F

Lesson Plan 10-1, Objective 2
Exploring Quadratic Graphs

Lesson Objective	NAEP 2005	Local Standards
▼ Graph quadratic functions of the form $y = ax^2 + c$	A1e, h; A2d	
	NCTM 2000 2, 8, 9, 10	
	Pacing Two Year: 1 day Two-Year Block: 0.5 day	

1. INTRODUCE

Check Skills You'll Need: Assign these exercises if not used with Objective 1.

Review: Use the Key Concepts box to review the standard form of a quadratic function.

Targeted Resources
☐ ✐ Transparency: Check Skills You'll Need 10-1

2. TEACH

▼ **Objective:** Teach Examples 4 and 5. Assign Check Understanding 4 and 5 after the appropriate example.

Targeted Resources
☐ ✐ Transparency: Additional Examples 10-1
☐ ✐ Presentation Pro CD-ROM 10-1
☐ 💻 iText 10-1: at **PHSchool.com**

3. PRACTICE

Assignment Guide: Give an assignment based on the ability levels of your students.

   ▼ **Objective:** Core: 14–26, 31–33, 38–39, 45;
   Extension: 46–47, 49
   Standardized Test Prep: 50–53
   Mixed Review: 54–66

Homework: _____

Targeted Resources
☐ ✐ Transparency: Student Answers 10-1
☐ Grab & Go File: Practice 10-1, Reteaching 10-1, Enrichment 10-1
☐ Practice Workbook 10-1
☐ Spanish Practice Workbook 10-1
☐ Reading and Math Literacy 10A
☐ Spanish Reading and Math Literacy 10A
☐ Reasoning & Puzzles 88: at **PHSchool.com**

4. ASSESS

Lesson Quiz: Assign the Lesson Quiz to assess students' mastery of the lesson content.

Targeted Resources
☐ ✐ Transparency: Lesson Quiz 10-1
☐ 💻 Online Lesson Quiz 10-1: at **PHSchool.com**
☐ ✐ Computer Test Generator CD-ROM 10-1

Teacher _____ Class _____ Date _____ M T W Th F

Lesson Plan 10-2, Objective 1
Quadratic Functions

Lesson Objective	NAEP 2005	Local Standards
▼ Graph quadratic functions of the form $y = ax^2 + bx + c$	A1e, h; A2d; A4c	
	NCTM 2000 2, 8, 9, 10	
	Pacing Two Year: 1 day Two-Year Block: 0.5 day	

1. INTRODUCE

Check Skills You'll Need: Assign these exercises to review the prerequisite skills of evaluating expressions and graphing quadratic functions.

Targeted Resources

☐ 🗲 Transparency: Check Skills You'll Need 10-2

2. TEACH

▼ **Objective:** Help students understand the property in the Key Concepts box. Teach Examples 1 and 2. Assign Check Understanding questions 1 and 2 after the appropriate example.

Targeted Resources

☐ 🗲 Transparency: Additional Examples 10-2
☐ ✐ Presentation Pro CD-ROM 10-2
☐ 📕 iText 10-2: at **PHSchool.com**

3. PRACTICE

Assignment Guide: Give an assignment based on the ability levels of your students.

▼ **Objective:** Core: 1–16, 23–35, 40–42; Extension: 43, 46
Standardized Test Prep: 47–50
Mixed Review: 51–62

Homework: _____

Targeted Resources

☐ 🗲 Transparency: Student Answers 10-2
☐ Grab & Go File: Practice 10-2, Reteaching 10-2, Enrichment 10-2
☐ Practice Workbook 10-2
☐ Spanish Practice Workbook 10-2

4. ASSESS

Lesson Quiz: Create a quiz on Objective 1 using the Computer Test Generator.

Targeted Resources

☐ ✐ Computer Test Generator CD-ROM 10-2

© Pearson Education, Inc., publishing as Pearson Prentice Hall.

120 Lesson 10-2, Objective 1   *Algebra 1A and 1B Lesson Plans*

Lesson Plan 10-2, Objective 2
Quadratic Functions

Lesson Objective	NAEP 2005	Local Standards
▼ Graph quadratic inequalities	A1e, h; A2d; A4c	
	NCTM 2000 2, 8, 9, 10	
	Pacing Two Year: 1 day Two-Year Block: 0.5 day	

1. INTRODUCE

Check Skills You'll Need: Assign these exercises if not used with Objective 1.

Review: Use the Key Concepts box to review the graph of a quadratic function.

Targeted Resources
- ☐ ✎ Transparency: Check Skills You'll Need 10-2

2. TEACH

▼ **Objective:** Teach Example 3. Assign Check Understanding question 3.

Targeted Resources
- ☐ ✎ Transparency: Additional Examples 10-2
- ☐ ✍ Presentation Pro CD-ROM 10-2
- ☐ ▣ iText 10-2: at **PHSchool.com**

3. PRACTICE

Assignment Guide: Give an assignment based on the ability levels of your students.

▼ **Objective:** Core: 17–22, 36–39; Extension: 44–45
Mixed Review: 51–62

Homework: _____

Targeted Resources
- ☐ ✎ Transparency: Student Answers 10-2
- ☐ Grab & Go File: Practice 10-2, Reteaching 10-2, Enrichment 10-2
- ☐ Practice Workbook 10-2
- ☐ Spanish Practice Workbook 10-2

4. ASSESS

Lesson Quiz: Assign the Lesson Quiz to assess students' mastery of the lesson content.

Targeted Resources
- ☐ ✎ Transparency: Lesson Quiz 10-2
- ☐ ▣ Online Lesson Quiz 10-2: at **PHSchool.com**
- ☐ ✍ Computer Test Generator CD-ROM 10-2

Lesson Plan 10-3, Objective 1
Finding and Estimating Square Roots

Lesson Objective ▼ find square roots **New Vocabulary:** square root, principal square root, negative square root, radicand	**NAEP 2005** N1d; N2d **NCTM 2000** 1, 2, 9, 10 **Pacing** Two Year: 0.5 day Two-Year Block: 0.5 day	**Local Standards**

1. INTRODUCE

Check Skills You'll Need: Assign these exercises to review the prerequisite skill of squaring rational numbers.

New Vocabulary: Help students pre-read the lesson by pointing out the new terms introduced in Objective 1.

Targeted Resources

☐ 🖳 Transparency: Check Skills You'll Need 10-3

2. TEACH

▼ **Objective:** Teach Examples 1 and 2. Assign Check Understanding questions 1 and 2 after the appropriate example.

Targeted Resources

☐ 🖳 Transparency: Additional Examples 10-3
☐ 🖉 Presentation Pro CD-ROM 10-3
☐ 🖳 iText 10-3: at **PHSchool.com**

3. PRACTICE

Assignment Guide: Give an assignment based on the ability levels of your students.

▼ **Objective:** Core: 1–16, 26–38, 49–51;
Extension: 56–59
Standardized Test Prep: 65
Mixed Review: 66–86

Homework: _____

Targeted Resources

☐ 🖳 Transparency: Student Answers 10-3
☐ Grab & Go File: Practice 10-3, Reteaching 10-3, Enrichment 10-3
☐ Practice Workbook 10-3
☐ Spanish Practice Workbook 10-3

4. ASSESS

Lesson Quiz: Create a quiz on Objective 1 using the Computer Test Generator.

Targeted Resources

☐ 🖉 Computer Test Generator CD-ROM 10-3

Teacher _____ Class _____ Date _____ M T W Th F

Lesson Plan 10-3, Objective 2
Finding and Estimating Square Roots

Lesson Objective	NAEP 2005	Local Standards
▿ Estimate and use square roots **New Vocabulary:** perfect squares	N1d; N2d **NCTM 2000** 1, 2, 9, 10 **Pacing** Two Year: 0.5 day Two-Year Block: 0.5 day	

1. INTRODUCE

Check Skills You'll Need: Assign these exercises if not used with Objective 1.

Review: Use the Key Concepts box to review square roots.

New Vocabulary: Help students pre-read the lesson by pointing out the new term introduced in Objective 2.

Targeted Resources
☐ ⌂ Transparency: Check Skills You'll Need 10-3

2. TEACH

▿ **Objective:** Teach Examples 3–5. Assign Check Understanding questions 3–5 after the appropriate example.

Targeted Resources
☐ ⌂ Transparency: Additional Examples 10-3
☐ ⊘ Presentation Pro CD-ROM 10-3
☐ ▣ iText 10-3: at **PHSchool.com**

3. PRACTICE

Assignment Guide: Give an assignment based on the ability levels of your students.

  ▿ **Objective:** Core: 17–25, 39–48; Extension: 52–55
  Standardized Test Prep: 60–64
  Mixed Review: 66–86

Homework: _____

Targeted Resources
☐ ⌂ Transparency: Student Answers 10-3
☐ Grab & Go File: Practice 10-3, Reteaching 10-3, Enrichment 10-3
☐ Practice Workbook 10-3
☐ Spanish Practice Workbook 10-3
☐ Reasoning & Puzzles 90: at **PHSchool.com**

4. ASSESS

Lesson Quiz: Assign the Lesson Quiz to assess students' mastery of the lesson content.

Targeted Resources
☐ ⌂ Transparency: Lesson Quiz 10-3
☐ ▣ Online Lesson Quiz 10-3: at **PHSchool.com**
☐ ⊘ Computer Test Generator CD-ROM 10-3

Lesson Plan 10-4, Objective 1
Solving Quadratic Equations

Lesson Objective	NAEP 2005	Local Standards
▼ Solve quadratic equations by graphing **New Vocabulary:** quadratic equation, standard form of a quadratic equation	A4a, c **NCTM 2000** 1, 2, 3, 9, 10 **Pacing** Two Year: 1 day Two-Year Block: 0.5 day	

1. INTRODUCE

Check Skills You'll Need: Assign these exercises to review the prerequisite skill of simplifying square roots.

New Vocabulary: Help students pre-read the lesson by pointing out the new terms introduced in Objective 1.

Targeted Resources

☐ 🖾 Transparency: Check Skills You'll Need 10-4

2. TEACH

▼ **Objective:** Have students work the Investigation to explore Finding *x*-intercepts. Go over the definition in the Key Concept box. Teach Example 1. Assign Check Understanding question 1.

Targeted Resources

☐ 🖾 Transparency: Additional Examples 10-4
☐ ✑ Presentation Pro CD-ROM 10-4
☐ 🖳 iText 10-4: at **PHSchool.com**

3. PRACTICE

Assignment Guide: Give an assignment based on the ability levels of your students.

▼ **Objective:** Core: 1–9, 36–38, 40
Standardized Test Prep: 46–47
Mixed Review: 51–70

Homework: _____

Targeted Resources

☐ 🖾 Transparency: Student Answers 10-4
☐ Grab & Go File: Practice 10-4, Reteaching 10-4, Enrichment 10-4
☐ Practice Workbook 10-4
☐ Spanish Practice Workbook 10-4
☐ Reading and Math Literacy 10B
☐ Spanish Reading and Math Literacy 10B
☐ Technology Activities 7, 24

4. ASSESS

Lesson Quiz: Create a quiz on Objective 1 using the Computer Test Generator.

Targeted Resources

☐ ✑ Computer Test Generator CD-ROM 10-4

Lesson Plan 10-4, Objective 2
Solving Quadratic Equations

Lesson Objective	NAEP 2005	Local Standards
▼ Solve quadratic equations using square roots	A4a, c **NCTM 2000** 1, 2, 3, 9, 10 **Pacing** Two Year: 1 day Two-Year Block: 0.5 day	

1. INTRODUCE

Check Skills You'll Need: Assign these exercises if not used with Objective 1.

Review: Use the Key Concepts box to review the standard form of a quadratic equation.

Targeted Resources
- ☐ 🖳 Transparency: Check Skills You'll Need 10-4

2. TEACH

▼ **Objective:** Teach Examples 2 and 3. Assign Check Understanding 2 and 3 after the appropriate example.

Targeted Resources
- ☐ 🖳 Transparency: Additional Examples 10-4
- ☐ ✐ Presentation Pro CD-ROM 10-4
- ☐ 🖳 iText 10-4: at **PHSchool.com**

3. PRACTICE

Assignment Guide: Give an assignment based on the ability levels of your students.

▼ **Objective:** Core: 10–35, 39, 41–42; Extension: 43–45
Standardized Test Prep: 48–50
Mixed Review: 51–70

Homework: _____

Targeted Resources
- ☐ 🖳 Transparency: Student Answers 10-4
- ☐ Grab & Go File: Practice 10-4, Reteaching 10-4, Enrichment 10-4
- ☐ Practice Workbook 10-4
- ☐ Spanish Practice Workbook 10-4
- ☐ Reading and Math Literacy 10B
- ☐ Spanish Reading and Math Literacy 10B
- ☐ Technology Activities 7, 24
- ☐ Reasoning & Puzzles 96, 97: at **PHSchool.com**

4. ASSESS

Lesson Quiz: Assign the Lesson Quiz to assess students' mastery of the lesson content.

Checkpoint Quiz: Use the Checkpoint Quiz to assess student progress over several lessons.

Targeted Resources
- ☐ 🖳 Transparency: Lesson Quiz 10-4
- ☐ 🖳 Online Lesson Quiz 10-4: at **PHSchool.com**
- ☐ Grab & Go File: Checkpoint Quiz 1
- ☐ ✐ Computer Test Generator CD-ROM 10-4

Lesson Plan 10-5, Objective 1
Factoring to Solve Quadratic Equations

Lesson Objective	NAEP 2005	Local Standards
▼ Solve quadratic equations by factoring	A4a	
New Vocabulary: zero-product property	**NCTM 2000** 1, 2, 3, 9, 10	
	Pacing Two Year: 2 days Two-Year Block: 1 day	

1. INTRODUCE

Check Skills You'll Need: Assign these exercises to review the prerequisite skills of solving linear equations and factoring quadratic expressions.

New Vocabulary: Help students pre-read the lesson by pointing out the new term introduced in Objective 1.

Targeted Resources

☐ 🖳 Transparency: Check Skills You'll Need 10-5

2. TEACH

▼ **Objective:** Help students understand the concept in the Key Concepts box. Teach Examples 1–4. Assign Check Understanding questions 1–4 after the appropriate example.

Targeted Resources

☐ 🖳 Transparency: Additional Examples 10-5
☐ 📀 Presentation Pro CD-ROM 10-5
☐ 🖳 iText 10-5: at **PHSchool.com**

3. PRACTICE

Assignment Guide: Give an assignment based on the ability levels of your students.

  ▼ **Objective:** Core: 1–46; Extension: 47–50
Standardized Test Prep: 51–56
Mixed Review: 57–64

Homework: _____

Targeted Resources

☐ 🖳 Transparency: Student Answers 10-5
☐ Grab & Go File: Practice 10-5, Reteaching 10-5, Enrichment 10-5
☐ Practice Workbook 10-5
☐ Spanish Practice Workbook 10-5

4. ASSESS

Lesson Quiz: Assign the Lesson Quiz to assess students' mastery of the lesson content.

Targeted Resources

☐ 🖳 Transparency: Lesson Quiz 10-5
☐ 🖳 Online Lesson Quiz 10-5: at **PHSchool.com**
☐ 📀 Computer Test Generator CD-ROM 10-5

Lesson Plan 10-6, Objective 1
Completing the Square

Lesson Objective	NAEP 2005	Local Standards
▼ Solve quadratic equations by completing the square	A4a	
	NCTM 2000	
New Vocabulary: completing the square	1, 2, 3, 9, 10	
	Pacing	
	Two Year: 2 days	
	Two-Year Block: 1 day	

1. INTRODUCE

Check Skills You'll Need: Assign these exercises to review the prerequisite skills of squaring binomials and factoring perfect-square trinomials.

New Vocabulary: Help students pre-read the lesson by pointing out the new term introduced in the lesson.

Targeted Resources

☐ 🖳 Transparency: Check Skills You'll Need 10-6

2. TEACH

▼ Objective: Teach Examples 1–4. Assign Check Understanding questions 1–4 after the appropriate example.

Targeted Resources

☐ 🖳 Transparency: Additional Examples 10-6
☐ 🖉 Presentation Pro CD-ROM 10-6
☐ 🖳 iText 10-6: at **PHSchool.com**

3. PRACTICE

Assignment Guide: Give an assignment based on the ability levels of your students.

▼ Objective: Core: 1–41; Extension: 42–44
Standardized Test Prep: 45–49
Mixed Review: 50–70

Homework: _____

Targeted Resources

☐ 🖳 Transparency: Student Answers 10-6
☐ Grab & Go File: Practice 10-6, Reteaching 10-6, Enrichment 10-6
☐ Practice Workbook 10-6
☐ Spanish Practice Workbook 10-6
☐ Hands-On Activities 23
☐ Reasoning & Puzzles 98, 99: at **PHSchool.com**

4. ASSESS

Lesson Quiz: Assign the Lesson Quiz to assess students' mastery of the lesson content.

Targeted Resources

☐ 🖳 Transparency: Lesson Quiz 10-6
☐ 🖳 Online Lesson Quiz 10-6: at **PHSchool.com**
☐ 🖉 Computer Test Generator CD-ROM 10-6

Lesson Plan 10-7, Objective 1
Using the Quadratic Formula

Lesson Objective	NAEP 2005	Local Standards
▼ Use the quadratic formula when solving quadratic equations **New Vocabulary:** quadratic formula	A4a **NCTM 2000** 1, 2, 3, 7, 9 **Pacing** Two Year: 1 day Two-Year Block: 0.5 day	

1. INTRODUCE

Check Skills You'll Need: Assign these exercises to review the prerequisite skill of completing the square.

New Vocabulary: Help students pre-read the lesson by pointing out the new term introduced in Objective 1.

Targeted Resources
- ☐ 🖳 Transparency: Check Skills You'll Need 10-7

2. TEACH

▼ **Objective:** Help students understand the quadratic formula in the Key Concepts box. Teach Examples 1–3. Assign Check Understanding questions 1–3 after the appropriate example.

Targeted Resources
- ☐ 🖳 Transparency: Additional Examples 10-7
- ☐ 🖉 Presentation Pro CD-ROM 10-7
- ☐ 🖳 iText 10-7: at **PHSchool.com**

3. PRACTICE

Assignment Guide: Give an assignment based on the ability levels of your students.

▼ **Objective:** Core: 1–17, 33–34, 36–38, 40; Extension: 41
Standardized Test Prep: 43–45
Mixed Review: 47–55

Homework: _____

Targeted Resources
- ☐ 🖳 Transparency: Student Answers 10-7
- ☐ Grab & Go File: Practice 10-7, Reteaching 10-7, Enrichment 10-7
- ☐ Practice Workbook 10-7
- ☐ Spanish Practice Workbook 10-7

4. ASSESS

Lesson Quiz: Create a quiz on Objective 1 using the Computer Test Generator.

Targeted Resources
- ☐ 🖉 Computer Test Generator CD-ROM 10-7

Lesson Plan 10-7, Objective 2
Using the Quadratic Formula

Lesson Objective	NAEP 2005	Local Standards
▿ Choose an appropriate method when solving a quadratic equation	A4a **NCTM 2000** 1, 2, 3, 7, 9 **Pacing** Two Year: 1 day Two-Year Block: 0.5 day	

1. INTRODUCE

Check Skills You'll Need: Assign these exercises if not used with Objective 1.

Review: Use the Key Concepts box to review the quadratic formula.

Targeted Resources
☐ 🖳 Transparency: Check Skills You'll Need 10-7

2. TEACH

▿ **Objective:** Teach Example 4. Assign Check Understanding question 4.

Targeted Resources
☐ 🖳 Transparency: Additional Examples 10-7
☐ 🖉 Presentation Pro CD-ROM 10-7
☐ 🖳 iText 10-7: at **PHSchool.com**

3. PRACTICE

Assignment Guide: Give an assignment based on the ability levels of your students.

> ▿ **Objective:** Core: 18–32, 35, 39; Extension: 42
> **Standardized Test Prep:** 46
> **Mixed Review:** 47–55

Homework: _____

Targeted Resources
☐ 🖳 Transparency: Student Answers 10-7
☐ Grab & Go File: Practice 10-7, Reteaching 10-7, Enrichment 10-7
☐ Practice Workbook 10-7
☐ Spanish Practice Workbook 10-7
☐ Reasoning & Puzzles 84: at **PHSchool.com**

4. ASSESS

Lesson Quiz: Assign the Lesson Quiz to assess students' mastery of the lesson content.

Targeted Resources
☐ 🖳 Transparency: Lesson Quiz 10-7
☐ 🖳 Online Lesson Quiz 10-7: at **PHSchool.com**
☐ 🖉 Computer Test Generator CD-ROM 10-7

Lesson Plan 10-8, Objective 1
Using the Discriminant

Lesson Objective	NAEP 2005	Local Standards
▼ Find the number of solutions of a quadratic equation **New Vocabulary:** discriminant	A4c **NCTM 2000** 1, 2, 3, 7, 9, 10 **Pacing** Two Year: 2 days Two-Year Block: 1 day	

1. INTRODUCE

Check Skills You'll Need: Assign these exercises to review the prerequisite skills of evaluating an expression and solving with the quadratic formula.

New Vocabulary: Help students pre-read the lesson by pointing out the new term introduced in the lesson.

Targeted Resources

☐ 🖳 Transparency: Check Skills You'll Need 10-8

2. TEACH

▼ **Objective:** Go over the concepts shown in the Key Concepts box. Teach Examples 1 and 2. Assign Check Understanding questions 1 and 2 after the appropriate example.

Targeted Resources

☐ 🖳 Transparency: Additional Examples 10-8
☐ 🖳 Transparency: Classroom Aid 3
☐ 💿 Presentation Pro CD-ROM 10-8
☐ 🖳 iText 10-8: at **PHSchool.com**

3. PRACTICE

Assignment Guide: Give an assignment based on the ability levels of your students.

▼ **Objective:** Core: 1–37; Extension: 38–42
Standardized Test Prep: 43–48
Mixed Review: 49–61

Homework: _____

Targeted Resources

☐ 🖳 Transparency: StudentAnswers 10-8
☐ Grab & Go File: Practice 10-8, Reteaching 10-8, Enrichment 10-8
☐ Practice Workbook 10-8
☐ Spanish Practice Workbook 10-8
☐ Reading and Math Literacy 10C
☐ Spanish Reading and Math Literacy 10C
☐ Hands-On Activities 24
☐ Reasoning & Puzzles 94: at **PHSchool.com**

4. ASSESS

Lesson Quiz: Assign the Lesson Quiz to assess students' mastery of the lesson content.

Checkpoint Quiz: Use the Checkpoint Quiz to assess student progress over several lessons.

Targeted Resources

☐ 🖳 Transparency: Lesson Quiz 10-8
☐ 🖳 Online Lesson Quiz 10-8: at **PHSchool.com**
☐ Grab & Go File: Checkpoint Quiz 2
☐ 💿 Computer Test Generator CD-ROM 10-8

Lesson Plan 10-9, Objective 1
Choosing a Linear, Quadratic, or Exponential Model

Lesson Objective	NAEP 2005	Local Standards
▼ Choose a linear, quadratic, or exponential model for data	A2g	
	NCTM 2000	
	2, 5, 9, 10	
	Pacing	
	Two Year: 2 days	
	Two-Year Block:	
	1 day	

1. INTRODUCE

Check Skills You'll Need: Assign these exercises to review the prerequisite skills of graphing linear, exponential, and quadratic functions.

Targeted Resources

☐ ✎ Transparency: Check Skills You'll Need 10-9

2. TEACH

▼ **Objective:** Go over the functions in the Key Concepts box. Teach Examples 1–3. Assign Check Understanding questions 1–3 after the appropriate example.

Targeted Resources

☐ ✎ Transparency: Additional Examples 10-9
☐ ✎ Transparency: Classroom Aid 27
☐ ✐ Presentation Pro CD-ROM 10-9
☐ 🖳 iText 10-9: at **PHSchool.com**

3. PRACTICE

Assignment Guide: Give an assignment based on the ability levels of your students.

▼ **Objective:** Core: 1–27; Extension: 28–29
Standardized Test Prep: 30–33
Mixed Review: 34–48

Homework: _____

Targeted Resources

☐ ✎ Transparency: Student Answers 10-9
☐ Grab & Go File: Practice 10-9, Reteaching 10-9, Enrichment 10-9
☐ Practice Workbook 10-9
☐ Spanish Practice Workbook 10-9
☐ Technology Activities 9
☐ Hands-On Activities 25

4. ASSESS

Lesson Quiz: Assign the Lesson Quiz to assess students' mastery of the lesson content.

Targeted Resources

☐ ✎ Transparency: Lesson Quiz 10-9
☐ 🖳 Online Lesson Quiz 10-9: at **PHSchool.com**
☐ ✐ Computer Test Generator CD-ROM 10-9

Lesson Plan 11-1, Objective 1
Simplifying Radicals

Lesson Objective	NAEP 2005	Local Standards
▼ Simplify radicals involving products	A3b, c	
New Vocabulary: radical expression	**NCTM 2000** 2, 8, 10	
	Pacing Two Year: 1 day Two-Year Block: 0.5 day	

1. INTRODUCE

Check Skills You'll Need: Assign these exercises to review the prerequisite skills of factoring powers and evaluating radicals.

New Vocabulary: Help students pre-read the lesson by pointing out the new term introduced in Objective 1.

Targeted Resources

☐ ✎ Transparency: Check Skills You'll Need 11-1

2. TEACH

▼ **Objective:** Go over the property in the Key Concepts box. Teach Examples 1–4. Assign Check Understanding questions 1–4 after the appropriate example.

Targeted Resources

☐ ✎ Transparency: Additional Examples 11-1
☐ ✐ Presentation Pro CD-ROM 11-1
☐ 💻 iText 11-1: at **PHSchool.com**

3. PRACTICE

Assignment Guide: Give an assignment based on the ability levels of your students.

▼ **Objective:** Core: 1–27, 54–58, 69–74; Extension: 75–76
Standardized Test Prep: 79–80, 82
Mixed Review: 84–93

Homework: _____

Targeted Resources

☐ ✎ Transparency: Student Answers 11-1
☐ Grab & Go File: Practice 11-1, Reteaching 11-1, Enrichment 11-1
☐ Practice Workbook 11-1
☐ Spanish Practice Workbook 11-1
☐ Reading and Math Literacy 11A
☐ Spanish Reading and Math Literacy 11A

4. ASSESS

Lesson Quiz: Create a quiz on Objective 1 using the Computer Test Generator.

Targeted Resources

☐ ✐ Computer Test Generator CD-ROM 11-1

Lesson Plan 11-1, Objective 2
Simplifying Radicals

Lesson Objective	NAEP 2005	Local Standards
☑ Simplify radicals involving quotients **New Vocabulary:** rationalize	A3b, c **NCTM 2000** 2, 8, 10 **Pacing** Two Year: 1 day Two-Year Block: 0.5 day	

1. INTRODUCE

Check Skills You'll Need: Assign these exercises if not used with Objective 1.

Review: Use the Key Concepts box to review the Multiplication Property of Square Roots.

New Vocabulary: Help students pre-read the lesson by pointing out the new term introduced in Objective 2.

Targeted Resources
- ☐ 🖳 Transparency: Check Skills You'll Need 11-1

2. TEACH

☑ **Objective:** Go over the property in the Key Concepts box. Teach Examples 5–7. Assign Check Understanding questions 5–7 after the appropriate example.

Targeted Resources
- ☐ 🖳 Transparency: Additional Examples 11-1
- ☐ ✐ Presentation Pro CD-ROM 11-1
- ☐ 🖳 iText 11-1: at **PHSchool.com**

3. PRACTICE

Assignment Guide: Give an assignment based on the ability levels of your students.

  ☑ **Objective:** Core: 28–53, 59–68; Extension: 77–78
  Standardized Test Prep: 81, 83
  Mixed Review: 84–93

Homework: _____

Targeted Resources
- ☐ 🖳 Transparency: Student Answers 11-1
- ☐ Grab & Go File: Practice 11-1, Reteaching 11-1, Enrichment 11-1
- ☐ Practice Workbook 11-1
- ☐ Spanish Practice Workbook 11-1
- ☐ Reading and Math Literacy 11A
- ☐ Spanish Reading and Math Literacy 11A
- ☐ Reasoning & Puzzles 91: at **PHSchool.com**

4. ASSESS

Lesson Quiz: Assign the Lesson Quiz to assess students' mastery of the lesson content.

Targeted Resources
- ☐ 🖳 Transparency: Lesson Quiz 11-1
- ☐ 🖳 Online Lesson Quiz 11-1: at **PHSchool.com**
- ☐ ✐ Computer Test Generator CD-ROM 11-1

Teacher _____ Class _____ Date _____ M T W Th F

Lesson Plan 11-2, Objective 1
The Pythagorean Theorem

Lesson Objective	NAEP 2005	Local Standards
▼ Solve problems using the Pythagorean Theorem **New Vocabulary:** hypotenuse, leg, Pythagorean Theorem	G3d, f **NCTM 2000** 2, 3, 4, 10 **Pacing** Two Year: 2 days Two-Year Block: 1 day	

1. INTRODUCE

Check Skills You'll Need: Assign these exercises to review the prerequisite skills of simplifying expressions with powers and solving quadratic equations.

New Vocabulary: Help students pre-read the lesson by pointing out the new terms introduced in Objective 1.

Targeted Resources

☐ 🖳 Transparency: Check Skills You'll Need 11-2

2. TEACH

▼ Objective: Have students work the Investigation to explore using the Pythagorean Theorem. Teach Examples 1 and 2. Assign Check Understanding questions 1 and 2 after the appropriate example.

Targeted Resources

☐ 🖳 Transparency: Additional Examples 11-2
☐ 🖳 Transparency: Classroom Aid 18
☐ Graphing Calculator Procedure 19: at **PHSchool.com**
☐ ✐ Presentation Pro CD-ROM 11-2
☐ 🖳 iText 11-2: at **PHSchool.com**

3. PRACTICE

Assignment Guide: Give an assignment based on the ability levels of your students.

▼ Objective: Core: 1–15, 26–32, 39–47, 52–53; Extension: 54–56
Standardized Test Prep: 60–61
Mixed Review: 66–85

Homework: _____

Targeted Resources

☐ 🖳 Transparency: Student Answers 11-2
☐ Grab & Go File: Practice 11-2, Reteaching 11-2, Enrichment 11-2
☐ Practice Workbook 11-2
☐ Spanish Practice Workbook 11-2
☐ Hands-On Activities 26

4. ASSESS

Lesson Quiz: Create a quiz on Objective 1 using the Computer Test Generator.

Targeted Resources

☐ ✐ Computer Test Generator CD-ROM 11-2

Algebra 1A and 1B Lesson Plans

Lesson Plan 11-2, Objective 2
The Pythagorean Theorem

Lesson Objective	NAEP 2005	Local Standards
☑ Identify right triangles **New Vocabulary:** conditional, hypothesis, conclusion, converse	G3d, f **NCTM 2000** 2, 3, 4, 10 **Pacing** Two Year: 1 day Two-Year Block: 1 day	

1. INTRODUCE

Check Skills You'll Need: Assign these exercises if not used with Objective 1.

Review: Use the Key Concepts box to review the Pythagorean Theorem.

New Vocabulary: Help students pre-read the lesson by pointing out the new terms introduced in Objective 2.

Targeted Resources
- ☐ Transparency: Check Skills You'll Need 11-2

2. TEACH

☑ Objective: Teach Examples 3 and 4. Assign Check Understanding questions 3 and 4 after the appropriate example.

Targeted Resources
- ☐ Transparency: Additional Examples 11-2
- ☐ Transparency: Classroom Aid 18
- ☐ Graphing Calculator Procedure 19: at **PHSchool.com**
- ☐ Presentation Pro CD-ROM 11-2
- ☐ iText 11-2: at **PHSchool.com**

3. PRACTICE

Assignment Guide: Give an assignment based on the ability levels of your students.

☑ Objective: Core: 16–25, 33–38, 48–51;
Extension: 57–59
Standardized Test Prep: 62–65
Mixed Review: 66–85

Homework: _____

Targeted Resources
- ☐ Transparency: Student Answers 11-2
- ☐ Grab & Go File: Practice 11-2, Reteaching 11-2, Enrichment 11-2
- ☐ Practice Workbook 11-2
- ☐ Spanish Practice Workbook 11-2
- ☐ Hands-On Activities 26
- ☐ Reasoning & Puzzles 94: at **PHSchool.com**

4. ASSESS

Lesson Quiz: Assign the Lesson Quiz to assess students' mastery of the lesson content.

Targeted Resources
- ☐ Transparency: Lesson Quiz 11-2
- ☐ Online Lesson Quiz 11-2: at **PHSchool.com**
- ☐ Computer Test Generator CD-ROM 11-2

Lesson Plan 11-3, Objective 1
The Distance and Midpoint Formulas

Lesson Objective	NAEP 2005	Local Standards
▼ Find the distance between two points on a coordinate plane **New Vocabulary:** distance formula	M1e **NCTM 2000** 2, 3, 4, 10 **Pacing** Two Year: 2 days Two-Year Block: 1 day	

1. INTRODUCE

Check Skills You'll Need: Assign these exercises to review the prerequisite skills of applying the Pythagorean Theorem and finding the mean of two numbers.

New Vocabulary: Help students pre-read the lesson by pointing out the new term introduced in Objective 1.

Targeted Resources
- ☐ ✎ Transparency: Check Skills You'll Need 11-3

2. TEACH

▼ **Objective:** Go over the distance formula in the Key Concepts box. Teach Examples 1 and 2. Assign Check Understanding 1 and 2 after the appropriate example.

Targeted Resources
- ☐ ✎ Transparency: Additional Examples 11-3
- ☐ ✎ Transparency: Classroom Aid 18
- ☐ ✐ Presentation Pro CD-ROM 11-3
- ☐ 🖥 iText 11-3: at **PHSchool.com**

3. PRACTICE

Assignment Guide: Give an assignment based on the ability levels of your students.

▼ **Objective:** Core: 1–8, 17–25, 30–31; Extension: 38
Standardized Test Prep: 41, 43, 45, 47
Mixed Review: 48–65

Homework: _____

Targeted Resources
- ☐ ✎ Transparency: Student Answers 11-3
- ☐ Grab & Go File: Practice 11-3, Reteaching 11-3, Enrichment 11-3
- ☐ Practice Workbook 11-3
- ☐ Spanish Practice Workbook 11-3
- ☐ Reading and Math Literacy 11B
- ☐ Spanish Reading and Math Literacy 11B
- ☐ Hands-On Activities 27

4. ASSESS

Lesson Quiz: Create a quiz on Objective 1 using the Computer Test Generator.

Targeted Resources
- ☐ ✐ Computer Test Generator CD-ROM 11-3

Teacher _____ Class _____ Date _____ M T W Th F

Lesson Plan 11-3, Objective 2
The Distance and Midpoint Formulas

Lesson Objective	NAEP 2005	Local Standards
☑ Find the coordinates of the midpoint of a line segment **New Vocabulary:** midpoint, midpoint formula	M1e **NCTM 2000** 2, 3, 4, 10 **Pacing** Two Year: 1 day Two-Year Block: 1 day	

1. INTRODUCE

Check Skills You'll Need: Assign these exercises if not used with Objective 1.

Review: Use the Key Concepts box to review the distance formula.

New Vocabulary: Help students pre-read the lesson by pointing out the new terms introduced in Objective 2.

Targeted Resources
- ☐ ◔ Transparency: Check Skills You'll Need 11-3

2. TEACH

☑ Objective: Go over the midpoint formula in the Key Concepts box. Teach Examples 3 and 4. Assign Check Understanding 3 and 4 after the appropriate example.

Targeted Resources
- ☐ ◔ Transparency: Additional Examples 11-3
- ☐ ◔ Transparency: Classroom Aid 18
- ☐ ⊘ Presentation Pro CD-ROM 11-3
- ☐ ▣ iText 11-3: at **PHSchool.com**

3. PRACTICE

Assignment Guide: Give an assignment based on the ability levels of your students.

☑ Objective: Core: 9–16, 26–29, 32–37; Extension: 39–40
Standardized Test Prep: 42, 44, 46
Mixed Review: 48–65

Homework: _____

Targeted Resources
- ☐ ◔ Transparency: Student Answers 11-3
- ☐ Grab & Go File: Practice 11-3, Reteaching 11-3, Enrichment 11-3
- ☐ Practice Workbook 11-3
- ☐ Spanish Practice Workbook 11-3
- ☐ Reading and Math Literacy 11B
- ☐ Spanish Reading and Math Literacy 11B
- ☐ Hands-On Activities 27

4. ASSESS

Lesson Quiz: Assign the Lesson Quiz to assess students' mastery of the lesson content.

Checkpoint Quiz: Use the Checkpoint Quiz to assess student progress over several lessons.

Targeted Resources
- ☐ ◔ Transparency: Lesson Quiz 11-3
- ☐ ▣ Online Lesson Quiz 11-3: at **PHSchool.com**
- ☐ Grab & Go File: Checkpoint Quiz 1
- ☐ ⊘ Computer Test Generator CD-ROM 11-3

Lesson Plan 11-4, Objective 1
Operations with Radical Expressions

Lesson Objective	NAEP 2005	Local Standards
▼ Simplify sums and differences	A3b	
New Vocabulary: like radicals, unlike radicals	**NCTM 2000** 1, 2, 10	
	Pacing Two Year: 2 days Two-Year Block: 1 day	

1. INTRODUCE

Check Skills You'll Need: Assign these exercises to review the prerequisite skill of simplifying radical expressions.

New Vocabulary: Help students pre-read the lesson by pointing out the new terms introduced in Objective 1.

Targeted Resources

☐ 🖳 Transparency: Check Skills You'll Need 11-4

2. TEACH

▼ **Objective:** Teach Examples 1 and 2. Assign Check Understanding questions 1 and 2 after the appropriate example.

Targeted Resources

☐ 🖳 Transparency: Additional Examples 11-4
☐ 🖉 Presentation Pro CD-ROM 11-4
☐ 🖥 iText 11-4: at **PHSchool.com**

3. PRACTICE

Assignment Guide: Give an assignment based on the ability levels of your students.

▼ **Objective:** Core: 1–15, 48–54, 62–63
Standardized Test Prep: 72–73
Mixed Review: 76–92

Homework: _____

Targeted Resources

☐ 🖳 Transparency: Student Answers 11-4
☐ Grab & Go File: Practice 11-4, Reteaching 11-4, Enrichment 11-4
☐ Practice Workbook 11-4
☐ Spanish Practice Workbook 11-4

4. ASSESS

Lesson Quiz: Create a quiz on Objective 1 using the Computer Test Generator.

Targeted Resources

☐ 🖉 Computer Test Generator CD-ROM 11-4

Lesson Plan 11-4, Objective 2
Operations with Radical Expressions

Lesson Objective	NAEP 2005	Local Standards
☑ Simplify products and quotients **New Vocabulary:** conjugates	A3b **NCTM 2000** 1, 2, 10 **Pacing** Two Year: 2 days Two-Year Block: 1 day	

1. INTRODUCE

Check Skills You'll Need: Assign these exercises if not used with Objective 1.

Review: Remind the students how to simplify sums and differences.

New Vocabulary: Help students pre-read the lesson by pointing out the new term introduced in Objective 2.

Targeted Resources
- ☐ 💻 Transparency: Check Skills You'll Need 11-4

2. TEACH

☑ **Objective:** Teach Examples 3–6. Assign Check Understanding questions 3–6 after the appropriate example.

Targeted Resources
- ☐ 💻 Transparency: Additional Examples 11-4
- ☐ 💿 Presentation Pro CD-ROM 11-4
- ☐ 💻 iText 11-4: at **PHSchool.com**

3. PRACTICE

Assignment Guide: Give an assignment based on the ability levels of your students.

☑ **Objective:** Core: 16–47, 55–61; Extension: 64–71
Standardized Test Prep: 74–75
Mixed Review: 76–92

Homework: _____

Targeted Resources
- ☐ 💻 Transparency: Student Answers 11-4
- ☐ Grab & Go File: Practice 11-4, Reteaching 11-4, Enrichment 11-4
- ☐ Practice Workbook 11-4
- ☐ Spanish Practice Workbook 11-4

4. ASSESS

Lesson Quiz: Assign the Lesson Quiz to assess students' mastery of the lesson content.

Targeted Resources
- ☐ 💻 Transparency: Lesson Quiz 11-4
- ☐ 💻 Online Lesson Quiz 11-4: at **PHSchool.com**
- ☐ 💿 Computer Test Generator CD-ROM 11-4

Lesson Plan 11-5, Objective 1
Solving Radical Equations

Lesson Objective	NAEP 2005	Local Standards
▼ Solve equations containing radicals **New Vocabulary:** radical equation	A3c, e **NCTM 2000** 1, 2, 10 **Pacing** Two Year: 2 days Two-Year Block: 1 day	

1. INTRODUCE

Check Skills You'll Need: Assign these exercises to review the prerequisite skills of evaluating and simplifying radical expressions.

New Vocabulary: Help students pre-read the lesson by pointing out the new term introduced in Objective 1.

Targeted Resources

☐ ⏚ Transparency: Check Skills You'll Need 11-5

2. TEACH

▼ **Objective:** Teach Examples 1–3. Assign Check Understanding questions 1–3 after the appropriate example.

Targeted Resources

☐ ⏚ Transparency: Additional Examples 11-5
☐ ⦸ Presentation Pro CD-ROM 11-5
☐ ▤ iText 11-5: at **PHSchool.com**

3. PRACTICE

Assignment Guide: Give an assignment based on the ability levels of your students.

▼ **Objective:** Core: 1–14, 29–30, 44–46; Extension: 53–54
Standardized Test Prep: 55–57
Mixed Review: 62–79

Homework: _____

Targeted Resources

☐ ⏚ Transparency: Student Answers 11-5
☐ Grab & Go File: Practice 11-5, Reteaching 11-5, Enrichment 11-5
☐ Practice Workbook 11-5
☐ Spanish Practice Workbook 11-5
☐ Technology Activities 25

4. ASSESS

Lesson Quiz: Create a quiz on Objective 1 using the Computer Test Generator.

Targeted Resources

☐ ⦸ Computer Test Generator CD-ROM 11-5

Lesson Plan 11-5, Objective 2
Solving Radical Equations

Lesson Objective	NAEP 2005	Local Standards
❷ Identify extraneous solutions **New Vocabulary:** extraneous solution	A3c, e **NCTM 2000** 1, 2, 10 **Pacing** Two Year: 1 day Two-Year Block: 1 day	

1. INTRODUCE

Check Skills You'll Need: Assign these exercises if not used with Objective 1.

Review: Remind the students how to solve radical equations

New Vocabulary: Help students pre-read the lesson by pointing out the new term introduced in Objective 2.

Targeted Resources
- ☐ 🖥 Transparency: Check Skills You'll Need 11-5

2. TEACH

❷ **Objective:** Teach Examples 4 and 5. Assign Check Understanding questions 4 and 5 after the appropriate example.

Targeted Resources
- ☐ 🖥 Transparency: Additional Examples 11-5
- ☐ 🖉 Presentation Pro CD-ROM 11-5
- ☐ 💻 iText 11-5: at **PHSchool.com**

3. PRACTICE

Assignment Guide: Give an assignment based on the ability levels of your students.

❷ **Objective:** Core: 15–28, 31–43, 47; Extension: 48–52
Standardized Test Prep: 58–61
Mixed Review: 62–79

Homework: _____

Targeted Resources
- ☐ 🖥 Transparency: Student Answers 11-5
- ☐ Grab & Go File: Practice 11-5, Reteaching 11-5, Enrichment 11-5
- ☐ Practice Workbook 11-5
- ☐ Spanish Practice Workbook 11-5
- ☐ Technology Activities 25

4. ASSESS

Lesson Quiz: Assign the Lesson Quiz to assess students' mastery of the lesson content.

Targeted Resources
- ☐ 🖥 Transparency: Lesson Quiz 11-5
- ☐ 💻 Online Lesson Quiz 11-5: at **PHSchool.com**
- ☐ 🖉 Computer Test Generator CD-ROM 11-5

Lesson Plan 11-6, Objective 1
Graphing Square Root Functions

Lesson Objective	NAEP 2005	Local Standards
▼ Graph square root functions	A2a, d	
New Vocabulary: square root function	**NCTM 2000** 2, 8, 10	
	Pacing Two Year: 2 days Two-Year Block: 1 day	

1. INTRODUCE

Check Skills You'll Need: Assign these exercises to review the prerequisite skills of graphing quadratic functions and evaluating radical expressions.

New Vocabulary: Help students pre-read the lesson by pointing out the new term introduced in Objective 1.

Targeted Resources

☐ ✎ Transparency: Check Skills You'll Need 11-6

2. TEACH

▼ **Objective:** Teach Examples 1 and 2. Assign Check Understanding questions 1 and 2 after the appropriate example.

Targeted Resources

☐ ✎ Transparency: Additional Examples 11-6
☐ ✎ Transparency: Classroom Aid 27
☐ ✐ Presentation Pro CD-ROM 11-6
☐ ▨ iText 11-6: at **PHSchool.com**

3. PRACTICE

Assignment Guide: Give an assignment based on the ability levels of your students.

▼ **Objective:** Core: 1–16, 30–33, 51–58; Extension: 59, 62
Standardized Test Prep: 67
Mixed Review: 70–87

Homework: _____

Targeted Resources

☐ ✎ Transparency: Student Answers 11-6
☐ Grab & Go File: Practice 11-6, Reteaching 11-6, Enrichment 11-6
☐ Practice Workbook 11-6
☐ Spanish Practice Workbook 11-6
☐ Reading and Math Literacy 11C
☐ Spanish Reading and Math Literacy 11C

4. ASSESS

Lesson Quiz: Create a quiz on Objective 1 using the Computer Test Generator.

Targeted Resources

☐ ✐ Computer Test Generator CD-ROM 11-6

Lesson Plan 11-6, Objective 2
Graphing Square Root Functions

Lesson Objective	NAEP 2005	Local Standards
▼ Translate graphs of square root functions	A2a, d	
	NCTM 2000	
	2, 8, 10	
	Pacing	
	Two Year: 1 day	
	Two-Year Block: 1 day	

1. INTRODUCE

Check Skills You'll Need: Assign these exercises if not used with Objective 1.

Review: Remind students how to graph a square root function.

Targeted Resources

☐ ✎ Transparency: Check Skills You'll Need 11-6

2. TEACH

▼ **Objective:** Teach Examples 3 and 4. Assign Check Understanding questions 3 and 4 after the appropriate example.

Targeted Resources

☐ ✎ Transparency: Additional Examples 11-6
☐ ✎ Transparency: Classroom Aid 27
☐ ❂ Presentation Pro CD-ROM 11-6
☐ ▣ iText 11-6: at **PHSchool.com**

3. PRACTICE

Assignment Guide: Give an assignment based on the ability levels of your students.

   ▼ **Objective:** Core: 17–29, 34–50; Extension: 60–61
Standardized Test Prep: 63–66, 68–69
Mixed Review: 70–87

Homework: _____

Targeted Resources

☐ ✎ Transparency: Student Answers 11-6
☐ Grab & Go File: Practice 11-6, Reteaching 11-6, Enrichment 11-6
☐ Practice Workbook 11-6
☐ Spanish Practice Workbook 11-6
☐ Reading and Math Literacy 11C
☐ Spanish Reading and Math Literacy 11C

4. ASSESS

Lesson Quiz: Assign the Lesson Quiz to assess students' mastery of the lesson content.

Checkpoint Quiz: Use the Checkpoint Quiz to assess student progress over several lessons.

Targeted Resources

☐ ✎ Transparency: Lesson Quiz 11-6
☐ ▣ Online Lesson Quiz 11-6: at **PHSchool.com**
☐ Grab & Go File: Checkpoint Quiz 2
☐ ❂ Computer Test Generator CD-ROM 11-6

Lesson Plan 11-7, Objective 1
Trigonometric Ratios

Lesson Objective	NAEP 2005	Local Standards
▼ Find trigonometric ratios **New Vocabulary:** trigonometric ratios, sine, cosine, tangent	M1m **NCTM 2000** 2, 3, 4, 8, 10 **Pacing** Two Year: 1 day Two-Year Block: 0.5 day	

1. INTRODUCE

Check Skills You'll Need: Assign these exercises to review the prerequisite skills of evaluating ratios and solving proportions.

New Vocabulary: Help students pre-read the lesson by pointing out the new terms introduced in Objective 1.

Targeted Resources

☐ 🖳 Transparency: Check Skills You'll Need 11-7

2. TEACH

▼ **Objective:** Have students work the Investigation to explore trigonometric ratios. Teach Examples 1–3. Assign Check Understanding questions 1–3 after the appropriate example.

Targeted Resources

☐ 🖳 Transparency: Additional Examples 11-7
☐ 🖳 Transparency: Classroom Aid 28, 29
☐ Graphing Calculator Procedure 10:
    at **PHSchool.com**
☐ ✐ Presentation Pro CD-ROM 11-7
☐ 🖳 iText 11-7: at **PHSchool.com**

3. PRACTICE

Assignment Guide: Give an assignment based on the ability levels of your students.

▼ **Objective:** Core: 1–17, 22–28, 34–37;
Extension: 45
Standardized Test Prep: 47–49
Mixed Review: 51–62

Homework: _____

Targeted Resources

☐ 🖳 Transparency: Student Answers 11-7
☐ Grab & Go File: Practice 11-7, Reteaching 11-7, Enrichment 11-7
☐ Practice Workbook 11-7
☐ Spanish Practice Workbook 11-7
☐ Hands-On Activities 28

4. ASSESS

Lesson Quiz: Create a quiz on Objective 1 using the Computer Test Generator.

Targeted Resources

☐ ✐ Computer Test Generator CD-ROM 11-7

Lesson Plan 11-7, Objective 2
Trigonometric Ratios

Lesson Objective	NAEP 2005	Local Standards
▼ Solve problems using trigonometric ratios **New Vocabulary:** angle of elevation, angle of depression	M1m **NCTM 2000** 2, 3, 4, 8, 10 **Pacing** Two Year: 1 day Two-Year Block: 0.5 day	

1. INTRODUCE

Check Skills You'll Need: Assign these exercises if not used with Objective 1.

Review: Remind the students how to find trigonometric ratios.

New Vocabulary: Help students pre-read the lesson by pointing out the new terms introduced in Objective 2.

Targeted Resources
- ☐ Transparency: Check Skills You'll Need 11-7

2. TEACH

▼ **Objective:** Teach Examples 4 and 5. Assign Check Understanding questions 4 and 5 after the appropriate example.

Targeted Resources
- ☐ Transparency: Additional Examples 11-7
- ☐ Transparency: Classroom Aid 28, 29
- ☐ Graphing Calculator Procedure 10: at **PHSchool.com**
- ☐ Presentation Pro CD-ROM 11-7
- ☐ iText 11-7: at **PHSchool.com**

3. PRACTICE

Assignment Guide: Give an assignment based on the ability levels of your students.

▼ **Objective:** Core: 18–21, 29–33, 38–42; Extension: 43–44, 46
Standardized Test Prep: 50
Mixed Review: 51–62

Homework: _____

Targeted Resources
- ☐ Transparency: Student Answers 11-7
- ☐ Grab & Go File: Practice 11-7, Reteaching 11-7, Enrichment 11-7
- ☐ Practice Workbook 11-7
- ☐ Spanish Practice Workbook 11-7
- ☐ Hands-On Activities 28

4. ASSESS

Lesson Quiz: Assign the Lesson Quiz to assess students' mastery of the lesson content.

Targeted Resources
- ☐ Transparency: Lesson Quiz 11-7
- ☐ Online Lesson Quiz 11-7: at **PHSchool.com**
- ☐ Computer Test Generator CD-ROM 11-7

Lesson Plan 12-1, Objective 1
Inverse Variation

Lesson Objective	NAEP 2005	Local Standards
▼ Solve inverse variations	A1e, h	
New Vocabulary: inverse variation, constant of variation	**NCTM 2000** 2, 6, 8, 9	
	Pacing Two Year: 1 day Two-Year Block: 0.5 day	

1. INTRODUCE

Check Skills You'll Need: Assign these exercises to review the prerequisite skills of writing and interpreting direct variations.

New Vocabulary: Help students pre-read the lesson by pointing out the new terms introduced in Objective 1.

Targeted Resources

☐ ⌂ Transparency: Check Skills You'll Need 12-1

2. TEACH

▼ **Objective:** Have students work the Investigation to explore inverse variation. Go over the definition in the Key Concepts box. Teach Examples 1–3. Assign Check Understanding 1–3 after the appropriate example.

Targeted Resources

☐ ⌂ Transparency: Additional Examples 12-1
☐ ✎ Presentation Pro CD-ROM 12-1
☐ ▆ iText 12-1: at **PHSchool.com**

3. PRACTICE

Assignment Guide: Give an assignment based on the ability levels of your students.

   ▼ **Objective:** Core: 1–23, 30–35, 39–40;
   Extension: 50
   Standardized Test Prep: 52–53
   Mixed Review: 56–70

Homework: _____

Targeted Resources

☐ ⌂ Transparency: Student Answers 12-1
☐ Grab & Go File: Practice 12-1, Reteaching 12-1, Enrichment 12-1
☐ Practice Workbook 12-1
☐ Spanish Practice Workbook 12-1
☐ Reading and Math Literacy 12A
☐ Spanish Reading and Math Literacy 12A

4. ASSESS

Lesson Quiz: Create a quiz on Objective 1 using the Computer Test Generator.

Targeted Resources

☐ ✎ Computer Test Generator CD-ROM 12-1

Lesson Plan 12-1, Objective 2
Inverse Variation

Lesson Objective	NAEP 2005	Local Standards
❷ Compare direct and inverse variation	A1e, h	
	NCTM 2000 2, 6, 8, 9	
	Pacing Two Year: 1 day Two-Year Block: 0.5 day	

1. INTRODUCE

Check Skills You'll Need: Assign these exercises if not used with Objective 1.

Review: Use the Key Concepts box to review inverse variation.

Targeted Resources

☐ 📖 Transparency: Check Skills You'll Need 12-1

2. TEACH

❷ **Objective:** Teach Examples 4 and 5. Assign Check Understanding 4 and 5 after the appropriate example.

Targeted Resources

☐ 📖 Transparency: Additional Examples 12-1
☐ 💿 Presentation Pro CD-ROM 12-1
☐ 💻 iText 12-1: at **PHSchool.com**

3. PRACTICE

Assignment Guide: Give an assignment based on the ability levels of your students.

❷ **Objective:** Core: 24–29, 36–38, 41–49;
Extension: 51
Standardized Test Prep: 54–55
Mixed Review: 56–70

Homework: _____

Targeted Resources

☐ 📖 Transparency: Student Answers 12-1
☐ Grab & Go File: Practice 12-1, Reteaching 12-1, Enrichment 12-1
☐ Practice Workbook 12-1
☐ Spanish Practice Workbook 12-1
☐ Reading and Math Literacy 12A
☐ Spanish Reading and Math Literacy 12A

4. ASSESS

Lesson Quiz: Assign the Lesson Quiz to assess students' mastery of the lesson content.

Targeted Resources

☐ 📖 Transparency: Lesson Quiz 12-1
☐ 💻 Online Lesson Quiz 12-1: at **PHSchool.com**
☐ 💿 Computer Test Generator CD-ROM 12-1

Lesson Plan 12-2, Objective 1
Graphing Rational Functions

Lesson Objective	NAEP 2005	Local Standards
▼ Graph rational functions **New Vocabulary:** rational function, asymptote	A1e; A2a **NCTM 2000** 2, 8, 9, 10 **Pacing** Two Year: 1 day Two-Year Block: 0.5 day	

1. INTRODUCE

Check Skills You'll Need: Assign these exercises to review the prerequisite skills of evaluating and graphing functions.

New Vocabulary: Help students pre-read the lesson by pointing out the new terms introduced in Objective 1.

Targeted Resources

☐ ⛭ Transparency: Check Skills You'll Need 12-2

2. TEACH

▼ **Objective:** Teach Examples 1–3. Assign Check Understanding 1–3 after the appropriate example. Review the summary in the Key Concepts box.

Targeted Resources

☐ ⛭ Transparency: Additional Examples 12-2
☐ ✆ Presentation Pro CD-ROM 12-2
☐ ▣ iText 12-2: at **PHSchool.com**

3. PRACTICE

Assignment Guide: Give an assignment based on the ability levels of your students.

▼ **Objective:** Core: 1–25, 35–52; Extension: 57–59
Standardized Test Prep: 64–67
Mixed Review: 68–77

Homework: _____

Targeted Resources

☐ ⛭ Transparency: Student Answers 12-2
☐ Grab & Go File: Practice 12-2, Reteaching 12-2, Enrichment 12-2
☐ Practice Workbook 12-2
☐ Spanish Practice Workbook 12-2
☐ Technology Activities 26

4. ASSESS

Lesson Quiz: Create a quiz on Objective 1 using the Computer Test Generator.

Targeted Resources

☐ ✆ Computer Test Generator CD-ROM 12-2

Lesson Plan 12-2, Objective 2
Graphing Rational Functions

Lesson Objective ⚐ Identify types of functions	**NAEP 2005** A1e; A2a **NCTM 2000** 2, 8, 9, 10 **Pacing** Two Year: 1 day Two-Year Block: 0.5 day	Local Standards

1. INTRODUCE

Check Skills You'll Need: Assign these exercises if not used with Objective 1.

Review: Use the Key Concepts box to review graphs of rational functions.

Targeted Resources
- ☐ ⬛ Transparency: Check Skills You'll Need 12-2

2. TEACH

⚐ **Objective:** Review the types of functions in the Key Concepts box. Teach Example 4. Assign Check Understanding 4.

Targeted Resources
- ☐ ⬛ Transparency: Additional Examples 12-2
- ☐ ⊘ Presentation Pro CD-ROM 12-2
- ☐ ⬛ iText 12-2: at **PHSchool.com**

3. PRACTICE

Assignment Guide: Give an assignment based on the ability levels of your students.

⚐ **Objective:** Core: 26–34, 53–56; Extension: 60–62
Standardized Test Prep: 63
Mixed Review: 68–77

Homework: _____

Targeted Resources
- ☐ ⬛ Transparency: Student Answers 12-2
- ☐ Grab & Go File: Practice 12-2, Reteaching 12-2, Enrichment 12-2
- ☐ Practice Workbook 12-2
- ☐ Spanish Practice Workbook 12-2
- ☐ Technology Activities 26

4. ASSESS

Lesson Quiz: Assign the Lesson Quiz to assess students' mastery of the lesson content.

Targeted Resources
- ☐ ⬛ Transparency: Lesson Quiz 12-2
- ☐ ⬛ Online Lesson Quiz 12-2: at **PHSchool.com**
- ☐ ⊘ Computer Test Generator CD-ROM 12-2

Teacher _____ Class _____ Date _____ M T W Th F

Lesson Plan 12-3, Objective 1
Simplifying Rational Expressions

Lesson Objective	NAEP 2005	Local Standards
▼ Simplify rational expressions	A3b	
New Vocabulary: rational expression	**NCTM 2000** 2, 8, 9, 10	
	Pacing Two Year: 2 days Two-Year Block: 1 day	

1. INTRODUCE

Check Skills You'll Need: Assign these exercises to review the prerequisite skills of simplifying fractions and factoring quadratic expressions.

New Vocabulary: Help students pre-read the lesson by pointing out the new term introduced in Objective 1.

Targeted Resources
☐ 🖳 Transparency: Check Skills You'll Need 12-3

2. TEACH

▼ **Objective:** Teach Examples 1–4. Assign Check Understanding questions 1–4 after the appropriate example.

Targeted Resources
☐ 🖳 Transparency: Additional Examples 12-3
☐ 🖉 Presentation Pro CD-ROM 12-3
☐ 🖳 iText 12-3: at **PHSchool.com**

3. PRACTICE

Assignment Guide: Give an assignment based on the ability levels of your students.

▼ **Objective:** Core: 1–41; Extension: 42–47
Standardized Test Prep: 48–53
Mixed Review: 54–64

Homework: _____

Targeted Resources
☐ 🖳 Transparency: Student Answers 12-3
☐ Grab & Go File: Practice 12-3, Reteaching 12-3, Enrichment 12-3
☐ Practice Workbook 12-3
☐ Spanish Practice Workbook 12-3
☐ Reading and Math Literacy 12B
☐ Spanish Reading and Math Literacy 12B
☐ Reasoning & Puzzles 32, 33: at **PHSchool.com**

4. ASSESS

Lesson Quiz: Assign the Lesson Quiz to assess students' mastery of the lesson content.

Checkpoint Quiz: Use the Checkpoint Quiz to assess student progress over several lessons.

Targeted Resources
☐ 🖳 Transparency: Lesson Quiz 12-3
☐ 🖳 Online Lesson Quiz 12-3: at **PHSchool.com**
☐ Grab & Go: Checkpoint Quiz 1
☐ 🖉 Computer Test Generator CD-ROM 12-3

Lesson Plan 12-4, Objective 1
Multiplying and Dividing Rational Expressions

Lesson Objective ▼ Multiply rational expressions	NAEP 2005 A3b NCTM 2000 2, 6, 8, 10 Pacing Two Year: 1 day Two-Year Block: 0.5 day	Local Standards

1. INTRODUCE

Check Skills You'll Need: Assign these exercises to review the prerequisite skills of multiplying and dividing monomials and factoring trinomials.

Targeted Resources
- ☐ 🖾 Transparency: Check Skills You'll Need 12-4

2. TEACH

▼ **Objective:** Teach Examples 1–3. Assign Check Understanding questions 1–3 after the appropriate example.

Targeted Resources
- ☐ 🖾 Transparency: Additional Examples 12-4
- ☐ 🖉 Presentation Pro CD-ROM 12-4
- ☐ 🖳 iText 12-4: at **PHSchool.com**

3. PRACTICE

Assignment Guide: Give an assignment based on the ability levels of your students.

▼ **Objective:** Core: 1–15, 29, 36, 41–45; Extension: 47–48
Mixed Review: 59–76

Homework: _____

Targeted Resources
- ☐ 🖾 Transparency: Student Answers12-4
- ☐ Grab & Go File: Practice 12-4, Reteaching 12-4, Enrichment 12-4
- ☐ Practice Workbook 12-4
- ☐ Spanish Practice Workbook 12-4

4. ASSESS

Lesson Quiz: Create a quiz on Objective 1 using the Computer Test Generator.

Targeted Resources
- ☐ 🖉 Computer Test Generator CD-ROM 12-4

Lesson Plan 12-4, Objective 2
Multiplying and Dividing
Rational Expressions

Lesson Objective	NAEP 2005	Local Standards
▼ Divide rational expressions	A3b	
	NCTM 2000	
	2, 6, 8, 10	
	Pacing	
	Two Year: 1 day	
	Two-Year Block:	
	0.5 day	

1. INTRODUCE

Check Skills You'll Need: Assign these exercises if not used with Objective 1.

Review: Remind the students how to multiply rational expressions.

Targeted Resources

☐ 🖳 Transparency: Check Skills You'll Need 12-4

2. TEACH

▼ **Objective:** Teach Examples 4 and 5. Assign Check Understanding questions 4 and 5 after the appropriate example.

Targeted Resources

☐ 🖳 Transparency: Additional Examples 12-4
☐ ✐ Presentation Pro CD-ROM 12-4
☐ 🖳 iText 12-4: at **PHSchool.com**

3. PRACTICE

Assignment Guide: Give an assignment based on the ability levels of your students.

   ▼ **Objective:** Core: 16–28, 30–35, 37–40, 46;
Extension: 49–53
Standardized Test Prep: 54–58
Mixed Review: 59–76

Homework: _____

Targeted Resources

☐ 🖳 Transparency: Student Answers12-4
☐ Grab & Go File: Practice 12-4, Reteaching 12-4, Enrichment 12-4
☐ Practice Workbook 12-4
☐ Spanish Practice Workbook 12-4

4. ASSESS

Lesson Quiz: Assign the Lesson Quiz to assess students' mastery of the lesson content.

Targeted Resources

☐ 🖳 Transparency: Lesson Quiz 12-4
☐ 🖳 Online Lesson Quiz 12-4: at **PHSchool.com**
☐ ✐ Computer Test Generator CD-ROM 12-4

Lesson Plan 12-5, Objective 1
Dividing Polynomials

Lesson Objective	NAEP 2005	Local Standards
▼ Divide polynomials	A3b	
	NCTM 2000 NC1, 2, 9	
	Pacing Two Year: 2 days Two-Year Block: 1 day	

1. INTRODUCE

Check Skills You'll Need: Assign these exercises to review the prerequisite skills of writing polynomials in standard form and multiplying binomials.

Targeted Resources

☐ ⚞ Transparency: Check Skills You'll Need 12-5

2. TEACH

▼ **Objective:** Teach Examples 1–4. Assign Check Understanding questions 1–4 after the appropriate example. Work though the summary in the Key Concepts box.

Targeted Resources

☐ ⚞ Transparency: Additional Examples 12-5
☐ ✏ Presentation Pro CD-ROM 12-5
☐ ▣ iText 12-5: at **PHSchool.com**

3. PRACTICE

Assignment Guide: Give an assignment based on the ability levels of your students.

▼ **Objective:** Core: 1–47; Extension: 48–52
Standardized Test Prep: 53–57
Mixed Review: 58–72

Homework: _____

Targeted Resources

☐ ⚞ Transparency: Student Answers 12-5
☐ Grab & Go File: Practice 12-5, Reteaching 12-5, Enrichment 12-5
☐ Practice Workbook 12-5
☐ Spanish Practice Workbook 12-5

4. ASSESS

Lesson Quiz: Assign the Lesson Quiz to assess students' mastery of the lesson content.

Targeted Resources

☐ ⚞ Transparency: Lesson Quiz 12-5
☐ ▣ Online Lesson Quiz 12-5: at **PHSchool.com**
☐ ✏ Computer Test Generator CD-ROM 12-5

Lesson Plan 12-6, Objective 1
Adding and Subtracting Rational Expressions

Lesson Objective	NAEP 2005	Local Standards
▼ Add and subtract rational expressions with like denominators	A3b **NCTM 2000** 1, 2, 6, 8, 9 **Pacing** Two Year: 2 days Two-Year Block: 1 day	

1. INTRODUCE

Check Skills You'll Need: Assign these exercises to review the prerequisite skills of adding and subtracting fractions and factoring quadratic expressions.

Targeted Resources
- ☐ 🖳 Transparency: Check Skills You'll Need 12-6

2. TEACH

▼ **Objective:** Teach Examples 1 and 2. Assign Check Understanding questions 1 and 2 after the appropriate example.

Targeted Resources
- ☐ 🖳 Transparency: Additional Examples 12-6
- ☐ 🖉 Presentation Pro CD-ROM 12-6
- ☐ 🖳 iText 12-6: at **PHSchool.com**

3. PRACTICE

Assignment Guide: Give an assignment based on the ability levels of your students.

▼ **Objective:** Core: 1–12, 30–33; Extension: None
Standardized Test Prep: 55
Mixed Review: 59–66

Homework: _____

Targeted Resources
- ☐ 🖳 Transparency: Student Answers 12-6
- ☐ Grab & Go File: Practice 12-6, Reteaching 12-6, Enrichment 12-6
- ☐ Practice Workbook 12-6
- ☐ Spanish Practice Workbook 12-6

4. ASSESS

Lesson Quiz: Create a quiz on Objective 1 using the Computer Test Generator.

Targeted Resources
- ☐ 🖉 Computer Test Generator CD-ROM 12-6

Teacher _____ Class _____ Date _____ M T W Th F

Lesson Plan 12-6, Objective 2
Adding and Subtracting Rational Expressions

Lesson Objective	NAEP 2005	Local Standards
✔ Add and subtract rational expressions with unlike denominators	A3b **NCTM 2000** 1, 2, 6, 8, 9 **Pacing** Two Year: 2 days Two-Year Block: 1 day	

1. INTRODUCE

Check Skills You'll Need: Assign these exercises if not used with Objective 1.

Review: Remind students how to add and subtract rational expressions.

Targeted Resources

☐ 🖳 Transparency: Check Skills You'll Need 12-6

2. TEACH

✔ **Objective:** Teach Examples 3–5. Assign Check Understanding questions 3–5 after the appropriate example.

Targeted Resources

☐ 🖳 Transparency: Additional Examples 12-6
☐ 💿 Presentation Pro CD-ROM 12-6
☐ 💻 iText 12-6: at **PHSchool.com**

3. PRACTICE

Assignment Guide: Give an assignment based on the ability levels of your students.

✔ **Objective:** Core: 13–29, 34–50; Extension: 51–54
Standardized Test Prep: 56–58
Mixed Review: 59–66

Homework: _____

Targeted Resources

☐ 🖳 Transparency: Student Answers 12-6
☐ Grab & Go File: Practice 12-6, Reteaching 12-6, Enrichment 12-6
☐ Practice Workbook 12-6
☐ Spanish Practice Workbook 12-6
☐ Reasoning & Puzzles 36: at **PHSchool.com**

4. ASSESS

Lesson Quiz: Assign the Lesson Quiz to assess students' mastery of the lesson content.

Targeted Resources

☐ 🖳 Transparency: Lesson Quiz 12-6
☐ 💻 Online Lesson Quiz 12-6: at **PHSchool.com**
☐ 💿 Computer Test Generator CD-ROM 12-6

Lesson Plan 12-7, Objective 1
Solving Rational Equations

Lesson Objective ▼ Solve rational equations New Vocabulary: rational equation	NAEP 2005 A2e; A4a NCTM 2000 1, 2, 8, 9 Pacing Two Year: 2 days Two-Year Block: 1 day	Local Standards

1. INTRODUCE

Check Skills You'll Need: Assign these exercises to review the prerequisite skills of solving simple proportions and finding least common denominators.

New Vocabulary: Help students pre-read the lesson by pointing out the new term introduced in Objective 1.

Targeted Resources
☐ ⬏ Transparency: Check Skills You'll Need 12-7

2. TEACH

▼ Objective: Teach Examples 1–3. Assign Check Understanding questions 1–3 after the appropriate example.

Targeted Resources
☐ ⬏ Transparency: Additional Examples 12-7
☐ ✐ Presentation Pro CD-ROM 12-7
☐ ▦ iText 12-7: at **PHSchool.com**

3. PRACTICE

Assignment Guide: Give an assignment based on the ability levels of your students.

▼ Objective: Core: 1–17, 24–32, 35–39; Extension: 42–45
Standardized Test Prep: 49–51
Mixed Review: 53–67

Homework: _____

Targeted Resources
☐ ⬏ Transparency: Student Answers 12-7
☐ Grab & Go File: Practice 12-7, Reteaching 12-7, Enrichment 12-7
☐ Practice Workbook 12-7
☐ Spanish Practice Workbook 12-7
☐ Hands-On Activities 29

4. ASSESS

Lesson Quiz: Create a quiz on Objective 1 using the Computer Test Generator.

Targeted Resources
☐ ✐ Computer Test Generator CD-ROM 12-7

Lesson Plan 12-7, Objective 2
Solving Rational Equations

Lesson Objective	NAEP 2005	Local Standards
▼ Solve proportions	A2e; A4a	
	NCTM 2000 1, 2, 8, 9	
	Pacing Two Year: 1 day Two-Year Block: 1 day	

1. INTRODUCE

Check Skills You'll Need: Assign these exercises if not used with Objective 1.

Review: Remind students how to solve rational equations.

Targeted Resources
- ☐ 📠 Transparency: Check Skills You'll Need 12-7

2. TEACH

▼ **Objective:** Teach Examples 4 and 5. Assign Check Understanding questions 4 and 5 after the appropriate example.

Targeted Resources
- ☐ 📠 Transparency: Additional Examples 12-7
- ☐ 🖉 Presentation Pro CD-ROM 12-7
- ☐ 🖳 iText 12-7: at **PHSchool.com**

3. PRACTICE

Assignment Guide: Give an assignment based on the ability levels of your students.

▼ **Objective:** Core: 18–23, 33–34, 40–41; Extension: 46–48
Standardized Test Prep: 52
Mixed Review: 53–67

Homework: _____

Targeted Resources
- ☐ 📠 Transparency: Student Answers 12-7
- ☐ Grab & Go File: Practice 12-7, Reteaching 12-7, Enrichment 12-7
- ☐ Practice Workbook 12-7
- ☐ Spanish Practice Workbook 12-7
- ☐ Hands-On Activities 29

4. ASSESS

Lesson Quiz: Assign the Lesson Quiz to assess students' mastery of the lesson content.

Targeted Resources
- ☐ 📠 Transparency: Lesson Quiz 12-7
- ☐ 🖳 Online Lesson Quiz 12-7: at **PHSchool.com**
- ☐ 🖉 Computer Test Generator CD-ROM 12-7

Lesson Plan 12-8, Objective 1
Counting Methods and Permutations

Lesson Objective	NAEP 2005	Local Standards
▼ Use the multiplication counting principle **New Vocabulary:** multiplication counting principle	D4e **NCTM 2000** 1, 2, 6, 8, 10 **Pacing** Two Year: 0.5 day Two-Year Block: 0.5 day	

1. INTRODUCE

Check Skills You'll Need: Assign these exercises to review the prerequisite skill of finding probabilities.

New Vocabulary: Help students pre-read the lesson by pointing out the new term introduced in Objective 1.

Targeted Resources

☐ 📧 Transparency: Check Skills You'll Need 12-8

2. TEACH

▼ **Objective:** Have students work the Investigation to explore determining order. Teach Example 1. Assign Check Understanding 1. Go over the principle in the Key Concepts box. Teach Example 2. Assign Check Understanding question 2.

Targeted Resources

☐ 📧 Transparency: Additional Examples 12-8
☐ Graphing Calculator Procedure 16: at **PHSchool.com**
☐ 🖉 Presentation Pro CD-ROM 12-8
☐ 📖 iText 12-8: at **PHSchool.com**

3. PRACTICE

Assignment Guide: Give an assignment based on the ability levels of your students.

▼ **Objective:** Core: 1–4, 27; Extension: 32
Standardized Test Prep: 36–38
Mixed Review: 40–45

Homework: _____

Targeted Resources

☐ 📧 Transparency: Student Answers 12-8
☐ Grab & Go File: Practice 12-8, Reteaching 12-8, Enrichment 12-8
☐ Practice Workbook 12-8
☐ Spanish Practice Workbook 12-8
☐ Reading and Math Literacy 12C
☐ Spanish Reading and Math Literacy 12C
☐ Hands-On Activities 30

4. ASSESS

Lesson Quiz: Create a quiz on Objective 1 using the Computer Test Generator.

Targeted Resources

☐ 🖉 Computer Test Generator CD-ROM 12-8

Lesson Plan 12-8, Objective 2
Counting Methods and Permutations

Lesson Objective	NAEP 2005	Local Standards
▼ Find permutations **New Vocabulary:** permutation	D4e **NCTM 2000** 1, 2, 6, 8, 10 **Pacing** Two Year: 0.5 day Two-Year Block: 0.5 day	

1. INTRODUCE

Check Skills You'll Need: Assign these exercises if not used with Objective 1.

Review: Use the Key Concepts box to review the multiplication counting principle.

New Vocabulary: Help students pre-read the lesson by pointing out the new term introduced in Objective 2.

Targeted Resources
- ☐ 🖵 Transparency: Check Skills You'll Need 12-8

2. TEACH

▼ **Objective:** Teach Examples 3–5, pointing out the notation in the Key Concepts box. Assign Check Understanding 3–5 after the appropriate example.

Targeted Resources
- ☐ 🖵 Transparency: Additional Examples 12-8
- ☐ Graphing Calculator Procedure 16: at **PHSchool.com**
- ☐ ✐ Presentation Pro CD-ROM 12-8
- ☐ 🖥 iText 12-8: at **PHSchool.com**

3. PRACTICE

Assignment Guide: Give an assignment based on the ability levels of your students.

   ▼ **Objective:** Core: 5–26, 28–31; Extension: 33–35
   Standardized Test Prep: 39
   Mixed Review: 40–45

Homework: _____

Targeted Resources
- ☐ 🖵 Transparency: Student Answers 12-8
- ☐ Grab & Go File: Practice 12-8, Reteaching 12-8, Enrichment 12-8
- ☐ Practice Workbook 12-8
- ☐ Spanish Practice Workbook 12-8
- ☐ Reading and Math Literacy 12C
- ☐ Spanish Reading and Math Literacy 12C
- ☐ Hands-On Activities 30

4. ASSESS

Lesson Quiz: Assign the Lesson Quiz to assess students' mastery of the lesson content.

Checkpoint Quiz: Use the Checkpoint Quiz to assess student progress over several lessons.

Targeted Resources
- ☐ 🖵 Transparency: Lesson Quiz 12-8
- ☐ 🖥 Online Lesson Quiz 12-8: at **PHSchool.com**
- ☐ Grab & Go File: Checkpoint Quiz 2
- ☐ ✐ Computer Test Generator CD-ROM 12-8

Lesson Plan 12-9, Objective 1
Combinations

Lesson Objective ▼ Find combinations **New Vocabulary:** combination	**NAEP 2005** D4e, f **NCTM 2000** 1, 2, 8, 9, 10 **Pacing** Two Year: 1 day Two-Year Block: 0.5 day	**Local Standards**

1. INTRODUCE

Check Skills You'll Need: Assign these exercises to review the prerequisite skills of evaluating permutation symbols and finding probabilities.

New Vocabulary: Help students pre-read the lesson by pointing out the new term introduced in Objective 1.

Targeted Resources

☐ ✍ Transparency: Check Skills You'll Need 12-9

2. TEACH

▼ **Objective:** Go over the notation in the Key Concepts box. Teach Examples 1 and 2. Assign Check Understanding questions 1 and 2 after the appropriate example.

Targeted Resources

☐ ✍ Transparency: Additional Examples 12-9
☐ ✐ Presentation Pro CD-ROM 12-9
☐ ▣ iText 12-9: at **PHSchool.com**

3. PRACTICE

Assignment Guide: Give an assignment based on the ability levels of your students.

　　▼ **Objective:** Core: 1–12, 16–23, 25–27; Extension: 31–33
Standardized Test Prep: 37–38
Mixed Review: 41–58

Homework: _____

Targeted Resources

☐ ✍ Transparency: Student Answers 12-9
☐ Grab & Go File: Practice 12-9, Reteaching 12-9, Enrichment 12-9
☐ Practice Workbook 12-9
☐ Spanish Practice Workbook 12-9

4. ASSESS

Lesson Quiz: Create a quiz on Objective 1 using the Computer Test Generator.

Targeted Resources

☐ ✐ Computer Test Generator CD-ROM 12-9

Teacher _____ Class _____ Date _____ M T W Th F

Lesson Plan 12-9, Objective 2
Combinations

Lesson Objective	NAEP 2005	Local Standards
❷ Find probability with counting techniques	D4e, f **NCTM 2000** 1, 2, 8, 9, 10 **Pacing** Two Year: 1 day Two-Year Block: 0.5 day	

1. INTRODUCE

Check Skills You'll Need: Assign these exercises if not used with Objective 1.

Review: Use the Key Concepts box to review combination notation.

Targeted Resources
- ☐ Transparency: Check Skills You'll Need 12-9

2. TEACH

❷ **Objective:** Teach Examples 3 and 4. Assign Check Understanding questions 3 and 4 after the appropriate example.

Targeted Resources
- ☐ Transparency: Additional Examples 12-9
- ☐ Presentation Pro CD-ROM 12-9
- ☐ iText 12-9: at **PHSchool.com**

3. PRACTICE

Assignment Guide: Give an assignment based on the ability levels of your students.

❷ **Objective:** Core: 13–15, 24, 28–30; Extension: 34–36
Standardized Test Prep: 39–40
Mixed Review: 41–58

Homework: _____

Targeted Resources
- ☐ Transparency: Student Answers 12-9
- ☐ Grab & Go File: Practice 12-9, Reteaching 12-9, Enrichment 12-9
- ☐ Practice Workbook 12-9
- ☐ Spanish Practice Workbook 12-9

4. ASSESS

Lesson Quiz: Assign the Lesson Quiz to assess students' mastery of the lesson content.

Targeted Resources
- ☐ Transparency: Lesson Quiz 12-9
- ☐ Online Lesson Quiz 12-9: at **PHSchool.com**
- ☐ Computer Test Generator CD-ROM 12-9

© Pearson Education, Inc., publishing as Pearson Prentice Hall.   All rights reserved.

Algebra 1A and 1B Lesson Plans   Lesson 12-9, Objective 2   **161**

Mid-Course Test, Algebra 1A

Form A

Chapters 1–3

1. Use an equation to model the relationship in the table.

Month	Cost
1	$12
2	$24
3	$36
4	$48

Simplify each expression.

2. $2\frac{1}{2} + \left(-3\frac{1}{8}\right)$

3. $-7.4 - 2.8$

4. $\dfrac{8 + 4(3)^2}{2^2 + 3}$

Evaluate each expression for $a = -4$, $b = 6$, and $c = 2.5$.

5. $2ab$

6. $b^2 - 2c$

Write an expression for each phrase.

7. eight less than 12 times x

8. negative five times the quantity three plus k

9. In which quadrant or on which axis would you find the point $(-8, -4)$?

Solve each equation. Then check.

10. $25.08 + 4k = 80.06$

11. $2(y + 5) = 16$

12. $9k - 2 = 43$

Solve. If the equation is an identity, write *identity*. If it has no solution, write *no solution*.

13. $2x - 8 + 3x = 4 + 5x - 12$

14. $7y - 9 = 3y + 11y$

15. Write an equation to model this situation. Then use your equation to solve. Jack has saved $16.50 to spend on fair ride tickets. Each ticket costs $0.75. How many tickets can Jack afford?

16. A taxicab company charges each person a flat fee of $2.25 plus an additional $0.60 per quarter-mile.

   a. Write a formula to find the total cost for each fare.

   b. Use the formula to find the cost for 1 person to travel 6 mi.

Mid-Course Test, Algebra 1A (continued)   **Form A**

Chapters 1–3

Solve and check each inequality.

17. $n - 9.4 \geq 15.6$

18. $|x - 6| \geq 8$

19. $-20 \leq -4x$

20. $8 + 6n \geq 2$ or $-10n \geq 50$

21. Find the difference. $\begin{bmatrix} -4 & 2 \\ 3 & 8 \end{bmatrix} - \begin{bmatrix} -2 & 1 \\ 6 & -5 \end{bmatrix}$

22. Write an inequality for the graph.

$$\leftarrow \!\!\!+\!\!-\!\!+\!\!-\!\!\bullet\!\!-\!\!+\!\!-\!\!+\!\!-\!\!+\!\!-\!\!+\!\!-\!\!+\!\!-\!\!+\!\!-\!\!+\!\!\rightarrow$$
$$-5\ -4\ -3\ -2\ -1\quad 0\quad 1\quad 2\quad 3\quad 4\quad 5$$

23. Which property is illustrated?

$6(3 + 1) = 6 \cdot 3 + 6 \cdot 1$

Solve each problem.

24. The perimeters of the rectangle and equilateral triangle shown are equal. Find the value of x.

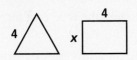

25. You remember bowling games of 116, 105, 109, and 113 however, you cannot remember your score for the fifth game. You know your bowling average is 109, what did you score the fifth game?

26. On four plays, a football team gained 15 yd, lost 6 yd, gained 12 yd, and lost 3 yd. What is the total number of yards gained or lost on the four plays?

Use the table below for Exercises 27–28.

Bus Riders

School	Number of Students	
	To School	Home
Elementary	201	186
Junior High	106	112
Senior High	80	68

27. Find the mean, median, and mode number of students who ride the bus to school.

28. Find the mean, median, and mode number of students who ride the bus home.

29. **Writing** Suppose a friend was absent from class and is having difficulty solving $3(x - 6) > 4(x + 3)$. Explain how to solve the inequality, showing all necessary steps.

30. Justify each step.

$$3(2x + 1) + 5x = 6x + 3 + 5x \quad \underline{\ ?\ }$$
$$= 6x + 5x + 3 \quad \underline{\ ?\ }$$
$$= (6 + 5)x + 3 \quad \text{Distributive Property}$$
$$= 11x + 3 \quad \underline{\ ?\ }$$

Mid-Course Test, Algebra 1A

Form B

Chapters 1–3

1. Use an equation to model the relationship in the table.

Month	Cost
1	$6
2	$12
3	$18
4	$24

Simplify each expression.

2. $-4\frac{1}{3} + \left(-2\frac{5}{6}\right)$

3. $1.8 - (-2.6)$

4. $\dfrac{2^3 \times 6 - 4^2}{5 - 1}$

Evaluate each expression for $a = -2$, $b = 3.4$, and $c = 8$.

5. $4ac$

6. $c^2 + 3b$

Write an expression for each phrase.

7. sum of 15 and twice x

8. negative six times the quantity four less than x.

9. In which quadrant or on which axis would you find each point $(3, -7)$?

Solve each equation. Then check.

10. $7.2x + 3.1 = 29.1$

11. $4(x + 2) = 36$

12. $\frac{7}{8}y - 2 = 3$

Solve. If the equation is an identity, write *identity*. If it has no solution, write *no solution*.

13. $3y - 8 = 6y + 4y$

14. $3x - 5 + 4x = 12 + 7x - 17$

15. Write an equation to model this situation. Then use your equation to solve. Emily has $6.00 to buy postcards for her friends. The postcards cost $0.75 each. How many postcards is she able to buy?

16. A taxicab company charges each person a flat fee of $2.50 plus an additional $0.40 per quarter-mile.

   a. Write a formula to find the total cost for each fare.

   b. Use the formula to find the cost for 1 person to travel 12 mi.

Mid-Course Test, Algebra 1A (continued) Form B

Chapters 1–3

Solve and check each inequality.

17. $n - 4.2 \geq 6.9$

18. $|x - 5| \geq 7$

19. $-62 \leq -2x$

20. $8 + 4n \geq 12$ or $-9n \geq 81$

21. Find the difference. $\begin{bmatrix} 3 & -9 \\ 6 & 4 \end{bmatrix} - \begin{bmatrix} 1 & 5 \\ -7 & 2 \end{bmatrix}$

22. Write an inequality for the graph.

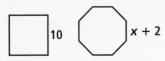

23. Which property is illustrated?

$(4 \cdot -7) \cdot 5 = 4(-7 \cdot 5)$

Solve each problem.

24. The perimeter of the square and the regular octagon are the same. Find the value of x.

10    $x + 2$

25. The mean of a set of data is 80. Five of the six data points are given as 91, 202, 56, 41, and 13. What is the value of the sixth point?

26. On four plays, a football team gained 12 yd, lost 7 yd, gained 20 yd, and lost 5 yd. What is the total number of yards gained or lost on the four plays?

Use the table below for Exercises 27–28.

School	Students	
	Buy Lunch	Pack Lunch
Elementary	132	90
Junior High	49	63
Senior High	86	63

27. Find the mean, median, and mode number of students who buy their lunch.

28. Find the mean, median, and mode number of students who pack their lunch.

29. **Writing** Suppose a friend was absent from class and is having difficulty solving $3(x - 8) > 4(x + 7)$. Explain how to solve the inequality, showing all necessary steps.

30. Justify each step.

$$\begin{aligned} 2(5x + 3) + 4x &= 10x + 6 + 4x & \underline{\quad ? \quad} \\ &= 10x + 4x + 6 & \underline{\quad ? \quad} \\ &= (10 + 4)x + 6 & \underline{\quad ? \quad} \\ &= 14x + 6 & \text{Addition} \end{aligned}$$

Final Test, Algebra 1A

Form A

Chapters 1–6

Simplify each expression.

1. $|-4.121|$

2. $22[5^2 \div (4^2 + 3^2) + 9]$

3. $-2\frac{1}{3} - 4\frac{5}{6}$

4. $(-6)^3(-3)$

5. Solve the proportion. $\frac{16}{9} = \frac{42}{x}$

6. The ratio of the number of right-handed students in school to the number of left-handed students in school is 9:1. There are 360 right-handed students in school. How many left-handed students are in school?

Evaluate the algebraic expression when $a = 3$, $b = 4.9$, and $c = -5$.

7. $a^2 - b$

8. $c^2 + 4ab$

9. In which quadrant or axis would you find the point $(0, -3)$?

Solve each equation or inequality.

10. $3x + 9 = 24$

11. $8(x - 5) = -40$

12. $-\frac{5}{6}y - 5 \geq 30$

13. $-5 < 2d - 1 < 3$

14. Which graph represents the real number solutions of $2x + 4 \geq 16$?

A.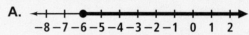

B.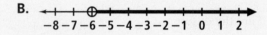

C.

D.

15. Solve and graph the inequality $|x + 3| \geq 7$.

16. Write a function rule to describe the amount of change $c(x)$ from a \$20 bill if you buy x pounds of grapes at \$1.29 per pound.

17. What is the range of $y = x^2 - 5$ when the domain is $\{-1, 0, 3.5\}$?

18. Find the sixth term in the sequence $8, -2, -12, -22, \ldots$.

Final Test, Algebra 1A (continued)   Form A

Chapters 1–6

Write an equation or inequality to model each situation. Then solve.

19. Mike withdrew $32 from his bank account at an ATM machine. The transaction slip said his balance was $289.14. What was his previous balance?

20. After you put 8 gallons of gas into an empty tank, the gas gauge reads $\frac{2}{3}$ full. What is the capacity of the tank?

21. The perimeter for the rectangle and the regular hexagon below are equal. Find x.

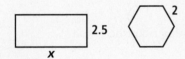

22. Fair tickets for 2 adults and 3 children cost $34. An adult ticket costs $2 more than a child ticket. What is the price of an adult ticket?

23. What is the greatest number of $0.25 gumballs you can buy with $2.20?

Solve.

24. 12 is what percent of 37.5?

25. 82% of 350 is what number?

26. A package delivery company handles 14 million packages per year in the Midwest. If this represents only 35% of their total business how many total packages do they handle in a year?

Find the slope of the line passing through each pair of points.

27. $(-3, 4)$ and $(6, 1)$

28. $(4, 16)$ and $(0, 8)$

Write the equation of the line for each of the following conditions.

29. through two points $(2, 4)$ and $(4, 7)$

30. a horizontal line passing through the point $(6, 18)$

31. parallel to the line $y = \frac{4}{9}x + 5$ through the point $(-2, 1)$

32. Write the equation of direct variation that includes the point $(-6, 2)$.

Write an expression for each phrase.

33. the quantity two times d minus five times the quantity six times d plus four

34. fifteen less than six times the square of x

35. Graph the function $y = |x| - 4$, by translating $y = |x|$.

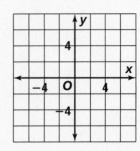

Final Test, Algebra 1A (continued)   Form A

Chapters 1–6

36. Which equation would translate $y = |x|$ 6 units to the left?

   A. $y = |x| + 6$ **B.** $y = |x + 6|$

   C. $y = |x| - 6$ **D.** $y = |x - 6|$

Solve.

37. Using the formula $C = \frac{5}{9}(F - 32)$, find the Fahrenheit temperature when the Celsius temperature is 45°.

38. Mr. Smith expects to pay \$19,400 in taxes. This is no more than $\frac{1}{3}$ of his salary. What is his least possible earned income?

39. Which property is illustrated?
$6(12 - 3) = 6(12) - 6(3)$

40. Which employee has the highest hourly rate? Keep in mind that they do not get paid for lunch.

	Total Hours Worked	Lunch Hour	Pay Before Taxes
Scott	42.5	3.5	\$645.60
Mike	38.75	2.75	\$629.70
Todd	40.5	3.25	\$641.25
Jason	41.25	4.0	\$647.50

41. Suppose you measure a piece of wood at 42.1 cm. Find the percent error in your measurement.

42. Suppose you have a bag that contains seven yellow, eight blue, and ten red marbles. You draw a marble. What is the probability that the marble is red?

43. Suppose you have a bag containing four red, seven green, and five yellow marbles. You choose two marbles. Find each probability.

   a. P(red and red) with replacing

   b. P(red and red) without replacing

44. Which story describes the graph?

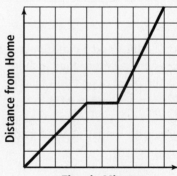

Time in Minutes

   A. You drive away from home, stop at a light, then continue at a slower rate.

   B. You drive away from home, stop at a light, then continue at a faster rate.

   C. You drive toward home, stop at a light, then continue at a slower rate.

   D. You drive toward home, stop at a light, then continue at a faster rate.

Final Test, Algebra 1A (continued)   Form A

Chapters 1–6

45. Joe started a new job in 2001. His salary was $32,600. At the beginning of the next year he will receive a raise of $1560. Assume he will receive the same raise every year.

   a. Write a function rule for finding Joe's salary after 2001.

   b. Find Joe's salary in 2007.

46. A boy 4 ft tall casts a shadow 6 ft long. He stands next to a monument that has a 52 ft long shadow. How tall is the monument?

47. You start a pet-sitting service. You spend $35 on advertising. You plan to charge $5 a day to watch each pet.

   a. Write an equation to relate your daily income *y* to the number of pets *x* you watch.

   b. Graph the equation. What are the *x*- and *y*-intercepts?

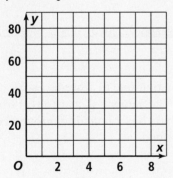

   c. How many days do you need to watch a pet to pay for advertising?

48. Write a function rule for the table of values.

x	y
−1	−3.5
0	0
1	3.5
2	7

49. As CEO of a company, you notice that your five executives have the following salaries: $85,000, $91,000, $70,000, $70,000, and $62,000. You are hiring a sixth executive. Which measure of central tendency would be the most attractive to people applying for the job? Justify your answer.

50. **Writing** James has saved $50. He wants to buy a DVD player for $149 in about 5 months. To find out how much he should save each week he wrote $50 + 20x = 149$. Explain his equation.

Final Test, Algebra 1A

Form B

Chapters 1–6

Simplify.

1. $|-3.412|$

2. $(10^2 - 4 \cdot 8) \div (10 + 7)$

3. $-3\frac{1}{2} - \left(-1\frac{7}{8}\right)$

4. $\dfrac{(-4)^5}{10 - 26}$

5. $\dfrac{104}{x} = \dfrac{8}{19}$

6. The ratio of the number of girls in Central High School to the number of boys in Central High School is $3 : 1$. If there are 420 girls in the school how many boys are at the school?

Evaluate each algebraic expression when $a = 3$, $b = 4.9$, and $c = -5$.

7. $a(a^2 - b)$

8. $4ac - c^2$

9. In which quadrant or axis would you find the point $(-4, 0)$?

Solve each equation or inequality.

10. $6x - 4 = 26$

11. $9(x + 3) = 108$

12. $-\dfrac{3}{4}y < -27$

13. $|x - 2| \leq 9$

14. Which graph represents the real number solutions of $5x + 3 \geq -12$?

A.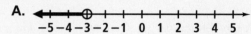

B.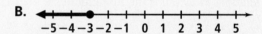

C.
```
  +--+--+--●--+--+--+--+--+--+--+--+
 -5 -4 -3 -2 -1  0  1  2  3  4  5
```

D.
```
  +--+--+--⊕--+--+--+--+--+--+--+--+
 -5 -4 -3 -2 -1  0  1  2  3  4  5
```

15. Solve and graph the inequality $2 \leq x - 3 < 9$.

16. Write a function rule to describe each statement. The amount of change $c(x)$ from a $100 bill if you buy x pounds of ground beef at $2.10 per pound.

17. What is the range $f(x) = x^2 - 3$ when the domain is $\{-1, 0, 3.5\}$?

18. Find the fifth term in the sequence $5, 22, 39, \ldots$.

Final Test, Algebra 1A (continued)   Form B

Chapters 1–6

Write an equation or inequality to model each situation. Then solve.

19. A mother holds her child and steps on the scale. Their total weight is 163 pounds. The child weighs 24 pounds. How much does the mom weigh?

20. You eat 4 pieces of a large pizza. There is $\frac{2}{3}$ of a pizza left. How many pieces make a large pizza?

21. The perimeter for the triangle and regular hexagon below are equal. Find *x*.

22. The rate to rent a moving truck is $65.00 per day and $0.26 per mile. Your friend gives you a check for $123.50 to cover the cost. How many miles did you drive?

23. What is the greatest number of $0.34 stamps you can buy with $4.40?

Solve.

24. What is 45% of 280?

25. 15 is what percent of 90.5?

26. A florist sells 1900 carnations in one month. This represents 42% of the flowers sold. Approximately how many total flowers does the florist sell?

Find the slope of the line passing through each pair of points.

27. $(4, 7)$ and $(-2, 3)$

28. $(-2, 7)$ and $(4, 1)$

Write the equation of the line for each of the following conditions.

29. through two points $(-6, 10)$ and $(3, 1)$

30. a vertical line passing through the point $(-2, 9)$

31. perpendicular to $y = 2x$, through point $(-1, 3)$

32. Write the equation of direct variation that includes the point $(2, -6)$.

Write an expression for each phrase.

33. the quantity *n* minus three-eighths times the quantity one-fifth plus *n*

34. three times the quantity *x* plus four squared

35. Graph the function $y = -|x| + 2$, by translating $y = |x|$.

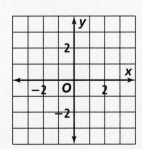

Final Test, Algebra 1A (continued)   Form B

Chapters 1–6

36. Which equation would translate $y = |x|$ 3 units to the right?

A. $y = |x| - 3$ **B.** $y = |x| + 3$

C. $y = |x + 3|$ **D.** $y = |x - 3|$

Solve.

37. Using the formula $C = \frac{5}{9}(F - 32)$, find the Fahrenheit temperature when the Celsius temperature is 35°.

38. Mrs. Rodriquez expects to pay $17,400 in taxes. This is no more than $\frac{3}{8}$ of her salary. What is her least possible earned income?

39. Which property is illustrated?

$5 \cdot \frac{1}{5} = 1$

40. Which employee has the highest hourly rate? Keep in mind that they do not get paid for lunch.

	Total Hours Worked	Lunch Hour	Pay Before Taxes
Jack	42	3.5	$539.00
Bill	38.5	2.75	$507.65
Joan	41.25	4.0	$510.33
Peggy	37.75	3.25	$503.70

41. The diameter of a pizza measures 12 inches, find the percent error in your measurement.

42. You have five dimes, eight nickels, and two quarters in a coin bank. Suppose you grab a coin from the coin bank. Find the probability that you select a quarter.

43. Suppose you have a coin bank with 3 quarters, 4 dimes, 2 nickels, and 1 penny. You choose two coins. Find each probability.

a. P(nickel and nickel) with replacing

b. P(nickel and nickel) without replacing

44. Which story describes the graph?

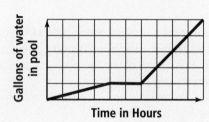

A. You drain a pool, stop the draining, and then continue draining it at a faster rate.

B. You drain a pool, stop the draining, and then continue draining it at a slower rate.

C. You fill a pool, stop filling it, and then continue filling it at a faster rate.

D. You fill a pool, stop filling it, and then continue filling it at a slower rate.

Final Test, Algebra 1A (continued)   Form B

Chapters 1–6

45. Maggie started a new job in 2001. Her salary was $34,200. She was promised a raise of $1750 each year.

    a. Write a function rule for finding Maggie's salary after 2001.

    b. Find Maggie's salary in 2006.

46. A girl 4 ft tall casts a shadow 5 ft long. She stands next to a monument that has a 13 ft long shadow. How tall is the monument?

47. You start a pet-sitting service. You spend $15 on advertising. You plan to charge $2 per day to watch each pet.

    a. Write an equation to relate your daily income y to the number of pets x you watch.

    b. Graph the equation. What are the x- and y-intercepts?

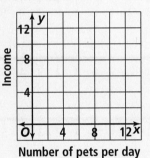

Number of pets per day

    c. How many days do you need to watch a pet to pay for advertising?

48. Write a function rule for the table of values.

x	y
−1	−3
0	−1
1	1
2	3

49. As head of the local union you are negotiating a new contract with a company. Which measure of central tendency will you use to persuade the company to support the raise you are asking for? A sampling of the hourly wages: $18.50, $19.10, $17.00, $17.00, and $16.20. Justify your answer.

50. **Writing** Natasha has saved $230. She wants to buy a new stereo for $550 in 4 months. To find how much she should save each week she wrote $230 + 16x = 550$. Explain her equation.

Diagnostic Test for Algebra 1B

Chapters 1–6

Simplify.

1. $-23 + 19$

2. $25 + (-8)$

3. $(10^2 - 4 \cdot 8) \div (10 + 7)$

4. $-3\frac{1}{2} - \left(-1\frac{7}{8}\right)$

5. $6.3 - 7.2$

6. $\dfrac{(-4)^5}{10 - 26}$

7. $(3n - 2m + 5)7$

8. $5x - 7y + 3x + 4y$

Evaluate each algebraic expression when $a = 5$, $b = 2.1$, and $c = -4$.

9. $a(a^2 - b)$

10. $4ac - c^2$

11. In which quadrant or axis would you find the point $(-3, -2)$?

12. What are the coordinates of A, B, and C?

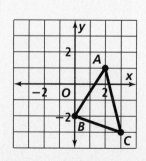

Solve each equation or inequality.

13. $6x - 4 = 26$

14. $9(x + 3) = 108$

15. $5x - 8 = 3x + 12$

16. $-\dfrac{3}{4}y < -27$

17. Which graph represents the real number solutions of $5x + 3 < -12$?

A.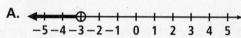

B.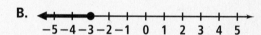

C.

D.
     −5 −4 −3 −2 −1   0   1   2   3   4   5

18. Solve and graph the inequality $5 - 2n \leq 3 - n$.

19. Write a function rule to describe the amount of change $c(x)$ from a \$100 bill you get if you buy x pounds of ground beef at \$2.10 per pound.

Diagnostic Test for Algebra 1B (continued)

Chapters 1–6

Write an equation or inequality to model each situation. Then solve.

20. A mother holds her twins and steps on the scale. Their total weight is 179 pounds. The mother weighs 141 pounds. How much does each twin weigh if they weigh the same amount?

21. The perimeter for the isosceles triangle and regular hexagon below are equal. Find x.

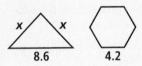

22. The rate to rent a moving truck is $65.00 per day and $0.26 per mile. Your friend gives you a check for $123.50 to cover the cost for one day. How many miles did you drive?

23. What is the greatest number of $0.34 stamps you can buy with $4.40?

Solve.

24. $-9x + 8 = 3x - 16$

25. $-\frac{6}{8} = \frac{x}{12}$

26. The ratio of the number of girls in Central High School to the number of boys in Central High School is $3:1$. If there are 420 girls in the school, how many boys are at the school?

Write the equation of the line for each of the following conditions.

27. slope $\frac{1}{3}$ and y-intercept 3

28. a line passing through $(-2, -7)$ with slope $-\frac{3}{2}$

29. through two points $(-6, 10)$ and $(3, 1)$

30. a vertical line passing through the point $(-2, 9)$

31. Find the x- and y-intercepts of $5x + 3y = 15$.

32. Graph $y = 2x + 1$.

33. Graph $5x - 4y = -15$.

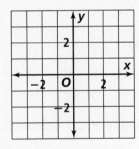

Mid-Course Test, Algebra 1B

Form A

Chapters 7–9

Solve each system by graphing.

1. $y = -x + 5$
   $y = 2x - 4$

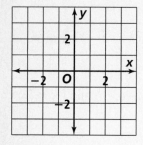

2. $y > 5x + 1$
   $y \leq -x + 3$

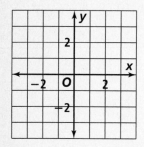

3. Solve the system using any method.
   $6x - 18y = 60$
   $9x + 2y = 32$

Write a system of equations to model each situation. Solve by any method.

4. Lisa charges $25 for private tutoring and $18 for a group tutoring session. One day in January, Lisa earned $265 from 12 students. How many students of each type did Lisa tutor?

5. A collection of quarters and nickels is worth $1.25. There are 13 coins in all. How many of each coin are there?

Simplify each expression.

6. $\dfrac{a^5 b^{-3}}{a^2}$

7. $4y^3 \cdot 7x^2 \cdot 9y^9$

8. $(x^2)^3 (6x^2 y^{-3})^2$

9. Write 3,463,000,000 in scientific notation.

10. Write the following in order from least to greatest. $4.72 \times 10^5, 42.7 \times 10^2, 472, 0.0427 \times 10^7$.

11. Which equation could you use to find the next term in the pattern $6, 18, 54, 162, \ldots$?
    A. $A(n) = 6n^2$ **B.** $A(n) = 6 \cdot 3n$
    C. $A(n) = 6^{n-1}$ **D.** $A(n) = 6(3)^{n-1}$

12. Evaluate $y = 3 \cdot 2^x$ for $x = 1, 2,$ and 3.

13. Use a table to graph the function $y = 3 \cdot 4^x$ with domain $\{-2, -1, 0, 1, 2\}$.

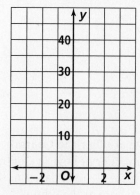

Mid-Course Test, Algebra 1B (continued)   Form A

Chapters 7–9

Simplify. Write each answer in standard form.

14. $(4x^3 + 3x^2 - 5x) - (x^3 - 11x^2 + 8)$

15. $(5x^4 - 3x^3 + 6x) + (3x^3 - 11x^2 - 8x)$

Simplify each product. Write in standard form.

16. $3x(4x^4 - 5x)$

17. $(x - 5)(x + 6)$

18. $(x + 3)(x^2 - 4x + 2)$

19. Write an expression for the situation as a product. Then, write in standard form. The height of a box is 4 in. less than its width w. The length of the box is 6 in. more than 8 times its width. What is the volume of the box in terms of w?

Factor each expression.

20. $x^2 + 5x - 6$

21. $x^2 - 625$

22. $8x^8 - 4x^4 + 12x^2$

23. $4x^2 - 16x - 84$

24. $2x^2 + 5x - 8x - 20$

25. Write an expression for the area of the shaded region. Write your answer in simplest form.

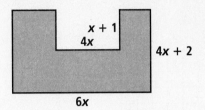

26. Open-Ended Write a trinomial with degree 5.

Solve.

27. Which value of b will make the graphs of $y = \frac{1}{2}x + 1$ and $y = -3x + b$ intersect at $(2, 2)$?

28. What would the value of n be, when $(x - n)^2$ are the factors of $x^2 - 12x + 36$?

29. An eighth grade class has planned a field trip to a local museum. If they take 4 vans and 1 car they can transport 28 students. If they take 2 vans and 5 cars they can transport 32 students.

  a. How many people can be transported in a van and in a car?

  b. Write a combination of cars and vans to transport the whole class of 40 students, taking the least number of full vehicles.

30. Writing Is $(3, 10)$ a solution of $y \geq 5x - 8$? Explain why or why not.

Mid-Course Test, Algebra 1B

Form B

Chapters 7–9

Solve each system by graphing.

1. $y = -\frac{1}{2}x + 3$

   $y = 3x - 4$

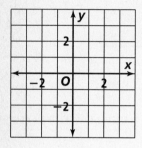

2. $y < 6x + 1$
   $y \geq -2x - 3$

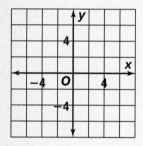

3. Solve the system using any method.
   $-x + 2y = -2$
   $3x + 6y = 12$

Write a system of equations to model each situation. Solve by any method.

4. Martin charges $30 for private tutoring and $22 for a group tutoring session. One day in February, Martin earned $378 from 15 students. How many students of each type did Martin tutor?

5. A collection of nickels and dimes is worth $1.85. There are 22 coins in all. How many of each coin are there?

Simplify each expression.

6. $\dfrac{a^4 b^{-5}}{ab^3}$

7. $6x \cdot 5y^4 \cdot 3x^7$

8. $(x^{-3})^6 (9xy^2)^3$

9. Write 0.000000724 in scientific notation.

10. Write the following in order from least to greatest. $0.039 \times 10^7, 319, 39.1 \times 10,$ 3.19×10^5.

11. Which equation could you use to find the next term in the pattern $4, 8, 16, 32, \ldots$?
    A. $A(n) = 4^{n-1}$ **B.** $A(n) = 4(2)^{n-1}$
    C. $A(n) = 4 \cdot 2n$ **D.** $A(n) = 4n^2$

12. Evaluate $y = 5 \cdot 2^x$ for $x = 1, 2,$ and 3.

13. Use a table to graph the function $y = 0.1 \cdot 3^x$ with domain $\{-2, -1, 0, 1, 2\}$.

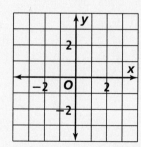

Mid-Course Test, Algebra 1B (continued)   Form B

Chapters 7–9

Simplify. Write each answer in standard form.

14. $(7x^3 - 3x^2 + 4) - (x^2 + 2)$

15. $(8x^5 + 6x^4 - 3x^2 - 5) + (7x^4 + 3x^2 - 2)$

Simplify each product. Write in standard form.

16. $5x(6x^5 - 3x^2)$

17. $(x - 8)(x - 9)$

18. $(2x + 3)(x^2 - 2x + 1)$

19. Write an expression for the situation as a product. Then, write in standard form. The height of a box is 5 in. less than its width w. The length of the box is 4 in. more than 5 times its width. What is the volume of the box in terms of w?

Factor each expression.

20. $x^2 + 2x - 24$

21. $x^2 - 324$

22. $12x^7 + 6x^4 - 30x^2$

23. $2x^2 - 2x - 12$

24. $5x^2 + 10x - x - 2$

25. Write an expression for the area of the shaded region. Write your answer in simplest form.

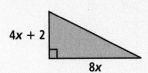

26. Open-Ended Write a trinomial with degree 7.

Solve.

27. Which value of b will make the graphs of $y = 2x + b$ and $y = x + 6$ intersect at $(-1, 5)$?

28. What would the value of n be, when $(x + n)^2$ are the factors of $x^2 + 8x + 16$?

29. A seniors group would like to take a trip. They have both buses and vans. If they take 2 buses and 2 vans they can transport 28 people. If they take 1 bus and 5 vans they can transport 30 people.

   a. How many people can be transported in each type of vehicle?

   b. Write a combination of cars and vans to transport the whole group of 68 seniors, taking the least number of full vehicles.

30. Writing Is $(-2, 1)$ a solution of $y \le 4x + 3$? Explain why or why not.

Final Test, Algebra 1B

Form A

Chapters 7–12

Graph.

1. $y = -x^2 - 2x + 1$

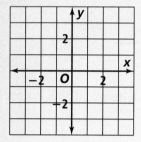

2. $y > \frac{1}{2}x^2$

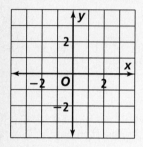

3. $y = \sqrt{x - 4}$

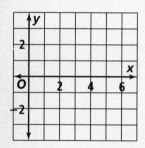

4. Which expression simplifies to -1?

A. $\dfrac{x + 5}{x - 5}$ B. $\dfrac{w - 3}{3 - w}$

C. $\dfrac{5 - y}{5 + y}$ D. $\dfrac{t + 6}{6 - t}$

Simplify.

5. $3\sqrt{4x^2} \cdot \sqrt{12x}$

6. $-8x(x - 3)$

7. $(6x^3 + 2x^2 - 5x) - (x^3 - 9x^2 + 4)$

Solve. If the equation is an identity or if it has no solution, write *identity* or *no* solution. Round to the nearest hundredth, if necessary.

8. $10 - 4\sqrt{y} = 5$

9. $\dfrac{8}{x + 3} = \dfrac{1}{x} + 1$

10. $\sqrt{7x - 1} = \sqrt{5x + 3}$

11. $\dfrac{x - 8}{3} + \dfrac{x - 3}{2} = 0$

12. $6x^2 + 7x - 20 = 0$

Simplify each expression.

13. $_5C_3$

14. $_8P_5$

Final Test, Algebra 1B (continued) # Form A

Chapters 7–12

Evaluate.

15. $f(3)$ when $f(x) = 45x^{-2}$

16. $f(3)$ when $f(x) = 2^x - 1$

Factor.

17. $x^2 + 6x - 27$

18. $2x^3 + x^2 - 14x - 7$

19. Find the number of real number solutions of $4x^2 + 16x + 15 = 0$.

20. What is the vertex of the graph of $y = x^2 - 4x - 3$?

Simplify each radical expression.

21. $\sqrt{75} + \sqrt{3}$

22. $\sqrt{75x^2} \cdot \sqrt{3x^3}$

Simplify each expression.

23. $\dfrac{5}{\sqrt{11} + \sqrt{7}}$

24. $7x^2y^{-1}(2xy^2)^3$

25. $\dfrac{4x^2y^5}{12x^3y^2z^{-3}}$

26. A landscaper has 15 different shrubs to choose from to complete a landscape job. In how many ways can the landscaper choose 8 different shrubs?

27. At a horse show, ribbons are given for first, second, third, and fourth places. There are 20 horses in the show. How many different arrangements of four winning horses are possible?

28. Approximate AB to the nearest hundredth. Then find the coordinates of the midpoint of $\overline{AB}$. $A(-3, 2)$ and $B(-15, 4)$.

Find each product. Write each answer in standard form.

29. $(x^2 + 4)(x + 3)$

30. $(3x - 4)(3x + 5)$

Final Test, Algebra 1B (continued)   Form A

Chapters 7–12

Solve.

31. Suppose the function $y = 25,000(1.06)^x$ models the annual starting salary for a small business x years after 2000.

    a. Find the starting salary in 2002.

    b. Find the starting salary in 2007.

32. Write 375,000 in scientific notation.

33. Which inequality describes the graph?

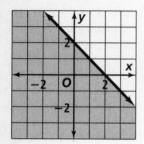

  A. $x + y > 2$ **B.** $x + y \geq 2$

  C. $-x + y \leq 2$ **D.** $x + y \leq 2$

34. Solve the system of equations by any method.
$$7x + 15y = 32$$
$$x = 3y + 20$$

35. Solve the system by graphing.
$$y = \frac{1}{2}x - 1$$
$$y = -x + 3$$

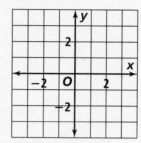

36. Write a system of equations to model this situation. Then use your system to solve. At a garage sale a CD costs three times as much as a book. You bought three books and 2 CDs. You spent $18. What is the price of a CD and the price of a book?

Solve.

37. A square picture frame occupies an area of 112 ft². What is the length of each side of the picture in simplified radical form?

38. One leg of a right triangle is 12. The hypotenuse equals 15. What is the length of the unknown leg?

39. The midpoint of the segment with endpoints at $(7, y)$ and $(-8, 6)$ is $\left(-\frac{1}{2}, 5\right)$. What is the value of y?

40. $\triangle LMN$ is a right triangle with right angle at N. Which of the given statements is false?

  A. $\cos L = \dfrac{NL}{LM}$ **B.** $\sin L = \dfrac{LM}{NL}$

  C. $\sin M = \dfrac{NL}{LM}$ **D.** $\tan M = \dfrac{NL}{NM}$

Final Test, Algebra 1B (continued)   Form A

Chapters 7–12

41. The graph of $y = \frac{3}{x}$ is translated 4 units up. What is the equation of the new graph?

46. Use a table to graph the function $y = 2x^2 - 5$. Estimate the value of the x-intercepts.

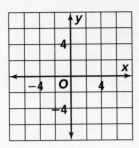

Solve.

42. In an inverse variation, when $x = 24, y = 6$. What is the equation of the inverse variation?

43. A construction worker drops a tool from the top of a building that is 300 feet high. The height of the tool above ground can be modeled by $h = -16t^2 + 300$, where h is height in feet and t is time in seconds.

   a. Use a table to graph this function.

   b. Use your graph to estimate the amount of time it takes for the tool to hit the ground. Round to the nearest tenth of a second.

47. a. Graph $y = \sqrt{x} + 2$.

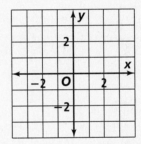

44. The sides of a triangular garden are 10 ft, 22 ft, and 18 ft. Is the garden in the shape of a right triangle? Justify your answer.

   b. Use the graph to decide if $y = \sqrt{x} + 2$ is a function. Explain why it is or is not.

45. Identify the asymptote(s) of the function. Then graph the function, $y = \frac{4}{x - 3}$.

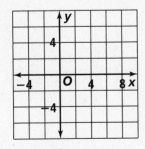

48. Subtract $\dfrac{y - 7}{y^2} - \dfrac{y + 7}{2y}$.

49. Writing Does $(x^2 + 4y)^2$ equal $x^4 + 16y^2$? Justify your answer.

50. Writing Explain the steps needed to simplify $\dfrac{8}{\sqrt{5} + \sqrt{23}}$.

Final Test, Algebra 1B

Form B

Chapters 7–12

Graph.

1. $y = x^2 - 4x + 3$

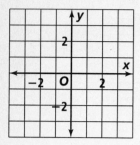

2. $y \leq \frac{1}{4}x^2$

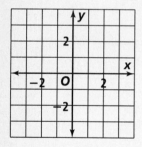

3. $y = \sqrt{x - 3}$

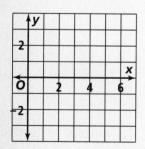

4. Which expression simplifies to -1?

A. $\frac{x + 6}{x - 6}$ B. $\frac{w - 5}{5 - w}$

C. $\frac{4 - y}{4 + y}$ D. $\frac{t + 7}{7 - t}$

Simplify.

5. $5\sqrt{6xy} \cdot \sqrt{8x^2y}$

6. $-7x(x + 3)$

7. $(9x^3 + 6x - 3) - (7x^3 + 4x^2 - 4x - 5)$

Solve. If the equation is an identity or if it has no solution, write *identity* or *no* solution. Round to the nearest tenth, if necessary.

8. $15 - 4\sqrt{y} = 10$

9. $\frac{6}{x^2} - \frac{5}{x} = 1$

10. $\sqrt{4x - 3} = \sqrt{2x + 8}$

11. $\frac{x + 1}{3} - \frac{x - 1}{5} = 0$

12. $5x^2 - 7x = 6$

Simplify each expression.

13. $_7C_4$

14. $_9P_5$

Final Test, Algebra 1B (continued)   Form B

Chapters 7–12

Evaluate.

15. $f(-5)$ when $f(x) = 200x^{-2}$

16. $f(2)$ when $f(x) = 3^x - 1$

Factor.

17. $x^2 - 5x - 24$

18. $5x^4 + 20x^3 + 6x + 24$

19. Find the number of real number solutions of $5x^2 + 6x + 7 = 0$.

20. What is the vertex of the graph of $y = 3x^2 + 12x - 5$?

Simplify each radical expression.

21. $\sqrt{63} + \sqrt{7}$

22. $\sqrt{2x^5} \cdot \sqrt{72x^2}$

Simplify each expression.

23. $\dfrac{6}{\sqrt{10} + \sqrt{8}}$

24. $8x^3y^{-2}(3x^2y^3)^2$

25. $\dfrac{3x^3y^{-2}z^4}{6x^2y^{-3}}$

26. For your birthday you receive a gift certificate from a local bookstore. There are 7 books you would like to have. If you select the books at random, how many different groups of 3 could you select?

27. At a horse show, ribbons are given for first, second, third, and fourth places. There are 18 horses in the show. How many different arrangements of four winning horses are possible?

28. Approximate AB to the nearest hundredth. Then find the coordinates of the midpoint of $\overline{AB}$. $A(5, -1)$ and $B(-3, 5)$.

Find each product. Write each answer in standard form.

29. $(x^2 + 5)(x - 6)$

30. $(5x - 3)(4x + 7)$

Final Test, Algebra 1B (continued)   Form B

Solve.

31. Suppose in the year 2000 a new car is worth $24,000. It depreciates by one tenth of its value each year. The function $y = 24,000(0.9)^x$ models the car's value after x years.

   a. Find the value of the car in 2002.

   b. Find the value of the car in 2007.

32. Write 425,000 in scientific notation.

33. Which inequality describes the graph?

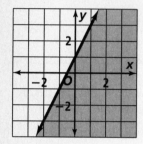

   A. $2x + y > 1$ **B.** $2x + y \geq 1$
   C. $-2x + y \geq 1$ **D.** $-2x + y \leq 1$

34. Solve the system of equations by any method.
$$y = 2x - 1$$
$$-6x + 5y = 3$$

35. Solve the system by graphing.
$$y = 3x - 1$$
$$y = -x + 3$$

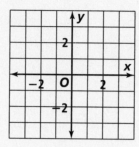

36. Write a system of equations to model this situation. Then use your system to solve. An elementary school is selling bulbs for a spring fundraiser. A package of tulip bulbs is $\frac{1}{3}$ the price of a package of iris bulbs. Your Aunt Molly buys 5 packages of tulip bulbs and 2 packages of iris bulbs for $33. Find the price of each package of bulbs.

Solve.

37. A square picture frame occupies an area of 216 ft². What is the length of each side of the picture in simplified radical form?

38. One leg of a right triangle is 8. The hypotenuse equals 15. What is the length of the unknown leg?

39. The midpoint of the segment with endpoints at $(2, y)$ and $(7, 9)$ is $\left(4\frac{1}{2}, 3\right)$. What is the value of y?

40. $\triangle PQR$ is a right triangle with right angle at R. Which of the given statements is false?

   A. $\cos P = \dfrac{PR}{PQ}$ **B.** $\sin Q = \dfrac{PR}{PQ}$

   C. $\sin P = \dfrac{RQ}{PQ}$ **D.** $\tan P = \dfrac{PR}{QR}$

Final Test, Algebra 1B (continued)

Form B

Chapters 7–12

41. The graph of $y = \frac{3}{x}$ is translated 4 units down. What is the equation of the new graph?

Solve.

42. The points $(6, 4)$ and $(8, y)$ are two points on the graph of an inverse variation. Find the missing value.

43. A construction worker drops a tool from the top of a building that is 500 feet high. The height of the tool above ground can be modeled by $h = -16t^2 + 500$, where h is height in feet and t is time in seconds.

   a. Use a table to graph this function.

   b. Use your graph to estimate the amount of time it takes for the tool to hit the ground. Round to the nearest tenth of a second.

44. The sides of a triangular garden are 15 ft, 39 ft, and 36 ft. Is the garden in the shape of a right triangle? Justify your answer.

45. Identify the asymptote(s) of the function. Then graph the function, $y = \frac{4}{x + 2}$.

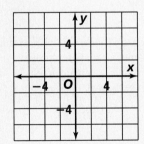

46. Use a table to graph the function $y = 4x^2 - 3$. Estimate the value of the x-intercepts.

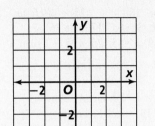

47. a. Graph $y = \sqrt{x} - 2$.

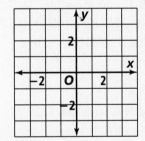

   b. Use the graph to decide if $y = \sqrt{x} - 2$ is a function. Explain why or why not.

48. Add $\dfrac{4x^2}{2(x^2 - 4)} + \dfrac{x}{x + 2}$.

49. **Writing** Does $(x^2 - 6y)^2$ equal $x^4 + 36y^2$? Justify your answer.

50. **Writing** Explain the steps needed to simplify $\dfrac{6}{\sqrt{3} + \sqrt{19}}$.

Answers

Mid-Course Test, Algebra 1A, Form A

1. $c = 12m$ **2.** $-\frac{5}{8}$ **3.** -10.2 **4.** $6\frac{2}{7}$ **5.** -48

6. 31 **7.** $12x - 8$ **8.** $-5(3 + k)$ **9.** III

10. 13.745 **11.** 3 **12.** 5 **13.** identity **14.** $-1\frac{2}{7}$

15. $0.75t = 16.50$; 22 tickets **16a.** $c = 2.25 + 4(0.60)m$
or $c = 2.25 + 2.40m$ **16b.** $16.65 **17.** $n \geq 25$
18. $x \geq 14$ or $x \leq -2$ **19.** $x \leq 5$ **20.** $n \geq -1$ or $n \leq -5$

21. $\begin{bmatrix} -2 & 1 \\ -3 & 13 \end{bmatrix}$ **22.** $x \geq -3$ **23.** Distributive Property

24. 2 **25.** 102 **26.** 18 yd gain **27.** mean: 129;
median: 106; mode: none **28.** mean: 122; median: 112;
mode: none **29.** Check students' work.
30. Distributive Property; Commutative Property of
Addition; Addition

Mid-Course Test, Algebra 1A, Form B

1. $c = 6m$ **2.** $-7\frac{1}{6}$ **3.** 4.4 **4.** 8 **5.** -64 **6.** 74.2

7. $15 + 2x$ **8.** $-6(x - 4)$ **9.** IV **10.** about 3.61 **11.** 7

12. $5\frac{5}{7}$ **13.** $-1\frac{1}{7}$ **14.** identity **15.** $0.75p = 6.00$; 8 postcards
16a. $2.50 + 4(0.4m)$ or $2.50 + 1.6m$ **16b.** $21.70
17. $n \geq 11.1$ **18.** $x \geq 12$ or $x \leq -2$ **19.** $x \leq 31$

20. $n \geq 1$ or $n \leq -9$ **21.** $\begin{bmatrix} 2 & -14 \\ 13 & 2 \end{bmatrix}$ **22.** $x \leq -5$

23. Associative Property of Multiplication **24.** 3 **25.** 77

26. 20 yd gain **27.** mean: 89; median: 86; mode: none
28. mean: 72; median: 63; mode: 63
29. Check students' work. **30.** Distributive Property;
Commutative Property of Addition; Distributive Property

Final Test, Algebra 1A, Form A

1. 4.121 **2.** 220 **3.** $-7\frac{1}{6}$ **4.** 648 **5.** 23.625
6. 40 left-handed students **7.** 4.1 **8.** 83.8 **9.** y-axis **10.** 5
11. 0 **12.** $y \leq -42$ **13.** $-2 < d < 2$ **14.** D
15. $x \leq -10$ or $x \geq 4$;

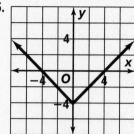

16. $c(x) = 20 - 1.29x$ **17.** $\{-4, -5, 7.25\}$ **18.** -42
19. $x - 32 = 289.14$; $321.14 **20.** $\frac{2}{3}x = 8$; 12 gallons
21. $2x + 5 = 12$; 3.5 **22.** $2(c + 2) + 3c = 34$; $8
23. $0.25x \leq 2.20$; 8 gumballs **24.** 32% **25.** 287
26. 40 million **27.** $-\frac{1}{3}$ **28.** 2 **29.** $y = \frac{3}{2}x + 1$
30. $y = 18$ **31.** $y = \frac{4}{9}x + \frac{17}{9}$ **32.** $y = -\frac{1}{3}x$
33. $(2d - 5)(6d + 4)$ **34.** $6x^2 - 15$

35.

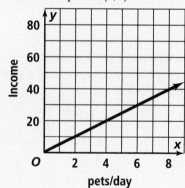

36. B **37.** 113°F **38.** $58,200 **39.** Distributive
Property **40.** Mike **41.** about 0.1%
42. $\frac{2}{5}$ **43a.** $\frac{1}{16}$ **43b.** $\frac{1}{20}$ **44.** B
45a. $f(x) = 1560x + 32,600$ **45b.** $41,960
46. $34\frac{2}{3}$ ft **47a.** $y = 5x$
47b. Both intercepts are $(0, 0)$.

47c. 7 days **48.** $y = 3.5x$
49. mean; Since you are trying to attract an employee, you
use the greatest value. **50.** James's equation represents the
amount of money he has ($50) plus how many weeks he has
to save (20) times the amount each week (x) is equal to the
amount he needs ($149).

Answers (continued)

Final Test, Algebra 1A, Form B

1. 3.412 **2.** 4 **3.** $-1\frac{5}{8}$ **4.** 64 **5.** 247

6. 140 boys **7.** 12.3 **8.** -85 **9.** x-axis **10.** 5

11. 9 **12.** $y > 36$ **13.** $-7 \le x \le 11$ **14.** C

15. $5 \le x < 12$;

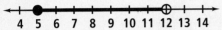

16. $c(x) = 100 - 2.10x$ **17.** $\{-2, -3, 9.25\}$ **18.** 73

19. $x + 24 = 163$; 139 lb **20.** $x - 4 = \frac{2}{3}x$; 12

21. $2x + 5 = 12$; 3.5 **22.** $65.00 + 0.26x = 123.50$; 225 miles

23. $0.34x \le 4.40$; 12 stamps **24.** 126 **25.** about 16.6%

26. 4524 flowers **27.** $\frac{2}{3}$ **28.** -1 **29.** $y = -x + 4$

30. $x = -2$ **31.** $y = -\frac{1}{2}x + \frac{5}{2}$ **32.** $y = -3x$

33. $\left(n - \frac{3}{8}\right)\left(\frac{1}{5} + n\right)$ **34.** $3(x + 4^2)$

35.

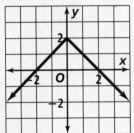

36. D **37.** 95°F **38.** $46,400 **39.** Inverse Property of Multiplication **40.** Peggy **41.** about 4.2%

42. $\frac{2}{15}$ **43a.** $\frac{1}{25}$ **43b.** $\frac{1}{45}$ **44.** C

45a. $f(x) = 1750x + 34,200$ **45b.** $42,950

46. 10.4 ft **47a.** $y = 2x$

47b. Both intercepts are $(0, 0)$.

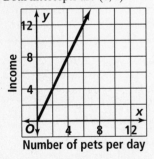

47c. 7.5 days **48.** $y = 2x - 1$

49. Mode or median since both are $17.00. Since you are negotiating for a higher salary you would use the measure of central tendency that is the lowest.

50. Natasha's equation represents the money she has ($230) plus the number of weeks she has to save (16) times the amount saved each week (x) is equal to the amount she needs ($550).

Diagnostic Test for Algebra 1B

1. -4 **2.** 17 **3.** 4 **4.** $-1\frac{5}{8}$ **5.** 0.9

6. 64 **7.** $21n - 14m + 35$ **8.** $8x - 3y$

9. 114.5 **10.** -64 **11.** IV quadrant

12. $A(2, 1)$; $B(0, -2)$; $C(4, -3)$ **13.** 5

14. 9 **15.** 10 **16.** $y > 36$ **17.** A

18. $n \le 1$;

19. $c(x) = 100 - 2.10x$ **20.** 19 pounds

21. 8.3 **22.** $65.00 + 0.26x = 123.50$; 225 miles

23. $0.34x < 4.40$; 12 stamps **24.** 2 **25.** -9

26. 140 boys **27.** $y = \frac{1}{3}x + 3$

28. $y = -\frac{3}{2}x - 10$ **29.** $y = -x + 4$ **30.** $x = -2$

31. x-intercept: 3; y-intercept: 5

32. 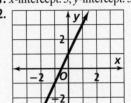 **33.**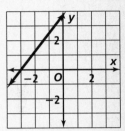

Answers (continued)

Mid-Course Test, Algebra 1B, Form A

1.

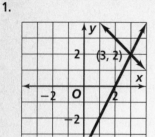

2.

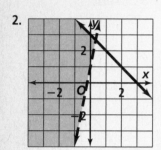

3. $(4, -2)$ **4.** $\begin{aligned} 25p + 18g &= 265 \\ p + g &= 12 \end{aligned}$; 7 private, 5 group

5. $\begin{aligned} 0.25q + 0.05n &= 1.25 \\ q + n &= 13 \end{aligned}$; 3 quarters, 10 nickels **6.** $\dfrac{a^3}{b^3}$

7. $252x^2y^{12}$ **8.** $\dfrac{36x^{10}}{y^6}$ **9.** 3.463×10^9 **10.** 472,

$42.7 \times 10^2, 0.0427 \times 10^7, 4.72 \times 10^5$ **11.** D **12.** 6, 12, 24

13.

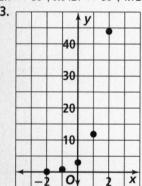

14. $3x^3 + 14x^2 - 5x - 8$ **15.** $5x^4 - 11x^2 - 2x$
16. $12x^5 - 15x^2$ **17.** $x^2 + x - 30$ **18.** $x^3 - x^2 - 10x + 6$
19. $w(w - 4)(8w + 6); 8w^3 - 26w^2 - 24w$ **20.** $(x + 6)(x - 1)$
21. $(x + 25)(x - 25)$ **22.** $4x^2(2x^6 - x^2 + 3)$
23. $4(x - 7)(x + 3)$ **24.** $(2x + 5)(x - 4)$ **25.** $20x^2 + 8x$
26. Answers will vary. Sample $7x^5 - x^2 + 4$ **27.** 8
28. 6 **29a.** 6 people in a van and 4 people in a car.
29b. 6 vans and 1 car **30.** Yes; $10 > 5(3) - 8$ is true.

Mid-Course Test, Algebra 1B, Form B

1.

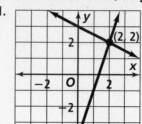

2.

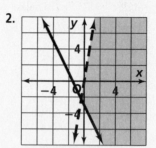

3. $\left(3, \dfrac{1}{2}\right)$ **4.** $\begin{aligned} 30p + 22g &= 378 \\ p + g &= 15 \end{aligned}$; 6 private, 9 group

5. $\begin{aligned} 0.05n + 0.10d &= 1.85 \\ n + d &= 22 \end{aligned}$; 7 nickels and 15 dimes

6. $\dfrac{a^3}{b^8}$ **7.** $90x^8y^4$ **8.** $\dfrac{729y^6}{x^{15}}$ **9.** 7.24×10^{-7} **10.** 319,

$39.1 \times 10, 3.19 \times 10^5, 0.039 \times 10^7$ **11.** B **12.** 10, 20, 40

13.

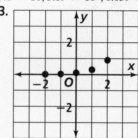

14. $7x^3 - 4x^2 + 2$ **15.** $8x^5 + 13x^4 - 7$
16. $30x^6 - 15x^3$ **17.** $x^2 - 17x + 72$
18. $2x^3 - x^2 - 4x + 3$ **19.** $w(w - 5)(5w + 4)$;
$5w^3 - 21w^2 - 20w$ **20.** $(x + 6)(x - 4)$
21. $(x + 18)(x - 18)$ **22.** $6x^2(2x^5 + x^2 - 5)$
23. $2(x - 3)(x + 2)$ **24.** $(5x - 1)(x + 2)$
25. $16x^2 + 8x$ **26.** Answers will vary. Sample:
$8x^7 - 5x^3 + 9x$ **27.** 7 **28.** 4 **29a.** 4 people in a van
and 10 people in a bus. **29b.** 6 buses and 2 vans
30. No; $1 \le 4(-2) + 3$ is false.

Answers (continued)

Final Test, Algebra 1A, Form A

1.

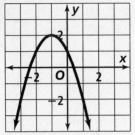

2.

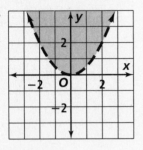

3.

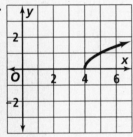

4. B **5.** $12x\sqrt{3x}$ **6.** $-8x^2 + 24x$

7. $5x^3 + 11x^2 - 5x - 4$ **8.** $\frac{25}{16}$ **9.** 3 or 1 **10.** 2

11. 5 **12.** $\frac{4}{3}, -\frac{5}{2}$ **13.** 10

14. 6720 **15.** 5 **16.** 7

17. $(x + 9)(x - 3)$ **18.** $(2x + 1)(x^2 - 7)$

19. two **20.** $(2, -7)$ **21.** $6\sqrt{3}$ **22.** $15x^2\sqrt{x}$

23. $\frac{5\sqrt{11} - 5\sqrt{7}}{4}$ **24.** $56x^5y^5$ **25.** $\frac{y^3z^3}{3x}$ **26.** 6435 ways

27. 116,280 arrangements **28.** 12.17; $(-9, 3)$

29. $x^3 + 3x^2 + 4x + 12$ **30.** $9x^2 + 3x - 20$

31a. $28,090 **31b.** $37590.76 **32.** 3.75×10^5 **33.** D

34. $(11, -3)$

35. $\left(\frac{8}{3}, \frac{1}{3}\right)$

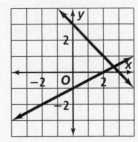

36. $y = 3x$ and $3x + 2y = 18$; book: $2.00; CD: $6.00

37. $4\sqrt{7}$ ft **38.** 9 **39.** 4 **40.** B **41.** $y = \frac{3}{x} + 4$

42. $y = \frac{144}{x}$

43a.

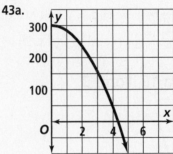

43b. 4.3 seconds

44. No, $10^2 + 18^2 \neq 22^2$.

45. vertical asymptote: $x = 3$; horizontal asymptote: $y = 0$

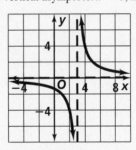

46. $-1.6, 1.6$;

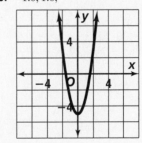

Answers (continued)

47a.

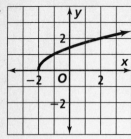

47b. The equation $y = \sqrt{x} + 2$ defines a function because any vertical line would only intersect the graph in one point.

48. $-\dfrac{y^2 + 5y + 14}{2y^2}$

49. No, each term was factored and the whole binomial needs to be multiplied by itself. There will be a middle term.

50. Rationalize the denominator by multiplying the numerator and denominator by the conjugate, $\sqrt{5} - \sqrt{23}$.

The resulting fraction can be reduced to $\dfrac{-4\sqrt{5} \ -4\sqrt{23}}{9}$.

Final Test, Algebra 1B, Form B

1.

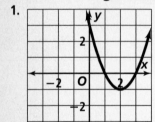

2.

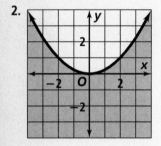

3.

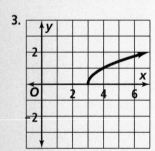

4. B **5.** $20xy\sqrt{3x}$ **6.** $-7x^2 - 21x$

7. $2x^3 - 4x^2 + 10x + 2$ **8.** $\dfrac{25}{16}$ **9.** $-6, 1$

10. 5.5 **11.** -4 **12.** $2, -\dfrac{3}{5}$ **13.** 35 **14.** 15, 120 **15.** 8

16. 8 **17.** $(x - 8)(x + 3)$ **18.** $(x + 4)(5x^3 + 6)$

19. none **20.** $(-2, -17)$ **21.** $4\sqrt{7}$ **22.** $12x^3\sqrt{x}$

23. $3\sqrt{10} - 6\sqrt{2}$ **24.** $72x^7y^4$ **25.** $\dfrac{xyz^4}{2}$

26. 35 groups of 3 **27.** 73,440 arrangements **28.** 10; $(1, 2)$

29. $x^3 - 6x^2 + 5x - 30$ **30.** $20x^2 + 23x - 21$

31a. \$19,440 **31b.** \$11479.13 **32.** 4.25×10^5

33. D **34.** $(2, 3)$

35. $(1, 2)$

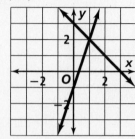

36. $y = \dfrac{1}{3}x$ and $2x + 5y = 33$; iris: \$9; tulips: \$3

37. $6\sqrt{6}$ ft **38.** about 12.7 **39.** -3 **40.** D

41. $y = \dfrac{3}{x} - 4$ **42.** 3

43a.

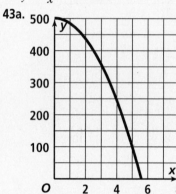

43b. 5.6 seconds

44. Yes; $15^2 + 36^2 = 39^2$.

45. vertical asymptote: $x = -2$; horizontal asymptote: $y = 0$

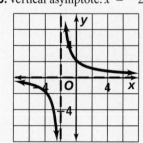

Answers (continued)

46. $-0.9, 0.9$

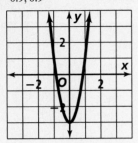

47a.

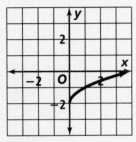

47b. The equation $y = \sqrt{x} - 2$ defines a function because any vertical line would only intersect the graph in one point.

48. $\dfrac{3x^2 - 2x}{x^2 - 4}$

49. No, the binomial needs to be multiplied by itself. This will result in a middle term. **50.** Rationalize the denominator by multiplying the numerator and denominator by the conjugate, $\sqrt{3} - \sqrt{19}$. The resulting fraction can be reduced to $\dfrac{-3\sqrt{3} - 3\sqrt{19}}{8}$.